STRATEGIC MANAGEMENT

SECOND EDITION
Previously published as
The Strategic Management Blueprint

STRATEGIC
MANAGEMENT
ISSUES AND CASES

**Paul Dobson, Kenneth Starkey
and John Richards**

Blackwell
Publishing

350 Main Street, Malden, MA 02148-5020, USA
108 Cowley Road, Oxford OX4 1JF, UK
550 Swanston Street, Carlton, Victoria 3053, Australia

First published as *The Strategic Management Blueprint* 1993 by Blackwell Publishers Ltd
This edition published 2004 by Blackwell Publishing Ltd

Library of Congress Cataloging-in-Publication Data

Dobson, Paul, 1962–
  [Strategic management blueprint]
  Strategic management : issues and cases / Paul Dobson, Ken Starkey, and John Richards. — 2nd ed.
      p. cm.
Previously published as: The strategic management blueprint.
Includes bibliographical references (p.) and index.
  ISBN 1-4051-1181-X (paperback : alk. paper)
  1. Strategic planning. 2. Organizational change. 3. Management.
I. Starkey, Ken, 1948– II. Richards, John. III. Title.

  HD30.28.D62 2004
  658.4'012—dc22

                                        2003016913

A catalogue record for this title is available from the British Library.

Set in Baskerville 10/12.5pt by Graphicraft Limited, Hong Kong
Printed and bound in the United Kingdom
by TJ International, Padstow, Cornwall

For further information on
Blackwell Publishing, visit our website:
http://www.blackwellpublishing.com

CONTENTS

List of figures	ix
List of tables	x
List of exhibits	xi
Preface	xii

1 Introduction: What is Strategic Management? — 1

What is strategy?	1
Two approaches to strategy	2
Elements of strategy	2
Our model of strategy	4
The growth vector	7
Mission statements	10
Identity	14
Theory of the business	15
Strategy evaluation	16
The book in brief	17

2 Situation Analysis: the Firm and its Environment — 18

What do we mean by 'environment'?	18
How does one analyse the environment?	19
Scanning the general environment	20
The nature of the environment	22

Gratis

117620

Structural analysis of the competitive environment 26

Identifying the firm's competitive position 32

The internal environment: resources and capabilities 41

SWOT analysis 46

Conclusion 49

3 Business-level Strategy 51

Strategic choice 51

Competitive strategies 52

Gaining competitive advantage 62

Competitive advantage through resources and capabilities 70

Market turbulence and hypercompetition 74

Dealing with the opposition 80

Conclusion 83

4 Corporate-level Strategy 86

Strategic considerations 86

Directional strategies 87

Methods of development 97

Portfolio strategies 100

Parenting strategies 104

Selecting appropriate strategies 111

Corporate objectives 112

5 Organization and Strategy 121

Organizational issues and strategy 121

Peters and Waterman's excellent organizations 122

Japanese organizations and strategic management 125

Strategic human resource management 128

Magic kingdoms? 134

Critical voices 137

New perspectives on excellence: *Built to Last* and *Good to Great* 138

Organization design: strategy and structure 140

Structuring for complexity 144

Parenting 146

Competition and co-operation 149

6 The Management of Strategic Change 151

Triggers for change 151

Radical change 152

The incremental approach to change 153

Radical and incremental change compared 154

Strategy subsystems 155

Managing change 157

The innovating organization 159

Organizational development and strategy 161

Change in service environments 163

Strategic management and leadership 165

Leaders and leadership 169

Leadership means change 173

7 The Future of Strategy: Competence and Responsibility 176

Competence 176

Competence, organization and human resources 178

Future excellence 180

The future of strategy 184

Software wars: Davids *v.* Goliath 184

Strategy and responsibility 187

Epilogue 191

Final thought 193

8 Case Studies 194

What business are we in? Boots: the journey to well-being 194

The sad fate of the dodo 197

Home Depot in the midst of transformation 198

The National Health Service: a case of too many trusts? 202

Nokia: a great company in a turbulent market   206

Rexam: a classic transformation   209

Sainsbury: stuck in the middle again   212

Sony: Idei's vision   217

GE: the leadership practices of Jack Welch   221

Xerox: capabilities discovered but not developed   225

References   229
Index   234

FIGURES

1.1	The strategic management process	4
1.2	Product, mission and market choices	8
1.3	Retailing product–market strategy options	9
1.4	Ford Motor Company's statement of mission, values and guiding principles	13
2.1	The organization and its environment	19
2.2	Situation analysis	20
2.3	The five forces of industry competition	26
2.4	Stages of the life cycle	35
2.5	The value chain	42
3.1	Three generic strategies	53
3.2	The virtuous circle	68
3.3	Positioning for success beyond the existing value-for-money frontier	69
4.1	Alternative directions for strategic development	88
4.2	Options for related diversification facing a manufacturer	91
4.3	The BCG growth–share business portfolio matrix	101
4.4	General Electric's nine-cell business portfolio matrix	103
4.5	Parenting fit matrix	105
5.1	The seven Ss framework	123
5.2	Type J versus Type A organizations	127
5.3	Key elements in manufacturing competitiveness	128
5.4	The Japanese management system	129
5.5	Eight excellent-management skills	135
5.6	The dynamic network	142
5.7	The flexible television/film production company	143
5.8	Industry requirements and company capabilities	146
6.1	Implementing strategic change	153
6.2	Strategic subsystems	155
6.3	Designing innovative organizations	160
6.4	The manager's roles	166
7.1	Stakeholder map of a very large organization	189

TABLES

3.1   Return on investment, by strategic position   67
3.2   Importance of strategic tools   82
3.3   Policies to achieve business success   84
4.1   Ranking of business goals: US and Japanese managers   113
4.2   Business objectives in the United Kingdom   114

EXHIBITS

1.1	Mission statements	11
1.2	Strategy	17
2.1	Could BT's number be up in fixed-line telephony?	21
2.2	*Déjà vu*: making the future feel familiar	24
2.3	Structural analysis of the UK carbonated soft drinks industry	29
2.4	Competitive standing of major grocery chains in relation to changing consumer profiles	33
2.5	Bad news: competition in a contracting market	36
2.6	Strategic food retailing groups in the United Kingdom	39
2.7	SWOT analysis of Safeway	48
3.1	Wal-mart: driving costs down to deliver superior value for customers	54
3.2	Cost leadership backfiring	57
3.3	Slater Menswear: is being upstairs a sensible strategic position?	60
3.4	Is Sainsbury's (terminally) 'stuck in the middle'?	65
3.5	Retaining market share by 'saving' customers at British Telecom	73
3.6	Razor-edged innovation: Gillette rewrites the rules of competition	76
3.7	The battle for supremacy in the PC industry	78
4.1	The internationalization of retailing	89
4.2	Diversifying the 'easy' way	94
4.3	Virgin territory	95
4.4	Unipart reborn	107
4.5	Whatever happened to retail conglomerates?	108
4.6	Value Based Management	114
4.7	McDonald's: time to return capital to shareholders?	117
5.1	Changing the culture of ICI	126
5.2	Canon parenting advantage statement	149
6.1	Leaders in action (I) Jan Carlzon and SAS	171
6.2	Leaders in action (II) Sir John Harvey-Jones: making it happen	172
7.1	What is David Beckham best at?	180

PREFACE

This book follows on from our previous book, *The Strategic Management Blueprint*, also published by Blackwell. It aims to provide a user-friendly introduction to the complexities of strategic management, analysing the key issue managers need to consider in taking strategic decisions – the relationship between the firm and its environment, choice of strategic direction, the importance of issues of organization for successful strategy, leadership and the management of strategic change, the current debate about the centrality of the concept of core competence to competitive advantage.

We have aimed to write a self-contained course, focusing upon current issues and techniques. We complement the focus on strategy theory with a wide variety of practical examples and we finish the book with a range of cases to illustrate the dynamics of strategy. We offer a model of strategy that we think has stood the test of time, both conceptually and in practical application.

We have directed our attention at issues and cases which we feel are of direct relevance to the day-to-day practice of strategy, and so of real use to managers, while grounding this in the consideration of strategy theory. We aim to encourage managers' and students' critical skills and to provide them with a synthesis of the key ideas in the field.

This should be a book that is accessible to the practising manager, involved in strategy, or who wants to know more about it. It should also be of use to a range of different student groups, undergraduate and postgraduate, MBAs and others. The book is also suitable for short courses in strategic management. Its use of concepts and cases should appeal to all those who are intrigued by the world of top management and by what we know of good strategic management principles.

We are grateful to those who have helped us develop our own thinking about strategy and have acted as guinea pigs for the ideas that appear in the following pages. We are grateful to the strategy experts, theorists, managers and consultants, with whom we have discussed and fine-tuned our ideas. Finally, we would like to thank all those at Blackwell Publishing who have helped us in the arduous process of bringing the text from concept to printed page, and, in particular, to Rosemary Nixon who has been an advocate for the project.

CHAPTER 1

INTRODUCTION: WHAT IS STRATEGIC MANAGEMENT?

What is Strategy?

The term 'strategy' proliferates in discussions of business. Scholars and consultants have provided myriad models and frameworks for analysing strategic choice (Hambrick and Fredrickson, 2001). For us, the key issue that should unite all discussion of strategy is a clear sense of an organization's objectives and a sense of how it will achieve these objectives. It is also important that the organization has a clear sense of its distinctiveness. For the leading strategy guru, Michael Porter (1996), strategy is about achieving competitive advantage through being different – delivering a unique value added to the customer, having a clear and enactable view of how to position yourself uniquely in your industry, for example, in the ways in which Southwest Airlines positions itself in the airline industry and IKEA in furniture retailing, in the way that Marks & Spencer used to. To enact a successful strategy requires that there is fit among a company's activities, that they complement each other, and that they deliver value to the firm and its customers. The three companies we have just mentioned illustrate that industries are fluid and that success is not guaranteed. Two of the firms came to prominence by taking on industry incumbents and developing new value propositions. The third was extremely successful and lost this position. While there is much debate on substance, there is agreement that strategy is concerned with the match between a company's capabilities and its external environment. Analysts disagree on how this may be done. John Kay (2000) argues that strategy is no longer about planning or 'visioning' – because we are deluded if we think we can predict or, worse, control the future – it is about using careful analysis to understand and influence a company's position in the market place. Another leading strategy guru, Gary Hamel (2000), argues that the best strategy is geared towards radical change and creating a new vision of the future in which you are a leader rather than a follower of trends set by others. According to Hamel, *winning strategy = foresight + vision.*

Two Approaches to Strategy

The idea of strategy has received increasing attention in the management literature. The literature on strategy is now voluminous and strategic management texts grow ever larger to include all the relevant material. In this book our aim is not to cover the whole area of strategy – that would require yet another mammoth tome – but to present a clear, logical and succinct approach to the subject that will be of use to the practising manager. We do not attempt a summary of the field, rather we present what we see as a useful framework for analysing strategic problems based on our own experience of teaching the subject on a variety of courses and to a variety of audiences over the years. Our premise is that a firm needs a well defined sense of its mission, its unique place in its environment and scope and direction of growth. Such a sense of mission defines the firm's strategy. A firm also needs an approach to management itself that will harness the internal energies of the organization to the realization of its mission.

Historically, views of strategy fall into two camps. There are those who equate strategy with planning. According to this perspective, information is gathered, sifted and analysed, forecasts are made, senior managers reflect upon the work of the planning department and decide what is the best course for the organization. This is a top-down approach to strategy. Others have a less structured view of strategy as being more about the process of management. According to this second perspective, the key strategic issue is to put in place a system of management that will facilitate the capability of the organization to respond to an environment that is essentially unknowable, unpredictable and, therefore, not amenable to a planning approach. We will consider both these views in this text. Our own view is that good strategic management actually encompasses elements of each perspective.

There is no one best way of strategy. The planning approach can work in a stable, predictable environment. Its critics argue that such environments are becoming increasingly scarce, events make the plan redundant, creativity is buried beneath the weight and protocols of planning and communication rules. Furthermore, those not involved in devising the plan are never committed to its implementation. The second approach emphasizes speed of reaction and flexibility to enable the organization to function best in an environment that is fast-changing and essentially unpredictable. The essence of strategy, according to this view, is adaptability and incrementalism. This approach has been criticized for failing to give an adequate sense of where the organization is going and what its mission is. Critics speak disparagingly of the 'mushroom' approach to management. (Place in a dark room, shovel manure/money on the seeds, close the door, wait for it to grow!)

Elements of Strategy

Definitions of strategy have their roots in military strategy, which defines itself in terms of drafting the plan of war, shaping individual campaigns and, within these, deciding on individual engagements (battles/skirmishes) with the enemy. Strategy in this military sense is the art of war, or, more precisely, the art of the general – the key decision maker. The analogy with business is that business too is on a war footing as competition becomes more and more fierce and survival more problematic. Companies and armies have much in common. They both, for example, pursue strategies of deterrence, offence, defence and alliance. One can think of a well developed business strategy in terms of probing opponents' weaknesses; withdrawing to consider how to act, given the knowledge of the opposition generated by such probing; forcing opponents to stretch their resources; concentrating one's own resources to attack an opponent's exposed position; overwhelming selected markets or market segments; establishing a leadership position of dominance in certain markets; then regrouping one's resources, deciding where to make the next thrust; then expanding from the base thus created to dominate a broader area.

Strategic thinking has been much influenced by military thinking about 'the strategy hierarchy' of goals, policies and programmes. Strategy itself sets the agenda for future action, strategic goals state what is to be achieved and when (but not how), policies set the guidelines and limits for permissible action in pursuit of the strategic goals, and programmes specify the step-by-step sequence of actions necessary to achieve major objectives and the timetable against which progress can be measured. A well defined strategy integrates an organization's major plans, objectives, policies and programmes and commitments into a cohesive whole. It marshals and allocates limited resources in the best way, which is defined by an analysis of a firm's unique strengths and weaknesses and of opportunities and threats in the environment. It considers how to deal with the potential actions of intelligent opponents.

Management is defined both in terms of its function as those activities that serve to ensure that the basic objectives of the enterprise, as set by the strategy, are achieved, and as a group of senior employees responsible for performing this function. Our working definition of strategic management is as follows: all that is necessary to position the firm a way that will assure its long-term survival in a competitive environment. A strategy is an organization's way of saying how it creates unique value and thus attracts the custom that is its lifeblood.

To understand the strategy of a particular firm we have to understand, unless we are in a start-up situation, what factors have made the firm what it is today. This involves answering questions such as: How did the organization reach its present state? Why is it producing its particular range of products and services? What kind of products or services does it intend to produce in the future – the same or different, and, if different, how different? If it is thinking of altering its current range, what are the reasons? Strategy usually reflects the thinking of a small group of senior individuals, or even one strong leader, the strategic apex of a company. Why are the people who make up the strategic apex in this position? How do they think? Are there other (more) fertile sources of strategic thinking elsewhere in the organization that could be usefully tapped? If necessary how can one go about learning from the 'collective wit' of the organization, the creative voice that so often remains silent? How are decisions made in the organization? What is its management style – top-down or bottom-up, autocratic or democratic? Why is the organization structured in a particular way? What is the link between strategy and structure?

TASK

Apply these questions to your own organization or to an organization that you know. (We will return to them later!)

Our Model of Strategy

Our working model of the strategic management process is set out in figure 1.1. This is a model that works for us in terms of organizing our thinking about strategy and our attempts to understand the strategic issues facing particular firms. We do not suggest that it is the only model that is useful or that this is the best. (We just think it is!) Hopefully, in the course of your reading of this book, and other work on the subject, you will be critically analysing the various models suggested

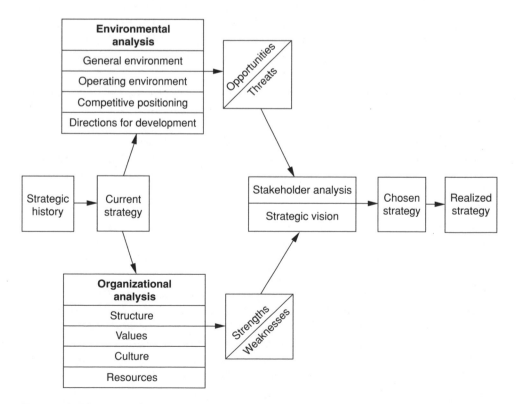

Figure 1.1 The strategic management process

and the concepts upon which they rest. You may come to this text with your own model, developed out of your own experience. We suggest that you try working with our model and examine the extent to which it complements or contradicts your own and others. The result of such a critical appraisal will be a model with which you are comfortable and find useful in practice. If you feel that the model you develop is far superior to our own, please tell us about it! Remember, there is no one best answer in strategic management. If a firm chooses a particular strategic direction and it works in the way that very successful firms like IBM or, on a smaller scale, Body Shop have, the fact that it is successful does not mean that the choice of strategy was optimal, that it was the best. Another strategic decision might have led to even greater success. Conversely, if a firm makes a choice that leads to disaster, this does not necessarily mean that it could have made a better choice (though, with better decision making, it hopefully could have done). The environmental conditions in its industry might have been such that this was the best choice, but that no choice, given its size or history, or the power of its competitors, could have changed its fate.

We will now explain our model, which provides the basis of subsequent chapters. *Current strategy* (italics indicate terms in the model) has its roots in the *strategic history* of a firm and its management and employees. We mention both management and employees here because, though in many cases senior management is the source of strategic decisions, it is the employees at the point of production or delivery of a product or service who are responsible for the actual implementation of a strategy. (Of course, in the final analysis it is management who are ultimately responsible for the performance of employees.) *Current strategy* is the result of the interaction of *intended strategy* and *emergent strategy*. The organization's actual strategy (its *realized strategy*) can be the direct result of strategic planning, the deliberate formulation and implementation of a plan. More often it is the outcome of the adaptation of such a plan to *emergent* issues in the environment. In some cases actual strategy can be very different from the strategy as planned or the firm may not have a very clear plan in the first place. In such cases the strategy can be described as *emergent* in the sense that strategy emerges from an ongoing series (sometimes described as a pattern or stream) of decisions.

Managers can decide that they are happy with their current strategy. They can take this decision in two ways. In a proactive sense they can scan their environment and the potential for change within their own organization and decide that to carry on doing what they are doing and what they are good at is the best way to face the future. In a less active, and far less satisfactory, way they can proceed on the basis of tradition – 'This is the way we have always done it. It has worked so far. That's good enough for us' – or inertia. Or management may decide that change is necessary. Again this can come about in a variety of ways. They may scan their environment and decide that there are major changes occurring in their business world to which they have to adapt. Or they might decide, through internal analysis, that they have the ability to develop a new way of doing business that will redefine the nature of the business they are in. Another stimulus to change can be the new manager appointed to a senior position who wants to leave his or her mark on the company and changes strategy primarily for this self-centred reason.

If change is the order of the day, then two issues need to be addressed: *environmental (external) analysis* and *organizational (internal) analysis*. (Remember, this is the ideal way of proceeding. In practice, managers may adopt only a partial solution and analyse only external or internal factors.) For a change of strategy to work there must be alignment between internal capability and external opportunity. This is described as 'strategic fit'. The ideal situation is where there is a fit between the environment, a business need arising out of that environment that is strongly felt by a firm that has the sense of purpose (*mission*) and a management *system* that enables it to respond to this need with a coherent and practicable strategy. The potential to act in this way depends upon managerial judgement, managerial skill to exploit windows of opportunity and management ability to motivate other employees to support and commit themselves to the firm's new strategic objectives.

The analysis of the environment can be segmented into four interactive elements. There is the issue of the firm's *general environment*, the broad environment comprising a mix of general factors such as social and political issues. Then there is the firm's *operating environment*, its more specific industry/business environment. What kind of industry is the firm competing in? What 'forces' make up its 'industry structure'? Having examined its business environment, the issue then arises: how is the firm to compete in its industry? What is to be the unique source of its *competitive positioning* that will give it an edge over its competitors? Will it go for a broad market position, competing on a variety of fronts, or will it look for niches? Will it compete on the basis of cost or on the basis of added value, differentiating its products and charging a premium? What is the range of *options* that managers have to choose from? How are they to prioritize between these options? Does the company have strategic vision, a strong sense of mission, a 'reason for being' that distinguishes it from others? If change is necessary, what is to be the firm's *direction for development*? Having identified the major forces affecting its environment, how is the firm to approach the future?

Organizational analysis can also be thought of as fourfold. How is the firm organized? What is the *structure* of the organization, who reports to whom, how are the tasks defined, divided and integrated? How do the management systems work, the processes that determine how the organization gets things done from day to day – for example, information systems, capital budgeting systems, performance measurement systems, quality systems? What do organizational members believe in, what are they trying to achieve, what motivates them, what do they *value*? What is the *culture* of the organization? What are the basic beliefs of organizational members? Do they have a shared set of beliefs about how to proceed, about where they are going, about how they should behave? We know, thanks to Peters and Waterman's *In Search of Excellence*, that the basic values, assumptions and ideologies (systems of belief) which guide and fashion behaviour in organizations have a crucial role to play in business success (or failure). What *resources* does the organization have at its disposal – for example, capital, technology, people?

Management's role is to try to 'fit' the analysis of externalities and internalities, to balance the organization's *strengths and weaknesses* in the light of environmental *opportunities and threats*. A concept that bridges internal and external analyses is that of *stakeholders*, the key groups whose legitimate interests have to be borne in mind when taking strategic decisions. These can be internal groups, such as managers themselves and employees, or the owners of the firm, shareholders. They can also be external groups: the stock market if it is a quoted company, banks, consumers, the government.

Senior management's task is to try and align the various interest groups in arriving at its *chosen strategy* in the light of the creation of an appropriate *strategic vision* for the organization. Increasingly important here is the issue of corporate responsibility, how the organization defines and acts upon its sense of responsibility to its stakeholders. The broad responsibility to society at large is important here in, for example, such areas as 'green' (ecological) issues. Sometimes the various interest groups may be at odds with each other and management will have to perform a delicate political balancing act between them.

Having chosen a strategy, there is the issue of implementation. Very few schemes go totally (or even approximately) according to plan. The business environment changes, new issues emerge – green ones, for example. Some demand to be taken on board so that in many, perhaps the majority, of cases emergent strategy asserts itself to the extent that the *realized strategy* differs markedly from the chosen/planned strategy. In time, the realized strategy becomes a part of the firm's strategic history . . . and the strategy process continues.

Strategic management in the public sector and the not-for-profit company

Most of what we will say in this book concerns the business firm looking to profit as the source of its survival. We would, however, contend that much of what we say can be applied to the public-sector organization or the not-for-profit firm. Similar principles of internal and external analysis apply.

The Growth Vector

Strategic management involves decisions concerning what a company might do, given the opportunities in its environment; what it can do, given the resources at its disposal; what it wants to do, given the personal values and aspirations of key decision makers; and what it should do, given the ethical and legal context in which it is operating. A firm needs a well defined sense of where it is going in the future and a firm concept of the business it is in. We can think of these in terms of the firm's 'product–market scope' and 'growth vector'. This specifies the particular products or services of the firm and the market(s) it is seeking to serve. A firm's 'growth vector' defines the direction in which the firm is moving with respect to its current product–market scope. The key components of the 'growth vector' are set out in figure 1.2. One qualification is necessary here. The use of the growth

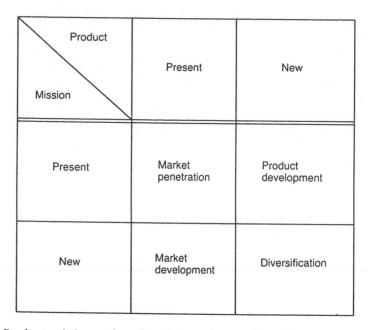

Product Mission	Present	New
Present	Market penetration	Product development
New	Market development	Diversification

Figure 1.2 Product, mission and market choices. *Source*: adapted from Ansoff (1965)

vector assumes that the firm is indeed growing. This is obviously not always the case, and strategic decision making may therefore involve 'downsizing' and with-drawal from some areas of business.

The *growth vector* illustrates the key decisions concerning the directions in which a firm may choose to develop. *Market penetration* comes about when the firm chooses as its strategy to increase its market share for its present product markets. If the firm pursues *product development* it sets out to develop new products to complement or replace its current offerings while staying in the same markets. It retains its current *mission* in the sense of continuing to attempt to satisfy the same or related consumer needs In *market development* the firm searches for new markets with its existing products. If a strategy of *diversification* is chosen, the firm has decided that its product range and market scope are no longer adequate, and it actively seeks to develop new kinds of products for new kinds of markets.

Let us illustrate the growth vector with an example concerning product–market strategy options in retailing. A retailing firm might decide to consolidate its posi-tion in its current markets by going for increased market share, perhaps through increased advertising. It might choose to develop new markets, perhaps expand-ing geographically into other areas, or even overseas, but retaining its current product range. It might choose to develop new retail products but stay in the same line of business – for example, increase its product range in clothing. It might choose to redefine the nature of these products. For example, the running shoe market was radically altered and expanded by redefining running shoes as leisure items, not merely as sports equipment. Finally, the firm might choose to move into

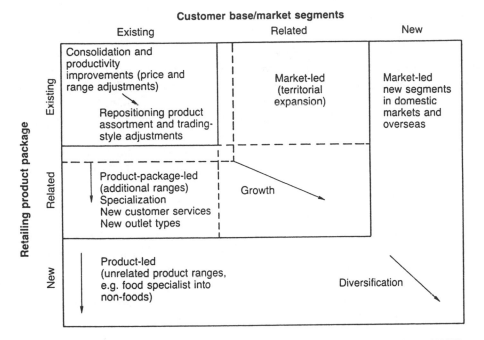

Figure 1.3 Retailing product–market strategy options. *Source*: Knee and Walters (1985)

totally different areas of business, for example, into financial services, as Marks & Spencer has done. The range of product–market strategy options in retailing is illustrated in figure 1.3.

Governing the choice between strategic options should be the notion of *competitive advantage*. The firm has to identify *unique* opportunities for itself in its chosen area(s). It has to identify particular characteristics within its approach to individual product–markets which will give it a strong competitive position. It might go for a large market share that would enable it to dominate particular markets and define the conditions of competition in them, for instance, as regards pricing policy. It might pursue technological dominance, looking for breakthrough products or a new manufacturing technology that would give it a technological edge over the competition, as Pilkington did, for example, with its development of the process for manufacturing float glass, which formed the foundation of the company's subsequent success. It might go for a better quality of product and service. In the automobile industry, Japanese manufacturers have rewritten the rules of the game regarding the quality of products and thus revolutionized consumer expectations. In the process they have made major inroads into Western markets historically dominated by Western firms. Or the firm might choose to combine some of these, as Sainsbury's has done with its 'good food' that 'costs less', an approach combining a low-cost advantage with a quality position in the world of supermarkets.

Mission Statements

The concept of mission has become increasingly fashionable in discussions of strategy. Indeed, some analysts go as far as asserting that a good 'mission statement' can provide an actual worthwhile alternative to the whole task of corporate planning. The definition of a firm's strategic *mission* encapsulated in the mission statement can be thought of as the first stage of the strategy process. Management guru Peter Drucker, the source of much contemporary thinking about the business mission, argues that asking the question 'What is our business?' is the same as asking the question 'What is our mission?' A business is defined by its mission. Only a clear definition of the mission of the organization makes possible clear and realistic business objectives, because the mission defines the purpose of the firm in terms of its enduring sense of its reason for being.

The mission defines the long-term vision of the organization in terms of what it wants to be and whom it wants to serve. A firm's mission should be clear and concise and distinguish it from any other firm. The mission statement has to be backed up with specific objectives and strategies, but these objectives and strategies are far more likely to be acted upon when there is a clear sense of mission informing action. A good mission statement will contain the following:

- the purpose of the organization – a statement of the principal activities of a business or organization;
- its principal business aims – its mission as regards the position it aims to achieve in its chosen business;
- the key beliefs and values of the company;
- definitions of who are the major stakeholders in the business;
- the guiding principles that define the code of conduct that tells employees how to behave.

Drucker illustrates the importance of a sense of mission with his story of three people working on a building site. All three were doing the same job but when asked what their job was gave very different answers. One answered, 'Breaking rocks,' another answered, 'Earning a living,' the third answered. 'Helping to build a cathedral.' There is a similar story told about three climbers. When asked what they were doing, one answered, 'Pitching camp,' the second answered, 'Collecting material for a film,' the third answered, 'Climbing Everest.' There are no prizes for deciding who was most committed to his/her task and who would be most motivated to perform to the best of his/her ability.

Drucker himself highlights the need to link a sense of mission with clear, achievable objectives. He makes the point when analysing the early success of Marks & Spencer:

> Marks & Spencer redefined its business as the subversion of the class structure of nineteenth-century England by making available to the working and lower middle classes upper-class goods of better than upper-class quality, and yet at prices the working

and lower middle-class customer could well afford. . . . What made Marks & Spencer unique and successful . . . was its conversion of the definition of 'what our business is, and should be' into clear, specific, operationally effective and multiple objectives. (Drucker, 1974: 96)

In the twentieth-century computer industry Apple set as its mission 'To make a contribution to the world by making tools for the mind that advance humankind'. Thornton's, a UK premium chocolate manufacturer and retailer, talks about itself in this way: 'Our aim is to *delight* our customers with *exceptional* products and *caring* service. Our goal is to be *widely* recognized as the *best specialist retailer* and *manufacturer* of quality confectionery.' Tesco, a major UK supermarket chain, has talked about its mission with a similar stress on service and the customer: 'The strategy is to make our stores, our products and our people the very best in the business in the opinion of our customers.' Other companies have a different emphasis. Levi Strauss, for example, talks about its aspirations in terms of the kind of company it wants to create for its employees: 'we want satisfaction from accomplishments and friendships, balanced personal and professional lives, and to have fun with our endeavors'.

Missions can be extremely visionary and challenging. For example, during its heyday Body Shop proclaimed the following in its annual report: 'Make compassion, care, harmony and trust the foundation stones of business. Fall in love with new ideas.'

QUESTION

1 Do you agree with the view expressed in exhibit 1.1?

EXHIBIT 1.1 MISSION STATEMENTS

A study of mission statements in the United States argued that every organization should have one to motivate its employees. It claimed that firms with clear motivating mission statements were likely to perform better than those without. Classic mission statements cited include the Peter Drucker example of the men on the cathedral building site, President Kennedy's 'Put a man on the moon,' Canon's 'Beat Xerox' and Komatsu's 'Encircle Caterpillar.' The trouble is that most mission statements tend to provoke cynicism and confusion rather than clarity and commitment by trying to combine statements of objectives with statements of values.

Source: adapted from *Financial Times*, 3 April 1989.

Ford Motor Company

Figure 1.4 contains the mission statement of a leading multinational company, the Ford Motor Company. Examine this statement and ask yourself the following questions:

1 Do you find it a satisfying statement of the company's mission?
2 Is there anything in the statement that you would wish to criticize?
3 Would you alter the statement in any way, either taking something out or adding more information to it?
4 What is the purpose of the mission statement for Ford?
5 Is it likely to fulfil this purpose?
6 The mission statement was devised by Ford in America. Is the very idea of a mission statement somehow inappropriate for the British context? Do the more reticent British, for example, feel uncomfortable with this kind of 'up-front' approach? Or is it equally useful in the United Kingdom and Europe? If you think it inappropriate, is there an alternative?
7 What would be an appropriate mission statement for your own firm or organization?
8 How are mission statements likely to differ in small and large firms?

There are four approaches to setting a mission (Collins and Porras, 1991):

- *Targeting.* Setting a clear, definable target for the organization to aim at, such as the moon (the NASA moon mission statement!), financial/growth targets or standards of excellence in product markets.
- *Focusing on a common enemy.* Defeat of the common enemy guides strategic choice, e.g. Pepsi's 'Beat Coke', Honda's 'Crush, squash, slaughter' Yamaha, Nike's attack on Adidas. Honda was so successful in its mission that Yamaha actually made a public apology for its claim that it would defeat Honda.
- *Role modelling.* Sometimes used by smaller companies that model themselves on dominant players in their industry. In the computer industry IBM and Apple have provided – at least, until recently – very different kinds of models.
- *Internal transformation.* Used by older organizations faced with the need for radical change. This kind of mission has as its starting point the admission that its current mission is out of tune with the new realities it is facing.

QUESTION

1 Which kind of mission do you think is best? Why?

Mission

Ford Motor Company is a worldwide leader in automotive and automotive-related products and services as well as in new industries such as aerospace, communications, and financial services. Our mission is to improve continually our products and services to meet our customers' needs, allowing us to prosper as a business and to provide a reasonable return for our stockholders, the owners of our business.

Values

How we accomplish our mission is as important as the mission itself. Fundamental to success for the Company are these basic values:

People – Our people are the source of our strength. They provide our corporate intelligence and determine our reputation and vitality. Involvement and teamwork are our core human values.

Products – Our products are the end result of our efforts, and they should be the best in serving customers worldwide. As our products are viewed, so are we viewed.

Profits – Profits are the ultimate measure of how efficiently we provide customers with the best products for their needs. Profits are required to survive and grow.

Guiding Principles

Quality comes first – To achieve customer satisfaction, the quality of our products and services must be our number one priority.

Customers are the focus of everything we do – Our work must be done with our customers in mind, providing better products and services than our competition.

Continuous improvement is essential to our success – We must strive for excellence in everything we do: in our products, in their safety and value – and in our services, our human relations, our competitiveness, and our profitability.

Employee involvement is our way of life – We are a team. We must treat each other with trust and respect.

Dealers and suppliers are our partners – The Company must maintain mutually beneficial relationships with dealers, suppliers, and our other business associates.

Integrity is never compromised – The conduct of our Company worldwide must be pursued in a manner that is socially responsible and commands respect for its integrity and for its positive contributions to society. Our doors are open to men and women alike without discrimination and without regard to ethnic origin or personal beliefs.

Figure 1.4 Ford Motor Company's statement of mission, values and guiding principles

The recent emphasis in strategy upon a sense of mission demonstrates the need companies feel to clarify their purpose and their values. In the large complex organization a sense of mission can serve as unifying factor. The mission tells employees what the company is about. It can also serve to give other stakeholders a sense that the company is clear about what it is doing and where it is going. The danger with missions is that they can come to be seen as empty rhetoric if senior management does not live according to their principles.

As the Ford case illustrates, strategy links with values when we consider mission. Public and private-sector organizations are likely to think of these differently.

Queen's Medical Centre, Nottingham, one of the United Kingdom's biggest providers of hospital-based medical services, defines its strategic aims in the following way:

- Provide quality services designed around the patient.
- Provide an environment in which the health care professional of tomorrow can be trained.
- Be knowledge organizations by promoting and investing in research and information.
- Be effective and supportive organizations for those working in both hospitals.
- Use our resources wisely.

Values support the achievement of these aims because 'values . . . drive the way we work and deliver care'. Queen's Medical Centre values include: care and service, striving for continuous improvement and supporting staff in delivering high-quality services and achieving a balance between their work and home lives.

CRITICAL VOICES

1 Some critics argue that the emphasis upon mission is misplaced, that mission statements are often more rhetoric than substance. Do you agree?

2 If a sense of mission is not the best way to give an organization a sense of direction, what is?

Identity

Mission and values are increasingly recognized as reflecting the identity of an organization – its central, enduring and distinctive character, and that which makes it unique. There is evidence that those organizations that do survive and prosper over the longer term do have a clear sense of identity, although they are also skilful enough to know when an existing identity needs to change as a result of major changes in the environment. For example, US railroads needed to recognize that the future was perilous if they clung to the identity of a railroad company. They could perhaps have coped better with a changing environment if they had refashioned themselves as a transport businesses, competing with the roads and the airlines. Such a change might have required major change, for new transport technologies might well have rendered their railroad identity obsolete. Firms can change too slowly and become increasingly vulnerable to change or lose out on major opportunities. Xerox is a case in point. It had all the knowledge and technical skills to become a major player in the computer industry but failed miserably (see chapter 8) because it could not see a way beyond its identity as a copier company. Other firms struggle to create a new identity at times of change. The Boots

Company, a major UK retailer, has struggled for a number of years to rethink its identity (see chapter 8).

Theory of the Business

In an influential *Harvard Business Review* article Peter Drucker argues that every organization has a 'theory of the business' (Drucker, 1994). When this theory fits the external reality, is internally coherent, and known and understood by everyone in the organization, then success follows – for example, in IBM in the 1950s, 1960s and 1970s; General Motors until the 1970s; Marks & Spencer until the mid-1990s. When external reality changes and the business model is taken for granted, then crisis and possibly failure ensue. Personal computers changed the driving force from hardware to software; lean manufacturing changed the economics of long runs, and the market for clothes became more of a lifestyle issue. In these situations adopting management recipes such as Total Quality Management, benchmarking, re-engineering and other management fads are not enough: the organization has to go back to re-examine its theory of the business.

Drucker argues that the theory of the business has three parts. While assumptions about the environment define what an organization is paid for, and assumptions about core competences define where an organization must excel, the assumptions about the specific mission 'define what an organization considers to be meaningful results; in other words they point to how it envisions itself making a difference in the economy and society at large'. This fits well with our model of strategy and with the resource-based view of the firm (see chapter 7).

This argument is taken up by Campbell and Gould (1994), who argue that 'people are more motivated and work more intelligently if they believe in what they are doing and trust the organization they are working with'. They acknowledge that motivation and commitment can also come from 'clear strategy, from the excitement of achievement, from the honour of being the best and the thrill of winning'. But strategy alone is not enough. It needs to be nested in a clear sense of mission and, in Drucker's terms, a viable and compelling theory of the firm.

Goold and Campbell define mission broadly as comprising:

- *a purpose*: some explanation of why the organization exists;
- *a strategy*: defining relevant product markets and the firm's positioning in them;
- *a set of values*: the beliefs that underpin the organization's management style, its relation to employees and other stakeholders and its ethics;
- *standards and behaviours*: a summary of some of the most important standards and behaviours in the organization.

This leaves top management with two main tasks in relation to mission:

- the intellectual task of defining purpose, developing strategies and values that reinforce each other and identifying the standards and behaviour that are the expression of the mission;

- a communication and management task of making the sense of mission come alive in the organization.

This is a theme we return to in chapter 6 when we consider Collins and Porras's work on organizations that were built to last. An enduring company's centre consists of core values ('the organization's essential and enduring tenets') and purpose ('the organization's fundamental reasons for existence beyond just making money').

Strategy Evaluation

Strategy can be neither formulated nor adjusted to changing circumstances without a process of strategy evaluation. Whether performed by an individual or as part of an organizational review procedure, strategy evaluation forms an essential step in the process of guiding an enterprise.

For many executives strategy evaluation is simply an appraisal of how well a business performs. Has it grown? Is the profit rate normal? If the answers to these questions are affirmative, it is argued that the firm's strategy must be sound. Despite its unassailable simplicity, this line of reasoning misses the whole point of strategy – that the critical factors determining the quality of current results are often not directly observable or simply measured, and that by the time strategic opportunities or threats do directly affect operating results it may well be too late for an effective response. Thus strategy evaluation is an attempt to look beyond the obvious facts regarding the short-term health of a business and appraise instead those more fundamental factors and trends that govern success in the chosen field of endeavour.

A strategy is a set of objectives, policies and plans that, taken together, define the scope of the enterprise and its approach to business. Rumelt suggests that three questions are central to the challenge of strategy evaluation:

1 Are the objectives of the business appropriate?
2 Are the major policies and plans appropriate?
3 Do the results obtained to date confirm or refute critical assumptions on which the strategy rests?

He further suggests that strategy must satisfy four broad criteria:

- *Consistency*. The strategy must not present mutually inconsistent goals and policies.
- *Consonance*. The strategy must represent an adaptive response to the external environment and to the critical changes occurring within it.
- *Advantage*. Strategy must provide for the creation and/or maintenance of a competitive advantage in the selected area of activity.
- *Feasibility*. The strategy must neither overtax available resources nor create insoluble problems.

EXHIBIT 1.2 STRATEGY

Inconsistency in strategy is not simply a flaw in logic. A key function of strategy is to provide coherence to organizational action. A clear and explicit concept of strategy can foster a climate of tacit co-ordination that is more efficient than most administrative mechanisms. Many high-technology firms, for example, face a basic strategic choice between offering high-cost products with high custom-engineering content and lower-cost products that are more standardized and sold at higher volume. If senior management does not enunciate a clear, consistent sense of where the corporation stands on these issues, there will be continuing conflict between sales, design, engineering and manufacturing people. A clear, consistent strategy, by contrast, allows a sales engineer to negotiate a contract with a minimum of co-ordination – the trade-offs are an explicit part of the firm's posture.

Source: Rumelt (1988).

A strategy must be evaluated against each of these criteria; if it fails to meet one or more of them, the strategy is flawed. We will have more to say about strategy evaluation in the chapters that follow.

The Book in Brief

Overall, the chapters that follow provide a brief history of the evolution of thinking about strategy. In chapters 2–4 we address the microeconomic aspects of strategic analysis, focusing on the structure of the firm's business environment, its internal resources and the range of strategic options open to it. In chapters 4–5 we turn to the management process aspects of strategy, looking first of all at organizational issues such as structure and culture, then the management of strategic change. In chapter 7 we focus on current major debates in strategy – core competence and management; chapter 8 consists of ten case studies which you may like to read first.

As in chapter 1, the following chapters are interspersed with examples, cases (historical and current) and questions. There is no 'one best way' of strategy. There is, therefore, no one right answer to the questions posed. Strategic management means coping with complexity and ambiguity. The examples, illustrations and questions are meant to foster critical thought on the issues under discussion and to help you reflect critically on your own experience of strategy in action. Hopefully, you will finish the book a little closer to a 'model' of strategic management, a way of thinking about strategy with which you personally feel comfortable, and able to discuss with others engaged in the same difficult but crucially important task of improving their understanding of strategic issues facing their businesses.

CHAPTER 2

SITUATION ANALYSIS: THE FIRM AND ITS ENVIRONMENT

Situation analysis is concerned with identifying the position of the firm in respect of the business environment it operates in and how well its resources and capabilities meet the demands of that business environment. Such analysis forms part of the background to which strategic decisions are made and provides insight into the difficulties of implementing strategic change. This chapter presents techniques for determining the firm's position in the environment. Applying these to one's own situation can help in identifying potential opportunities and threats facing the organization based on its strengths and weaknesses.

What do we mean by 'Environment'?

Figure 2.1 illustrates the organization in the context of various levels of its environment. The diagram represents the position of the organization relative to its external and internal environments – the greater the distance from the organization, the less direct effect there is on it. At the extreme the general environment concerns factors that not only affect the organization and its industry, but also the general business sector. More closely related to the organization is the competitive environment, which is concerned with issues like the position of suppliers, buyers and direct rivals. At the centre of the diagram we see the internal environment with organization-specific factors.

While figure 2.1 illustrates the degree to which different environmental factors affect the organization, conversely it also gives some indication of the extent to which the organization can affect (even manipulate) the environment by its behaviour and strategy. The environment should not simply be viewed as given (i.e. exogenous). Rather the organization may be in a position deliberately to change the environment to its benefit – particularly the internal and the competitive environment.

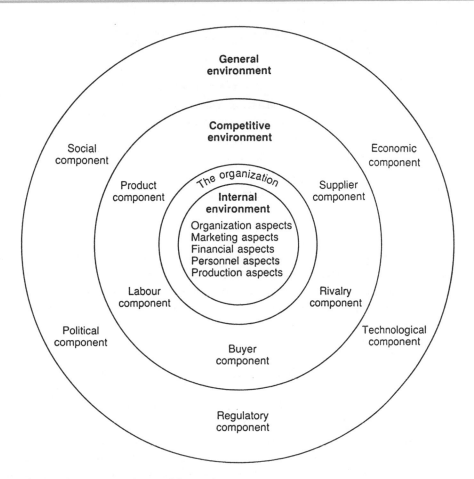

Figure 2.1 The organization and its environment

How does one Analyse the Environment?

Figure 2.2 presents a six-step procedure for analysing the external and internal environment to identify the firm's strategic position (or standing):

1 Undertake a general audit of environmental influences; the aim is to identify which of the many different sorts of general environmental factors have influenced the past performance and development of the organization along with some consideration as to which will in the future.
2 Consider the nature of the organization's environment in terms of how uncertain it is. Is it (a) static/simple, (b) dynamic or (c) complex?
3 Undertake a structural analysis to identify the key forces operating in the competitive environment.
4 Analyse the organization's position relative to its competitors (either for resources or customers).

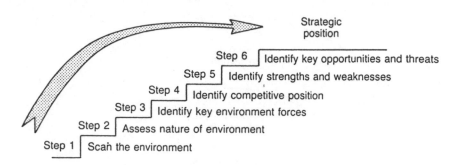

Figure 2.2 Situation analysis

5 Consider the internal environment with the aim of identifying the strengths and weaknesses of the organization.
6 Undertake SWOT (Strengths, Weaknesses, Opportunities and Threats) analysis where the understanding of the external environment (steps 1–4) is specifically related to the organization and its internal environment (step 5). This analysis is intended to identify opportunities and/or threats facing the organization and suggest how well positioned it is to meet these developments.

Scanning the General Environment

The first step is to undertake a general audit of environmental influences affecting the organization. This involves the strategist 'sensing the environment', trying to get a general feel for which environmental forces are currently or in the future going to be more or less important to the organization. This process should be on-going and give initial indication of changes in the environment that may signal the need for changes in strategy. The process can throw up opportunities and warn of threats. Obviously different organizations will face different key forces. The intention is to consider how environmental forces affect the organization, and give some initial thought to how the firm might try to use these forces. The audit requires two related questions to be addressed:

- What factors in the general (wider) environment are affecting the firm?
- Which of these are the most important either at present or in the future?

Each set of environmental factors should be considered in turn. The following list may be useful as a checklist for identifying key forces:

1 *Economic* factors: (a) disposable income, (b) interest rates, (c) exchange rates, (d) business cycles, (e) economy growth rates, (f) unemployment levels, (g) energy and basic raw material prices.
2 *Technological* factors: (a) new discoveries/developments in own or related (e.g. supplier) industry, (b) speed of technology transfer (diffusion), (c) government spending on research, (d) rates of obsolescence.

3 *Legal* factors: (a) employment law, (b) competition legislation, (c) environmental protection laws, (d) foreign trade regulations, (e) planning regulations.

4 *Political* factors: (a) government stability, (b) taxation policy, (c) government spending, (d) government relations with other countries, (e) industrial policy (e.g. towards privatization and regulation).

5 *Social and cultural* factors: (a) population demographics, (b) income distribution, (c) levels of education, (d) lifestyle changes, (e) attitudes to work and leisure, (f) consumerism, (g) social mobility.

Initially the scope should be broad. Once key changes have been identified, more detailed analysis should follow to determine the importance of the factor.

Developments in the broad environment cannot be underestimated in regard to the impact they can have on competition in an industry. As an illustration of this, exhibit 2.1 shows how a technological development combined with a move by an industry regulator offers the potential for a sudden shift in the nature and intensity of competition. In this case BT appears relatively secure in its position as the dominant player in fixed-line telephony in the United Kingdom. However, new developments pose a substantial challenge to this position as rivals gear themselves up for an onslaught on BT's dominant position.

EXHIBIT 2.1 COULD BT'S NUMBER BE UP IN FIXED-LINE TELEPHONY?

Twenty years after competition was introduced into the UK telecommunications industry, British Telecom still commands 73 per cent of the £8 billion residential telecoms market. However, all that could be about to change as new entrants take advantage of a technical innovation that makes it simple to switch telecom supplier. Customers will no longer need to dial a prefix number or install an auto-dialler box to make cheaper calls. The new 'carrier pre-selection' (CPS) services require BT to connect calls to cheaper firms automatically.

According to the industry regulator OfTel, about 1.1 million customers had already switched to the cheaper services by May 2003 – but this is still a small number compared with the 18.6 m residential customers controlled by BT. Many of the customers that have already switched have moved to services offered by other telecoms companies such as Centrica (owner of One.tel and British Gas Communications) and mobile handset retailers like Phones 4U and Carphone Warehouse. However, the UK's two largest supermarket retailers have announced their intention to enter the fray – proposing to offer cut-price phone services that will cut home phone bills by 30 per cent. Both will enter with joint ventures – in Sainsbury's case with Carphone Warehouse and in Tesco's case with Cable & Wireless. In addition it appears that other utility, financial services and technology companies are planning to enter the CPS market.

In the past, most of BT's rivals have concentrated their efforts on the business market, where the savings they could offer customers were much larger, in line with the larger company phone bills. Residential competition has been led by the cable television companies, principally Telewest and NTL. However, their growth has stalled. Initially fragmented, they developed a poor reputation for customer service and, in recent years, have been distracted by the financial problems caused by debt and over-expansion.

Cheap deals have also been available, particularly on international and mobile calls, from 'resellers' such as One.tel and Swiftcall, which buy wholesale capacity from BT and other network operators. However, to access these services customers need to dial a prefix number or install an auto-dialler. This has posed a sufficient obstacle to deter many potential customers. The associated hassle, along with consumer ignorance of the potential cost savings, has thus far limited the success of resellers. However, with the introduction of hassle-free CPS services and intense marketing effort by some of the best known companies in the United Kingdom, all could be about to change. BT's number may be up. It faces the choice of maintaining its price structure but losing market share or cutting prices to keep market share but in the process losing revenue. Either way its profits from the traditional residential market look set to fall. But it still has opportunities to expand other services to consumers, notably through rolling out its broadband high-speed Internet services and wi-fi services (high-speed wireless technology for laptop users), and thereby keep one step ahead of the chasing pack.

Source: 'Battle lines', *Sunday Times*, 11 May 2003.

EXERCISE

Identify the key forces in your organization's general environment. Which set of factors do you consider to be most influential (a) at present (b) in five years' time?

The Nature of the Environment

Since strategic decisions are made in situations of uncertainty, the strategist must attempt to understand the nature of the environment facing the organization. By reducing the many environmental influences to a coherent pattern, strategic analysis aids understanding of the nature of uncertainty and provides guidance as to which methods are most appropriate for monitoring and evaluating strategic options.

The more dynamic (rapidly changing) or complex the environmental conditions are, the more uncertainty increases. Modern organizations are increasingly finding that they are facing both a dynamic and highly complex environment. Complexity comes in different forms. First, it can result from the sheer diversity of environmental influences faced by an organization (e.g. multinationals). Second, it can arise because of the amount of knowledge required to handle environmental influences. Third, it can be due to the different environmental influences which are, in themselves, interconnected (e.g. economic factors affecting and in turn being affected by technological, socio-cultural and political changes – particularly a problem for multinationals operating in the pharmaceutical, electronic, computer or automobile industries).

Lowest uncertainty exists where the conditions are static and simple (e.g. raw material suppliers or in a traditional trade or profession, say a blacksmith or solicitor). Here technical progress is straightforward, competition may be limited and markets may operate the same over time. In these circumstances if change occurs it is likely to be fairly predictable.

Different methods are required for handling each type of environment.

Simple/static environment

Here the past acts as a good predictor of the future and thus environmental scanning is likely to be a more continuous and systematic exercise than in more dynamic situations where it is more intermittent. In a fairly static and simple situation it makes sense to undertake a detailed analysis of past environmental influences and use (quantitative) forecasting techniques to predict changes (with reasonable certainty).

Dynamic environment

The more the situation becomes dynamic, the less that can be learned from past circumstances, and therefore the focus should switch to considering the future and use of judgemental forecasting methods involving scenario planning. Here, the strategist constructs 'alternative futures', which consider the likely behaviour of suppliers, competitors and consumers so that an overall picture of possible competitive environments can be built up. Strategic analysis can then be undertaken on each of the scenarios, with different strategies developed for the different possible futures. Monitoring of the environment then provides the insight into which of the scenarios is likely to be most appropriate. However, a common problem with scenario (contingency) planning is escaping myopic perceptions – it is often difficult to conceive of scenarios and responses markedly different from familiar ones. The challenge is 'thinking the unthinkable' – identifying different possibilities in the environment and considering strategic responses.

Scenario planning is essentially a qualitative approach. It should involve detailed planning for at least three situations:

- the worst-case scenario (environment turns very unfriendly);
- the best-case scenario (where the operating and general environments are extremely favourable);
- the most likely case scenario (between the two extremes).

The analysis should show how the organization would respond to each scenario and formalize this in terms of *contingency plans* (see exhibit 2.2). The organization must regularly scan the environment, checking for signals that suggest the onset of a particular scenario. This monitoring acts as an early warning device so that the appropriate strategies can be implemented in good time.

Complex environment

In a complex environment the aim is simply to reduce the complexity! At the organizational level this may involve divisionalization when diversity is a problem, enabling each division/department to focus on its own environment. Structural analysis can involve sophisticated techniques such as model building and simulation. These techniques focus directly on the key influences and attempt to model the relations between them, with the aim of simulating the effects on an organization of different environmental conditions.

EXHIBIT 2.2 *DÉJÀ VU*: MAKING THE FUTURE FEEL FAMILIAR

In today's global and fast-changing environment, extrapolating from historical performance using medium and long-term forecasting techniques has not proved very reliable. Companies are increasingly replacing forecasts with a range of scenarios against which to test their plans for the future. One of the earliest converts was Royal Dutch Shell, one of the world's most profitable companies.

Traditionally, Shell planners would forecast refining plant requirements for several years ahead by extrapolating from current demand. However, the volatility in the oil market makes accurate prediction difficult. The diagram shows how Shell underestimated oil demand in the 1950s and 1960s, and overestimated it in the 1970s. Rather than relying on a single projection, Shell now develops a range of possible scenarios for managers to explore and imagine how they might act in

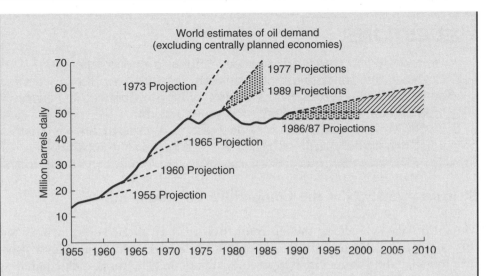

World estimates of oil demand
(excluding centrally planned economies)

differing conditions, so that when the future comes it 'feels' familiar. Forecasting is still used, but only to suggest possible scenarios – as seen in the 1980s projections.

According to Kees van der Heijden (1996), a former Shell planner, the benefits of scenario planning for Shell have been more robust strategic decisions, better thinking about the future, enhancing corporate perception of events as an emerging pattern, improving communication throughout the company, and as a means to provide decision making and leadership for the organization.

At a practical level, it is claimed that scenario planning has helped Shell to respond more quickly and effectively to major events and crises because of its prior examination of such situations, or at least similar ones, in respect of scenario analysis. According to Adam Kahane, former head of socio-political economic and technological planning for Shell International, 'scenarios alert you to what was previously invisible'. In his view this is very important, since 'the ability to learn faster than your competitors may be a company's only sustainable competitive advantage'. As an example, he cites how Shell's scenario analysis aided its strategic decision making in response to the Gulf War in 1990, when the oil market was exceptionally volatile. When the war came, according to Mr Kahane, there was little effect on Shell: 'None of our scenarios had involved such a violent clash, but we had considered a situation in which there was a serious disruption to oil supplies in the Gulf. Whether this came by war, or accident, or by religious fundamentalism, did not really matter to us, as the net effect is the same.'

Sources: Van der Heijden (1996); 'Scenarios make the future feel familiar', *Independent on Sunday*, 24 March 1991.

> ## *QUESTIONS*
>
> 1 How would you categorize your organization's environment?
> 2 Consider the conditions that (plausibly) describe your firm's worst-case scenario and best-case scenario. What probability do you assign to likelihood of them arising? (Are you worried?)
> 3 If your organization is one that operates in a complex environment, what measures would you propose to reduce this complexity?

Structural Analysis of the Competitive Environment

The third stage in analysing the environment is to place all the key influences and their degree of relevance within a framework of analysis which provides a structure to gauge the nature and intensity of competition. The framework commonly adopted is Michael Porter's, as shown in figure 2.3. Porter's (1979, 1980) framework is essentially a structured means of examining the competitive environment of an organization so as to provide a clear understanding of the forces at work. Note that 'competition' is taken not to mean just product (or resource) competition, rather it is the broader notion of 'competition for profits'. The framework is based on the view that forces facing the industry play a key role in determining the profitability and success of an organization. Porter argues that 'the intensity of competition in an industry is neither a matter of coincidence nor bad luck. Rather it is rooted in its underlying structure' (1980). Understanding the industry structure and how the forces operate can aid performance if the organization can take

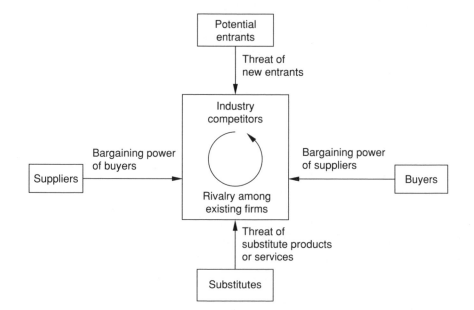

Figure 2.3 The five forces of industry competition. *Source*: Porter (1980)

action to avoid them or influence them. Then the task of the strategist is to determine which of the forces are of greatest importance to the organization and which can be influenced by the strategic decisions of the management.

There are five key forces to be considered:

1 *Entry barriers.* How easy is it for a new firm to enter the industry? New entry into the industry invariably reduces the existing firms' profitability. Therefore, existing firms should be concerned with how easy it is to entry the industry. High entry barriers are generally required to maintain high industry profits. When possible, firms should seek to prevent (deter) new entry. The following conditions make entry difficult:
   (a) *Significant economies of scale.* What is minimum efficient size and what are the consequences of operating below this level?
   (b) *Product differentiation.* The industry is characterized by a high degree of product differentiation (either technical or perceived, say through advertising).
   (c) *High switching costs.* Are buyers and/or suppliers 'locked in' to dealing with the existing firms? Are there significant costs if they decide to switch?
   (d) *High capital requirements.* Are initial investment costs high?
   (e) *Access to distribution is blocked.* New firms often face this problem in vertically integrated industries, e.g. petroleum, brewing.
   (f) *Entry cost.* Established firms have (absolute) cost advantages over a new entrant, e.g. due to the learning (experience) curve, access to inputs, technological know-how, highly trained employees).
   (g) *Retaliation.* Existing firms would retaliate aggressively against a new entrant. For example, a firm contemplating entry may be put off entering the industry if it believes that the existing firms would react with a price or advertising war.

2 *Competitive rivalry.* How intense is competition in the industry? The following are industry conditions usually associated with very intense rivalry and, in turn, low profitability:
   (a) *Slow growth.* This can lead to a 'market share game' and result in intense price and non-price (especially advertising) competition.
   (b) *Large number of firms.* With many competitors, each may fight aggressively for sales to gain scale and gain efficiency – avoidance of competition is very difficult.
   (c) *High fixed costs.* This creates pressure to use capacity, which encourages industry to overproduce, leading to lower prices (possibly through price wars).
   (d) *Lack of product differentiation.* In this situation competition is head-to-head, nothing distinguishes one firm from another so price becomes the chief weapon used in competition – which invariably proves very destructive to profits for the whole industry. In industries characterized by significant product differentiation (e.g. cars, pharmaceuticals, computer software) less aggressive forms of competition are used (e.g. advertising, research and development, quality differentiation).
   (e) *High exit barriers.* If it is difficult to leave the industry, excess capacity may be a problem in the industry and result in low profitability. These exit

barriers can be due to firms having specialized assets that they can sell, government intervention to maintain employment levels, or emotional barriers often associated with long-established family firms.

3 *Substitute products.* What substitutes pose a threat to industry profitability? Pressure on an industry will be stronger the more close substitutes (i.e. demand-related products) there are. In considering their influence, the strategist needs to examine substitutes on their price–performance, their mark-ups and costs of production. Pressure will be greatest when:

(a) Firms producing substitutes are reducing costs (e.g. investing in new machinery).
(b) Substitute producers are increasing their demand by continued product innovation.
(c) Buyers' switching costs are low (i.e. easy to transfer custom).
(d) There is intense competition between the substitute producers (leading to low prices and/or high levels of advertising).

4 *Power of buyers.* How much bargaining power do buyers possess? Profit margins will be squeezed if the buyers have a strong bargaining hand. Buyer power is likely to be strong in the following situations:

(a) There are only a few buyers, each of which buys in large volume.
(b) Buyers can switch suppliers more easily than sellers can switch buyers.
(c) Buyers have full information on demand and costs.
(d) Buyers have the threat of integrating backwards.
(e) There are plenty of substitute products.
(f) Buyers are particularly sensitive to price, e.g. consumers, or buyers for whom the product purchase constitutes a large portion of its total costs.
(g) Quality is not important.
(h) Buyers' profits are low and they therefore want to reduce costs.
(i) Buyers have selling influence, e.g. the power of retailers and wholesalers to promote a company's products by influencing consumers (so-called gatekeeper power).

5 *Power of suppliers.* How much bargaining power do suppliers possess? The points here are similar to those of buyer power. The power of suppliers is likely to be strong in the following circumstances:

(a) There are only a few suppliers. This may give them the power to dictate prices, quality and terms of trade.
(b) Highly differentiated inputs, e.g. good quality inputs giving buyers cost savings via improved efficiency.
(c) Lack of available substitute inputs.
(d) The industry is not an important customer of the supplier group.
(e) Cost relative to total purchases is high.
(f) Suppliers have the threat of forward integration.
(g) The work force (which, of course, 'supplies' labour) is organized in a trade union.

The strength of these five forces will vary between industries, and consequently so do levels of industry profitability. As Porter (1980) puts it, the collective strength of these forces determines the ultimate profit potential in the industry. . . . The forces range from intense in industries like tyres, paper and steel – where no firms earn spectacular returns – to relatively mild in industries like oilfield equipment and services, cosmetics, and toiletries – where high returns are quite common.

Exhibit 2.3 shows a structural analysis of the UK carbonated soft drinks industry, examining the impact the various forces have on this industry. This exhibit highlights the competitive significance of the power of retail grocery chains. The intensity of competition within the industry is quite high, with regular advertising wars taking place; on the other hand sales are increasing and the products are (perceived as) differentiated. On the plus side there are quite high barriers to entry due to the high capital requirements required for production and distribution, increasingly advanced and specialized technology, lack of access to distribution, and strong consumer loyalty to recognized brands.

A final, but very critical point to bear in mind is that the forces themselves change over time – sometimes in a predictable way, other times not. But it is usually possible for the firms to have some influence over these changes. If action no action is taken to counter the forces, it is extremely likely that the forces will grow stronger over time. Strategic action is called for. Each firm needs to consider the actions that it could take to counter the forces, or position itself in such a way as not to face their full impact. For example, merging with a rival not only eliminates a competitor but also reduces the number of competitors in the market as a whole – something that can benefit all rivals by reducing competitive intensity. Another

EXHIBIT 2.3 STRUCTURAL ANALYSIS OF THE UK CARBONATED SOFT DRINKS INDUSTRY

Background
Carbonated soft drinks are an important constituent of the beverage industry. Sales of such products account for around 15 per cent of all beverages consumed and almost 50 per cent of all soft drinks sold in the United Kingdom. The market for these products is worth some £5 billion at retail prices. The products are sold to consumers through over 250,000 outlets.

It is estimated that over 100 firms operate in the production and distribution of carbonated drinks. However, two companies, Coca-cola Enterprises (maker of Coca-cola, with 15 per cent market share) and Britvic Soft Drinks (maker of Pepsi, with 11 per cent market share), dominate the industry, with 40 per cent and 20 per cent of the total market (by volume) respectively. In addition to these major brand producers, a number of smaller producers exist making well known brands, including A. G. Barr (maker of Irn-bru, with 5 per cent market share), Hall & Woodhouse and Matthew Clarke. In addition to sales of branded products, own-label sales (mainly belonging to the major supermarket groups) account for some 26 per cent of total sales (by volume), mostly made by specialist own-label producers such as Cott, Prince's and Macaw. The remainder of the industry is made up of mainly small specialist producers, perhaps promoting a specialist product line (such as Vimto) or providing a local speciality.

Threat of entry
Entry into the market on a large scale is difficult. The major companies have essentially tied up the distribution channels in major grocers, public houses and fast food outlets (that collectively account for most sales). Furthermore, because the products are 'experience' goods, and reputation matters, very heavy advertising would be a necessity to gain a foothold as a brand producer. Entry as an own-label producer might be possible, but it would demand a large-scale operation to keep costs down and be as competitive as the existing large own-label producers. Even with the removal of trade barriers and generally greater harmonization (such as the move towards a single currency) within the European Union, major Continental firms have appeared reluctant to plan an assault on the UK market, at least not via 'green field' entry (that is, totally new entry, as opposed to entry through the acquisition of an existing UK operation).

Threat of substitutes
There are a number of substitutes for carbonated soft drinks, e.g. mineral water, fruit juice, tea, coffee, beer (especially low or non-alcoholic), wine and other alcoholic beverages such as 'f.a.b.s' (flavoured alcoholic beverages, like Hooch and Reef). However, carbonates have generally been gaining market share at their expense and this trend does not appear set to reverse. In addition, carbonated soft drinks have a particularly strong appeal to the youth market (ten to eighteen-year-olds), where much of the sales comes from. Overall, the threat appears relatively weak, especially to the core youth market.

Power of suppliers
Again, relatively weak pressure with the exception of sugar producers and plastic suppliers (e.g. Du Pont). The work force is not highly organized, nor is it militant.

Power of buyers
Over 65 per cent of sales are sold through multiple grocers. The top five grocery chains account for nearly 70 per cent (and increasing) of all grocery sales and are thus in a strong bargaining position. Some 8 per cent of sales are through fast food restaurants (such as

McDonald's) and 6 per cent of sales are through public houses (which are mainly controlled by large pub companies). The remainder of sales are to relatively weak buyers, including off-licences, confectioners, tobacconists and newsagents (CTNs) and restaurants/cafeterias.

Competitive rivalry

Rivalry is intense, particularly between the two dominant companies. But, rather than (damaging) price competition, the rivalry is usually in terms of very heavy promotion (including advertising and sponsorship), which serves to increase the size of the market. Industry advertising expenditure in 2002 was £43 million. Segmentation is a key feature of the market, with the products falling into distinct categories such as colas, lemonade, mixers and others (such as fruit-based, cream sodas and ginger beer), type (regular *v.* diet), and packaging form (e.g. 2 l PET bottles, 330 ml cans, 250 ml glass bottles and draught). Such segmentation, backed with brand promotion, tends to reduce price sensitivity in the market. Competition is also in terms of new product development, which occurs regularly in most categories, such as in the cola segment, where brand introductions have included vanilla and lemon. Again, this form of competition extends the size of the whole market. Thus segmentation and differentiation are key aspects of rivalry in the market and particular firms dominate particular segments, lessening the intensity of (direct head-to-head price) competition overall.

Conclusion

The strongest pressures come from the power of buyers and the fairly intense non-price competition within the industry. Nevertheless, overall the industry looks to be in a fairly healthy position: the leading firms are very profitable and industry growth is expected to be steady at around 8 per cent (by value) over the period 2002–7. Cola as a product appears to be reaching maturity but other segments offer prospects of development and growth. At the same time, the firms are actively competing on quality and bringing new products to market, as well as being innovative in terms of reducing costs by investing in new technology and machinery, developing new forms of packaging and offering better distribution services. The danger is that the firms may not be able to sustain this route to growth and instead may seek growth through undercutting rivals' prices in a market share game. In this situation profits are likely to deteriorate rapidly if destructive head-to-head price competition becomes the main competitive instrument.

Source: 'Carbonates in the UK', Mintel International Group, February 2003; authors' own research.

example would be successful lobbying for enhancing institutional barriers to entry
– e.g. tighter planning regulations in out-of-town retailing or higher (minimum)
capital requirements in bank authorization (as a regulatory requirement). A further example would be credibly threatening to support alternative suppliers to counter
supplier power, e.g. the development of own-label grocery products to counter producer brands power. Also, countering consumer buyer power might be achieved
by limiting their willingness or ability to switch providers, such as introducing penal-
ties in mortgage redemption policies or encouraging repeat purchases with store
loyalty cards. All these and a raft of other measures may lessen the impact of the
forces taking profits away from the industry.

EXERCISE

Consider the key pressures facing your industry (both currently and
in the near future). Rank order (1–5) each category from the most
to the least significant. State your reasons for this choice. What measures might the firms be capable of making to weaken the significance
of these forces?

Identifying the Firm's Competitive Position

Step 4 in environmental analysis is to identify the organization's competitive position. The first exercise might be to compare the effect environmental influences
(identified by the audit) have on the firm and its main competitors. Exhibit 2.4
is a competitive assessment of the major grocery chains in terms of changes
in consumer profiles. It assesses the overall impact the changes are likely to have
on the companies. Overall they appear to be in a reasonably good position to meet
the changes.

Such an exercise serves a useful introduction to understanding the positions
of competitors. Beyond this the strategist requires a more thorough yardstick by
which to gauge competition, and in turn the firm's position. We briefly outline
three frameworks commonly used: the life-cycle model, strategic group analysis and
market share (segmentation) analysis.

The life-cycle model

This represents a relatively simple way of conceiving the firm's position in terms
of the stage of development of its markets (i.e. their position in the life cycle of
such markets). The model is based on the view that conditions in the market place,
in terms of growth and maturity of markets, fundamentally affect market conditions and competitive behaviour. Figure 2.4 summarizes some of the conditions
that can be expected at different stages in the life cycle. Generally, different strategies are required at different stages in the life cycle to cope with the different

EXHIBIT 2.4 COMPETITIVE STANDING OF MAJOR GROCERY CHAINS IN RELATION TO CHANGING CONSUMER PROFILES

Store	Increasing affluence	Car ownership	Value-conscious	Snacking/ prepared meals	One-stop shopping	Top-up shopping	Overall impact
Tesco	+ Improving quality perception	++ Good edge-of-town locations	++ Generally low prices	++ Good range	+++ Large format inc. non-food	+ Tesco Metro expanding	++/+++ Very good
Sainsbury	++ High-quality service and products	++ Many edge-of-town locations	+ 'Good food costs less'	++ Good range	++ Large-format stores	+ Some city convenience stores	++ Good
Asda	O Questionable quality perception	+++ Edge/out-of-town locations	+++ 'Everyday low prices'	+ Growing reputation	+++ Hyper-market inc. non-food	– Only large format	++ Good
Safeway	++ High-quality service and products	++ Many edge-of-town locations	O 'High-low' pricing strategy	+ Solid range	++ Large-format stores	O Only a few convenience stores	+ Fair

EXHIBIT 2.4 (cont'd)

Store	Increasing affluence	Car ownership	Value-conscious	Snacking/prepared meals	One-stop shopping	Top-up shopping	Overall impact
Somerfield/Kwiksave	-/-/- Target less mobile/poor consumers	-/- Town-centre locations	-/+ High/discount prices	O/- Limited range	O/- Limited range	+/+ Handy town-centre locations	-/- Both formats weak
Morrison	O Stores tend to be in less affluent areas	++ Edge-of-town stores	++ Generally low prices	+ Solid range	++ Large format stores	- Only large format	+/++ Fair to good
Co-ops	- Little appeal to affluent consumers	- Neighbourhood location	- High prices for quality	O Limited range	- Small stores	++ Focus on convenience	- Weak
M&S	+++ Top quality perception	- Town centre locations	-- Rather pricey foods	+++ Excellent range	- Limited lines and only own label	+ Convenient locations	O/+ Neutral to fair

Key: +++ excellent, ++ good, + fair, O neutral, - weak, -- very weak.

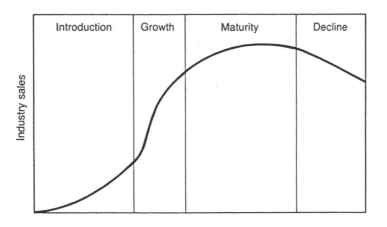

	Introduction	Growth	Maturity	Decline
Growth rate	Rising slowly	Accelerating	Levelling	Declining
Sales	Low	Rising	Peak	Declining
Unit costs	High	Declining	Low	Low
Product line	Very short	Growing	Diversified	Shrinking
Profits	Negative	Increasing	High but declining	Declining
Competitors	Few	Increasing	More but stable	Declining
Typical pricing	Cost-plus	Penetration	Competitive	Cut
Entry barriers	Technology	Start-up costs	Competitors	Overcapacity
Typical advertising	Information and education	Mass-market awareness	Persuasion and differentiation	Reduced

Figure 2.4 Stages of the life cycle

competitive conditions. For instance, the nature of the game changes substantially when one moves from the growth phase, where firms develop independently, to the mature phase, where growth can come about only at the expense of rivals. In the decline phase this problem is even more pronounced and it will be difficult for firms avoiding price wars when there is excess capacity and marginal firms are reluctant to leave the industry or face exit barriers due to costs associated with exiting – see exhibit 2.5.

The model is designed to be of use in considering the life cycle of a firm but more often the life cycle of the product(s) it produces. The picture is, of course, only a stylized representation. Some products may experience explosive growth then sudden collapse, e.g. fad items over the last few decades such as hula-hoops, pogo sticks, space hoppers and slinkies. Meanwhile, other products may have very long stages of development (possibly over hundreds of years) and have yet to enter the decline phase, e.g. beer and wine. It is also possible that rather than entering the decline phase, some mature products can receive a sudden impetus due to further product differentiation and innovation, which leads to further industry growth – the so-called rejuvenation phase. An example might be ice cream: once mainly the preserve of children, the product category received a boost in sales with the introduction of up-market brands (Haagen Das, Mars, etc.) targeted at adults.

EXHIBIT 2.5 BAD NEWS: COMPETITION IN A CONTRACTING MARKET

The British newspaper industry sustains eleven national titles, and unusually high readership levels in international terms. It is a surprisingly well managed industry, especially in managing distribution, wholesale and retailer relations to maximize circulation. Yet the newspapers are facing a troubled future. Even the present offers gloomy news, with the publishing groups reporting deteriorating financial performance. For instance, Pearson reported that its flagship title, the *Financial Times*, lost money in the second half of 2002, and just scraped a £1 million (US$1.6 million) full-year operating profit, 92 per cent down on 2001. Meanwhile operating profit at the market leader, News International, publisher of the *Sun*, the *Times* and the *Sunday Times*, fell 37 per cent in the last quarter of 2002 compared with the same period of 2001. Circulation revenue at the *Sun*, the largest national daily, has been battered by a price war with the *Mirror*. All this against a background where journalists are being fired, pay packets and expense accounts frozen and pension schemes slimmed.

One reason for the deteriorating financial performance is a slump in advertising revenue, the mainstay of income for newspapers. Following a bumper year in 2000, when advertising revenue across the British newspaper industry soared by 12 per cent, it dropped by 2 per cent in 2001 and a further 3 per cent in 2002. Some newspapers have fared worse than others. For example, advertising revenue at the *Financial Times* fell by 23 per cent in 2002, after a 20 per cent decline in 2001.

Newspapers are losing readers, too. In the second half of 2002 circulation fell from the same period of 2001 at all but three of the national titles, and at every one of the broadsheet newspapers. This is part of an apparent long-term trend that appears to set to continue. Overall national newspaper readership has dropped by a fifth since 1990, according to the National Readership Survey (NRS). With declining newspaper readership, advertising spend is slowly going elsewhere. For example, the share of all advertising spending taken by newspapers shrank from 21 per cent in 1985 to 19 per cent in 2001, while radio's share grew from 2 per cent to 5 per cent, and billboards' from 5 per cent to 7 per cent.

Most worrying of all for the industry, young people are just not buying newspapers the way previous generations did. The number of newspaper readers under the age of twenty-four has declined by over a third since 1990, while the number of those over sixty-five has fallen by only 6 per cent. The *Daily Telegraph* boasts the oldest average readership, 29 per cent of which is now over the age of sixty-five. But the share of older readers is growing faster at other papers, including the *Independent*, the *Times* and the *Mirror*. Instead of buying and reading

newspapers, it appears, young Britons are increasingly turning to alternative news sources, online, television or radio, and to 'news grazing'
in snatches through the day rather than sitting down for a daily read.
The worrying implication is that the industry is simply not nurturing its
future readers. A generation is growing up with no particular brand
loyalty to any newspaper, nor any entrenched habit of reading daily over
the breakfast table.

In the face of apparent long-run decline, what strategies should the
industry participants pursue? For some, like Richard Desmond, the owner
of Express Newspapers and the *Daily Star*, it has been about finding
a new market position, a low-cost one that dispenses with broad news
gathering, instead emphasizing celebrity 'news'. This has yielded some
success. Of the three daily tabloids that bucked the circulation decline
in the second half of 2002, two (the *Express* and the *Star*) were his;
the other was the *Sun*. Circulation at the *Star* increased by 17 per cent.

However, pulling off a shift to a new market position is far from easy.
While the *Sun* is trying to recapture younger readers with brash celebrity
news, the *Mirror*'s effort to desert the celebrity game and go up market has not been rewarded. It is now hunting readers in the overcrowded
middle ground, where the line between broadsheet and tabloid is
blurring. Finding a position where there is little direct competition yet
sufficient demand to make the position viable is difficult in such a crowded
market.

A second option, which comes to pass in many declining markets,
is to fight on price, treating competition as a market share game or
dog-eat-dog attrition battle. But as the ongoing tussle between the *Sun*
and the *Mirror* shows, and previously between the *Times* and the
Telegraph, this simply risks bleeding revenue (where the loss of cover-
price income is not compensated for by additional advertising income
even if circulation increases).

A third idea is to launch new titles. However, there have been notable
and costly launches in the past, such as the *European*, which have
failed badly. Accordingly, this seems an unlikely strategy to consider,
especially in a declining market. However, it can work. *Metro*, a free
sheet launched in 1999 by Associated Newspapers, publisher of the
Daily Mail and the *Evening Standard*, has started to make a profit. Others
may follow suit.

But the inevitable conclusion appears to be that there will be too
many papers chasing fewer and fewer readers, and something will
have to give. Commentators have questioned whether it is indeed sustainable to have nearly a dozen national newspapers in the United
Kingdom, given the decline in circulation. If one or more does ultimately
exit, it will certainly be big news. Sadly for the industry, fewer people
than at present will read about it in a national newspaper.

Source: 'Fading', *Economist*, 8 March 2003.

QUESTIONS

1 What stage of the life cycle would you consider your company's main product/service to be in?
2 Consider possible courses of action that your company could reasonably take when its main product reaches the end of its life cycle.

Strategic group analysis

The aim here is to focus on the group of firms that are the closest rivals to the organization in respect of the strategic positions they find themselves in. Specifically, a strategic group will generally share similar strategic characteristics, follow similar strategies and compete on similar bases. An industry could be composed of many, some or just one strategic group, depending on the extent to which firms are clustered together, pursuing the same strategies as, or different strategies from, others in the industry.

It is usual to define groups using two sets of characteristics as a basis of competition. Exhibit 2.6 identifies strategic groups in the UK grocery retail industry, in this case in terms of the degree of average store size and pricing policy – ranging from very low ('hard discount'), to every day low pricing (EDLP), to promotional pricing ('high–low'), to distinctly high. When constructing such a map the characteristics should be chosen to show distinct groupings of firms (i.e. to differentiate groupings clearly) as well as key defining industry characteristics. These characteristics will depend to a large extent on the history and development of the industry and the competitive forces at work in the industry.

The following is a list of characteristics that might be considered:

(a) extent of product diversity;
(b) number of market segments covered;
(c) extent of vertical integration;
(d) size of organization;
(e) product or service quality;
(f) marketing effort (size of sales force, budget or advertising spread);
(g) ownership structure (independent or owned by parent);
(h) R&D capability (extent of product or process innovation);
(i) extent of geographical coverage;
(j) pricing policy;
(k) extent of product branding;
(l) perceived value of product (price/quality).

As well as giving a good understanding of the competitive characteristics of competitors, this form of analysis allows one to ask how likely or possible it is to move from one strategic group to another. For example, in the grocery retail industry (exhibit 2.6) there is an important barrier to mobility – lack of available sites for large stores and general difficulty in gaining planning permission for new stores,

EXHIBIT 2.6 STRATEGIC FOOD RETAILING GROUPS IN THE UNITED KINGDOM

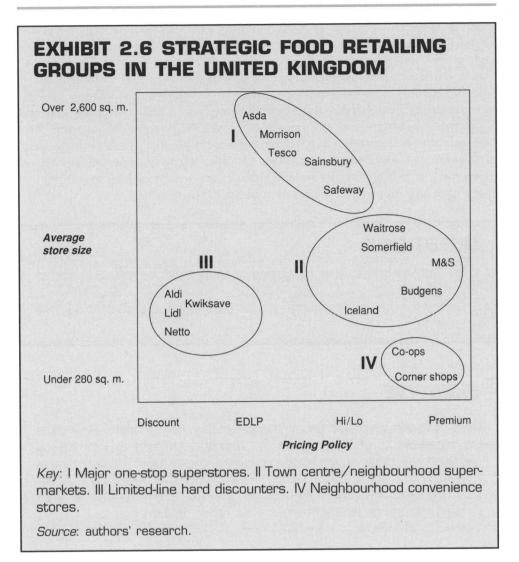

Key: I Major one-stop superstores. II Town centre/neighbourhood supermarkets. III Limited-line hard discounters. IV Neighbourhood convenience stores.

Source: authors' research.

meaning that it can be difficult to change average store size quickly, especially upwards. Even pricing policy has an important barrier to mobility element. It might be thought that pricing policy could simply be changed and that would allow a firm to join a different group. But it is not quite as straightforward as may appear. First, pricing policy is a key aspect of the retail brand (i.e. what the retailer represents to its customers), which takes investment and time to build up. Changing pricing policy may necessitate wholesale change of the brand image – something that will prove expensive and take time. Second, the stores themselves in respect of location and appearance may not be suited to a different pricing policy, e.g. down-market stores being used with up-market prices, and vice versa. Third, pricing policy might be conditioned by a retailer's operations and image in other markets (e.g., for Marks & Spencer, pricing policy on food reflects its overall image for clothing, furnishings, etc).

Just as barriers to entry may protect an industry from new entrants stripping profits away from incumbent firms, barriers to mobility can protect members of a strategic group from new entry to the group, making it easier for group members to maintain distinct positions (even within the group). But for a firm wanting to escape a group, barriers to mobility work against the firm wanting to change its position in the industry. It is not just the desire of moving to a different group that may appeal; moving to an area of strategic space not yet covered by any other firm may offer the prospect of establishing a unique and potentially highly valuable position. But not all 'white space' is desirable. Consider the areas unoccupied in regard to exhibit 2.6. Is it barriers to mobility that prevent a firm moving to unoccupied space or simply that such a position would not be profitable?

QUESTIONS

1 Do you consider the groupings identified in exhibit 2.6 to be reasonable?
2 Consider other combinations of characteristics. Do other groupings emerge?

EXERCISE

Construct two strategic group maps for your own industry. Which is the more useful of these maps for strategic considerations? Having identified the most appropriate groupings, give a brief assessment of how easy it is for a firm to enter your group and how easy it is for your organization to move to another group or even move to an area of strategic space where there are no other firms.

Market share analysis

It is widely held, and with much justification, that market share is a measure of market power. A high market share bestows benefits on a firm in the form of reduced costs due to economies of scale, buying power and experience. A firm's position relative to its competitors should then be viewed in terms of its market share in the market as a whole and also its share in the various segments of the market.

Market share analysis attempts to map out the relative power of competitors according to shares held in market segments. This should help the strategist identify where its strengths and weaknesses lie. Breaking the market into segments should also help in identifying opportunities open to the firm (and its competitors!), and may give further insight into the strategies that competitors are following.

A market can be segmented in various ways. The strategist may want to experiment with different classifications, since each basis could give rise to a different assessment of environmental opportunities. For example, segmentation could be *customer*-related (e.g. with consumers, social/income class, sex, age, size, culture) *product*-related (e.g. appearance, purpose, quality, price) or *firm*-related (e.g. size, location, experience).

Having identified the segments, the relative sizes (in percentage terms) and likely growth rates then need to be estimated along with the market segment position of each firm (in terms of rankings or 'weak'/'middling'/'dominant') for each segment identified. As with strategic group analysis, the basis of segmentation should hopefully discriminate between the firms. The firm's overall position is assessed in terms of the intensity of competition it faces in its main market segments and how difficult it is expand or to move into growing and/or profitable segments.

EXERCISE

1 Consider different classifications of segments for your industry. Which classification appears to be most appropriate? Why?
2 Identify those segments that your firm is dominant in and particularly weak in.
3 Which segments are rapidly growing and/or highly profitable? Are rivals in a stronger position to exploit these? If yes, what do you think your company should do?

The Internal Environment: Resources and Capabilities

Having gained an understanding of the external environment facing the firm, the next stage is to assess the firm's resources with the intention of identifying its strategic capability based on understanding its strengths and weaknesses. This should then provide guidance for assessing the suitability of particular strategies (i.e. can they be sustained?) as well as for resource planning and deployment.

The capability of any organization is fundamentally determined by how well it links together its various activities – such as designing, marketing, delivering, and supporting its products and services. Figure 2.5 shows how activities are linked together to form the *value chain*. Here the amount of value added, rather than costs, is assigned to each activity. Value chain analysis considers where and how a firm adds value (i.e. the internal factors that drive profitability). The diagram represents the linkages between 'primary' activities and the 'supporting' activities. The primary (i.e. the main value-adding) activities are grouped into five main areas:

- *inbound logistics* – concerned with receiving, storing, and distributing inputs;
- *operations* – transforming the inputs into the final product/service;
- *outbound logistics* – moving the product to buyers (including warehousing and distribution);
- *marketing and sales* – bringing the product to buyers and inducing them to buy and use it;
- *service* – activities to enhance or maintain the value of the product service (including installation, repairs, maintenance, training and other services).

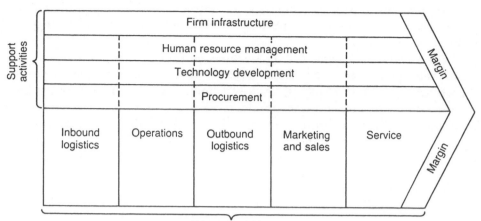

Figure 2.5 The value chain. *Source*: Porter (1985)

The primary activities are generally quite distinct, having different economies and, in large organizations, separate cost centres. Each of these five primary activities is linked with four supporting activities:

- *procurement*: processes for acquiring resources;
- *technology development*: covering product, process and raw material development and 'know-how';
- *human resource management*: including recruitment, training, development and rewards;
- *firm infrastructure*: chiefly the management systems, e.g. planning, finance accounting and quality control.

The capability of the organization depends on the quality of co-ordination across these activities, not just on competence in each individual activity. The linkages are harder to identify than the separate activities. Porter (1985) defines such linkages as 'relationships between the way one activity is performed and the cost and performance of another'. A good example is provided by just-in-time production, where parts procurement and assembly are tightly linked. It is often such linkages that provide competitive advantage. Building further linkages will increase value added. This provides a further mechanism to differentiate your company from its competitors, and thereby create 'margin' (as indicated on the right hand side of the value chain, figure 2.5).

To determine the firm's internal position we then need to assess these activities, which in turn depend on the resources at hand in the organization. The process begins with an audit of the firm's resources. This should enable management to decide on how well the resources are being utilized – i.e. how efficiently and effectively they are being used and how well they are being controlled. This analysis, in the context of the firm's activities, will hopefully identify the company's key strengths (i.e. good attributes) as well as identify missing or 'poor' resources that need to be attended to.

The following resources should be considered:

- *Physical resources.* These include buildings, materials, production facilities, production techniques, information systems, distribution networks, research facilities. Efficiency will concern capacity fill, unit costs, yield, layout and materials flow. Effectiveness should be measured by the match between the various resources. Relative position will be in respect of benchmarking against rivals, e.g. over values of fixed assets, age of capital equipment, scale of plant and flexibility of plant and equipment.
- *Human resources.* This is in terms of the number of employees, their productivity (set against wages and salaries), the extent and balance of technical and other skills (also competence, versatility, flexibility, adaptability), knowledge (awareness), experience, attitudes (commitment, loyalty, degree of interest and effort, team spirit, management style) and their demographic characteristics (age structure). Key indicators include educational, technical and professional qualifications of employees, compensation and pay relative to the industry, record on labour disputes and employee turnover rate.
- *Financial resources.* The financial capability depends on factors like financial size, growth pattern, profitability, use of working capital, price–earnings ratio, asset structure and capital structure. Key indicators will be the debt to equity ratio, the ratio of net cash to capital expenditure and the company's credit rating. The analyst will need to assess the costing system, budgets and investment appraisal procedures.
- *Technological resources.* These cover two aspects: the stock of technology and the resources for innovation. The former is concerned with the form of proprietary technology (e.g. patents, copyright, trade secrets) and expertise in the application of technology (i.e. know-how). The latter relates to research facilities and technical and scientific employees. Key indicators for the firm might include the number and significance of patents, revenue from patent licences and R&D staff as a percentage of total firm employment.
- *Intangibles.* This category is especially important for firms in the service sector, where value depends on 'goodwill' arising from brand names, company image, reputation, good contacts, etc. Effectiveness depends on how well this exploited, e.g. by public relations. Key indicators of reputation with customers might include brand recognition, premium over competing brands, percentage of repeat buying and the level and consistency of company performance. In addition the company might consider objective measures of company performance with respect to other interested parties, such as suppliers (including material suppliers, banks and other lenders, and employees), government and regulatory bodies, and with the community.

Assessing the resources and activities of the firm relies on various criteria, most notably:

1 historical experience;
2 competitors and other comparable firms ('industry or business norms');
3 personal opinions (involving value judgements) of management and consultants;
4 specific targets accomplished, e.g. budgets.

The assessment of the individual resources and activities then forms the background to judging the organization as a whole. This process should take into account the efficiency and effectiveness of the organization's form and structure, its standard operating procedures, the control system, the planning system and top management.

'But where does one obtain the information?' we hear you cry! The following should prove to be the most useful:

- personal observation and experience;
- customer contacts;
- accounts and planning and control system documents;
- managers, other employees, board members;
- competitive intelligence;
- consultants;
- published information (books, journals, magazines, newspapers, business/ market databases, the Internet).

The main problem will not be lack of data; rather, it will concern turning all the quantitative (especially the financial) measures into a meaningful (i.e. comprehensible) qualitative assessment!

The end result of the analysis should be the identification of the key issues – the major strengths and weaknesses – and their strategic importance. In terms of developing suitable competitive strategies the analysis should identify the areas where the firm has 'distinctive competence', arising from its strengths, giving it an edge over its rivals and give guidance where particular weaknesses are to be avoided.

In considering the core competence of the organization one should not forget the links with external parties which provide key services to the organization, as these links can provide a useful source of competitive advantage if they are successfully organized and controlled. The firm should examine whether these business services are more usefully carried out externally to the organization (i.e. contracted out) or should be 'internalized' and carried out within the organization (i.e. performed 'in house'). Even for manufacturing firms the range of business services used can now be extensive, and service activities are important at all stages of the value chain. Many companies choose to contract out some services that could be handled equally well in-house so that they can focus on the core business. These services would now typically include building maintenance services, order processing, payroll processing and direct marketing, among others, where 'dedicated' service providers may be able to provide superior services at a lower cost simply through specialization – in terms of both personnel and technology. As Porter (1990) argues, the drive to de-integrate business services appears to be growing (with the exception of legal services). The reason for this is the increasing capital intensity of service firms, which were traditionally extremely labour-intensive. Information technology and the use of computers and computerized techniques have revolutionized the manner in which functions are undertaken, leading to better control operations and increased employee productivity. The once highly fragmented service sector is now rapidly consolidating and an increasing number of large, even international, companies are emerging (e.g. Saatchi & Saatchi in advertising).

The advantage of using the specialized service firm over an in-house unit is essentially twofold. First, the specialist provider faces competition for the account and has the incentive to raise productivity and quality while keeping costs down. The (captive) in-house service department, on the other hand, is a cost centre and does not face such competitive pressures to ensure that productivity and quality is optimum. Second, the service provider, being specialized and concentrating its efforts, can often hire and train people more effectively, employ better methods, use more up-to-date equipment and perform the service cheaper and better. Meanwhile, the in-house service department may be regarded as of peripheral concern to the core activities of the business and lack the necessary flexibility if it is constrained to the guidelines of the other functions of the organization. This ultimately leads to an inefficient and ineffective service compared with what could be provided by an independent firm.

The one potential disadvantage with using outside service providers concerns communication and thus effective control. The development of large, specialist firms has, however, led to a more professional relationship with clients, and technology has allowed communication to become more instantaneous. The difficulties of dealing with outside service suppliers have thus been significantly reduced. Indeed, for many firms the links with outside suppliers, where a high level of co-operation and co-ordination has been effected, are a chief source of competitive advantage over rivals.

QUESTIONS

1 Consider how your firm assesses its capabilities. Is there a formal procedure for monitoring the internal environment?

2 Apply the concept of the value chain to your organization. Which is your (a) strongest and (b) weakest activity? Are there good links across the activities? Can you identify any room for improvement?

3 (a) Identify any activities the organization undertakes that could be more fruitfully contracted out to specialist service providers. (b) Similarly, identify any activities that would probably be better carried out by the organization, i.e. internalized.

4 The value chain approach is also extremely useful for comparing your own position against that of your rivals. Firms producing the same product or service for the same market will often have different competences in and across the various activities, which results in the different competitive standings amongst the firms. Consider the internal environment of your main rivals. Which areas are they strong and weak in? What are their strengths and weaknesses? Does this suggest any opportunities and/or threats?

SWOT Analysis

The final step in situation analysis is to determine the firm's strategic position by considering whether or not the present strategy of the firm is capable of dealing with the changes taking place in the business environment. The method typically used is SWOT analysis, which aims to relate the strengths and weaknesses of the organization (based on an internal audit of the firm's capabilities – see the next chapter for more detail) against the opportunities and threats thrown up by the analysis of the external environment. In order to conduct this type of analysis the management must have a clear view of what the current strategy is. This is not always obvious!

Essentially one wants to identify opportunities and threats, while at the same time identifying key aspects of organizational capability that provide strengths and weakness in dealing with these environmental changes. Opportunities and threats facing firms will not only differ across industries but also in the same industry. The following list gives some suggestions to help identify the main opportunities and threats facing a particular firm:

Opportunities – these should be exploited!

1 market share;
2 experience;
3 financial strength;
4 technological leadership;
5 good products (especially trade names);
6 low cost;
7 economies of scale or scope;
8 distribution system;
9 skilled personnel;
10 favourable public image.

Threats – these must be overcome by reviewing and appraising them realistically:

1 market saturation;
2 changes in consumer tastes;
3 demographic shifts;
4 shortages in factor-input supplies (including skilled labour);

5 economic uncertainty (inflation? recession? exchange rates?);
6 competitors' market power;
7 government regulations (including European Union);
8 pressure groups;
9 political uncertainty (change in the government?);
10 change in trade policy (breakdown of free-trade agreement?).

Let us then look at a simple procedure for matching up the identified opportunities and threats against the strengths and weakness of the organization (which emerge from analysing the firm's internal environment). The following five-step procedure is adapted from Johnson and Scholes (2002):

1 Identify the current or prevailing strategy or strategies in the organization.
2 Identify the key changes in the firm's environment.
3 Identify the key capabilities (strengths) and key limitations (weaknesses) of the organization (i.e. consider its resources).
4 List the key environmental issues against the relevance of the current strategy and the strengths and weaknesses of the organization.
6 Then examine the statements against each other, and score either a + (or a weighted + +) or a − (or a − −) or 0, as follows:
   (a) Mark + if there would be a benefit to the organization, i.e. a strength that would enable the firm either to take advantage of, or counteract, a problem from an environmental change, or offset a weakness caused by the change.
   (b) Mark − if there would be an adverse effect on the firm, i.e. either a strength would be reduced by the change or a weakness would prevent the firm from overcoming the problems associated with an environmental change.
   (c) Score 0 if there is no (or only a minimal) effect.

Exhibit 2.7 is a completed SWOT analysis for Safeway at a point (in 2003) where it was subject to a number of potential bids to take it over (including those from its four chief rivals in the grocery trade, Tesco, Sainsbury, Asda and Morrison, along with the entrepreneur and owner of Arcadia Group and BhS, Philip Green). The SWOT analysis gives some insights into why it was a take-over target. Its No. 4 position in the market meant that it did not possess the scale advantages of its rivals, nor did its high-price image fit well with a market where consumers are increasingly becoming value-conscious. However, its emphasis on quality and 'best at fresh' and availability look sensible in relation to the business environment, especially if it could clearly distinguish itself in this regard. Nevertheless, a major weakness compared with rivals appears to be its focus on just food, rather than moving into non-food, as its three main rivals had done to good effect. It seemed possible but by no means certain that all five prospective bidders could add value, through consolidations or a different business model, if they managed to achieve a take-over (subject to a Competition Commission inquiry).

EXHIBIT 2.7 SWOT ANALYSIS OF SAFEWAY

Key issues in the environment	Importance of reputation and brand image	Industry sales growing slowly	Consumer preference for diversified one-stop shopping	Increasing importance of scale for efficiency	Increasing emphasis on price competition	Health conscious consumers	+	-
Current strategies								
Grow food market share	0	+	−	+	−	0	2	2
Best at fresh and availability	++	+	0	0	0	++	5	0
Retail-tainment	++	+	0	−	− −	0	3	3
Main strengths								
Reputation for quality	++	+	0	0	−	+	4	1
Good relations with local suppliers	+	0	0	0	−	+	2	1
Good logistical support	+	0	0	++	0	+	3	0
Financially sound	+0	0+	00	++	0+	+0	3	0
Main weaknesses								
No. 4 player	0	−	−	− −	− −	0	0	6
Perceived as a high pricer	+	−	0	−	− −	+	2	4
Weak on non-food offer	0	−	− −	− −	0	+	1	5
Very mixed store sizes	0	−	−	−	−	0	0	4
+	9	5	0	3	1	7		
−	0	4	5	7	10	0		

Source: authors' research.

Conclusion

Armed with a sound knowledge of the firm's environment, the strategist can begin to contemplate strategic options. In evaluating these options SWOT analysis may prove useful as a simple ready-reckoner, though there are a number of other more sophisticated and specialized methods for evaluating options.

We end this chapter with two points to bear in mind. The first is the need for environmental/situation analysis to be viewed as a continuous process and not to be neglected. Sudden radical shifts in the broad or operating environments have been known to catch leading players out in a number of industries. In particular where there has been a major upheaval in an industry, especially through government intervention in deregulating the market, some firms are noticeably more able to cope with such changes than others.

Finally, even though we have emphasized, through Porter's (1980) structural analysis, that the firm's direction and performance (especially profitability) is likely to depend on the structure of the industry (where performance is likely to be stronger the fewer the competitors, the fewer substitutes available, the fewer the potential entrants and the weaker the buyers and the suppliers), all those factors may in fact actually work against the long-term position of the firm and the industry where lack of competition stifles the incentive to innovate and the firms cease to be dynamic and instead sit back and rest on their laurels.

Porter (1990) suggests that the lack of domestic competition and the weakness of related and supporting industries may have been a significant factor in accounting for the decline of many UK industries that once dominated world trade. In contrast, intense competition, e.g. in the Japanese consumer durable product industries (computers, electronics, cars, etc.) has spurred firms on to innovate new products, develop new processes and implement new management techniques to try to maintain their position and stay ahead of the competition. In terms of the 'competitive advantage of nations' the United Kingdom has lost all but a handful of its leading positions. While it still retains the dominant or at least a strong position in a number of service industries, including finance, insurance and auctioneering, most of the manufacturing side has declined, with the exception of pharmaceuticals, chemicals, cosmetics and some food and drink industries (e.g. whisky, confectionery, biscuits). The dominant position has been handed to other countries where domestic competition has been much stronger and consumers and other users have been far more demanding in terms of quality requirements.

A further study by Porter for the DTI in 2003 highlighted that UK industry needs to develop clusters of businesses located together to facilitate the build-up of a competitive infrastructure. The argument was most forcefully made for the high-tech and biotechnology industries, where the UK has had some success but lacks scale in global terms to ensure the long-term success of these businesses.

The upshot is that, no matter how good the business plan/strategy may be in principle, the firm may be hampered by the ineffectiveness of supporting industries (i.e. the chief suppliers of equipment, inputs and business services) and the lack of suitably trained personnel. Thus ironically the long-term position of a firm may be enhanced by very tough competition, as a nasty-tasting medicine, rather than the sweet situation of facing little or no competition.

REVIEW EXERCISE

Undertake a SWOT analysis of your company's position. What are the main opportunities facing the firm? Are current strategies appropriate to take advantage of these? Comment on the chief weaknesses of your organization. Suggest possible courses of action to remedy these.

CHAPTER 3

BUSINESS-LEVEL STRATEGY

Strategic Choice

The strategic options facing management are numerous – what markets to operate in, what resources to deploy, how to organize procurement, production and distribution, how to compete, etc. In all these respects, management faces not only the problem of identifying options, but also evaluating each of them and then implementing the chosen ones. In this chapter we consider strategic options at the business unit level, where a company or business unit is focused on a particular market or group of similar markets (related by either geographical proximity or product/service similarity). We look to see the ways in which the business can gain strategic success at this level – measured in respect of building competitive advantage over industry rivals to gain long-term superior performance. This calls for an understanding of *competitive strategies* – deciding the basis on how the firm will compete in its chosen market.

As will become apparent from our discussion, the range of possible competitive strategies is wide. This is evident from the different routes to success we observe in different markets. Different companies make different offers to their customers, with different product specifications or service levels, while having different cost implications for themselves and the prices they can command. For the fortunate few, it is their particular offer and mode of business operation that allow them to gain long-term superior performance. There is no magic formula to this, available to all. For, if there were, then all would seek to follow it and in the process the resulting offer would cease to be distinct, being copied by all, thus offering no firm any differential advantage.

This points to perhaps the key theme of this chapter – the importance of being *distinct* and having your own *unique* formula; being different from all other rivals in respect of what is offered and how it is offered. This is never easy to achieve. Some propositions will either not be sufficiently attractive to the market or be too costly to undertake, while rivals would too easily copy others. The challenge is to develop a position that is attractive, unique and defendable. This chapter demonstrates the guidance that is available, and its limits, to assist the strategist in meeting this challenge.

Market positioning is a key element in developing a competitive strategy, and this can be defined in several ways, as we explore in the first part of this chapter. Here, there would appear to be many options available. However, in practice, it is the resources and capabilities that a firm is able to develop that will greatly restrict its realistic options. Moreover, once adopted, the competitive strategy will considerably influence if not determine the character of the business operation – but equally the character of the business operation, once established, will largely determine what is possible in respect of developing a competitive strategy. The reason for this lies not only with resources being developed in accordance with the chosen competitive strategy but also with the culture of the organization gearing itself up to best fit the strategy. Nevertheless, while this appears restrictive, it is in fact these very resources and capabilities which are often the foundation of competitive advantage – they give the firm its distinctiveness and protect it from others copying its position.

The emphasis in this chapter is about building long-term, sustainable advantage over rivals. Having the vision to identify and then move to a novel market position is important in developing distinctiveness. Yet while such a move could offer immediate advantages and rewards through superior performance these will not be sustained unless the firm can defend the uniqueness of its position and build on its position in order to prevent it being outflanked or outmanoeuvred by rivals moving to even more desirable market positions. The important point is that positioning in the market is just the first stage – building and utilizing unique strategic resources and capabilities must follow in order for the firm to sustain that advantage.

The chapter begins with the market positioning options facing firms before considering in more detail the issues involved in sustaining competitive advantage. In respect of strategic choice, the central issue is about deciding on which *competitive* strategy to pursue. We begin by considering positioning in respect of what and how the firm can supply products/services to customers in contrast to rivals' products/services. This calls for an understanding of the attributes (both physical and intangible) that can be attached to a product/service and the method by which it can be produced and supplied. This approach, principally associated with Michael Porter (1980, 1985), is clearly a *supply-side* perspective and is explained in the next section. However, this is not the only way to look at how one stands relative to the competition. We can also conceive of a *demand-side* perspective, looking at how customers view different rival offers – for example, in respect of the price charged and the perceived value that these offers them. Our view is that using both perspectives is important in respect of choosing an appropriate competitive strategy.

Competitive Strategies

The objective in selecting and following a well defined 'competitive strategy' is to achieve *competitive advantage* – i.e. sustained superior profits compared with rivals.

This comes from positioning a firm in the market place so that it has an edge in coping with competitive forces (outlined in the previous chapter) and in attracting buyers. The essential aspect to competitive advantage is that a viable number of buyers end up preferring the firm's product offering because of the 'superior value' they perceive it has. Superior value is created in two ways: either by offering buyers a 'standard' product at a lower price, or by using some differentiating technique to provide a 'better' product (i.e. higher perceived quality than rivals') that consumers are willing to pay a higher price for.

According to Michael Porter (1985), to achieve competitive advantage management is faced with a choice between one of three strategies, which he calls 'generic competitive strategies' (generic in the sense that they can be pursued in *any* market):

- *Cost leadership strategy.* The firm strives to be the lowest-cost supplier and thus achieve superior profitability from an above-average price–cost margin.
- (*Product*) *differentiation strategy.* The firm strives to differentiate its product (or service) from rivals' products, such that it can raise price more than the cost of differentiating and thereby achieve superior profitability.
- *Focus strategy.* The firm concentrates on a particular segment of the market and applies either a cost leadership or a differentiation strategy.

These options are represented in figure 3.1, where the firm has the choice between operating across the market – a broad-based strategy – or operating only in a limited part of the market – a focus strategy. In each case the firm should seek

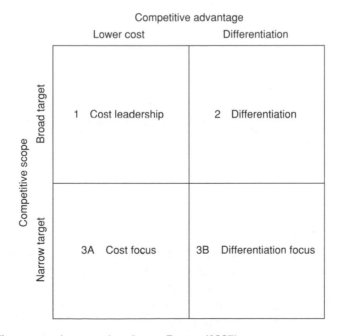

Figure 3.1 Three generic strategies. *Source*: Porter (1985)

either a cost leadership strategy or a differentiation strategy. Porter stresses that firms should not try to undertake more than one of these options.

Cost leadership strategies

Examples of successful implementation of this strategy in the United Kingdom include BiC in ballpoint pens and disposable razors, easyJet in low-cost passenger air travel, Matalan in discount clothes retailing, Aldi in the retail grocery trade and Egg in Internet banking. In each case the firm has kept costs to a minimum and products basic.

The rules for following this strategy are that the firm should seek to 'cover the bases' (i.e. emulate the quality of other products available to the consumer at each quality–price level), 'trim the fat' (i.e. reduce costs by trimming the product down to its bare essentials required at each price–quality level) and use resources fully (e.g. fully utilize capacity). In addition, producing several brand names at once may allow the firm to gain a larger share of the market and subsequently reduce costs if economies of scale are available.

Striving for an overall low-cost position typically entails the firm being the leader in constructing the most efficient plant, implementing cost-reducing technological advances, keeping overhead and administrative costs to a minimum and containing costs in R&D, advertising, service and distribution, while maintaining product quality. In particular, the firm should seek superior co-ordination across linkages in the value chain, while keeping costs to a minimum in each activity. Repositioning the firm may entail a fundamental internal shake-up, with working practices changed, automation extended, even relocation (closer to suppliers and/or customers). This applies equally across all industries, from utilities to manufacturing to services. For example, see exhibit 3.1 in regard to how Wal-mart drives costs down.

EXHIBIT 3.1 WAL-MART: DRIVING COSTS DOWN TO DELIVER SUPERIOR VALUE FOR CUSTOMERS

Wal-mart's sheer size is difficult to comprehend. With global sales around the US$250 billion mark, it is not only the largest retailer in the world, it is the world's largest company, measured by revenue. It has in excess of 1.3 million staff, making it the biggest private-sector employer in the world. It has more than 4,300 stores worldwide, all ultimately overseen by its headquarters in tiny Bentonville, Arkansas, in a building the size of twenty-four football fields. It handles supplies from 30,000 suppliers and it takes the world's second most powerful computer (after the Pentagon's) to support its logistics requirements.

Yet, for all these impressive statistics, Wal-mart tries to remain close to original its roots and the ideals of its founder, Sam Walton. Sam Walton's personal frugality appears to be a feature that the company has tried to maintain since its inception in 1962. While its profits are vast there appear few signs of opulence or ego at the company's austere headquarters. Executives have small offices, take out their own rubbish, pay for their own coffee, fly economy class and are told to bring pens back from conferences.

The company's small-town values supposedly carry over to its treatment of employees, who are called 'associates'. Most own shares and are on profit-share. They enjoy a degree of autonomy unseen in many other retailers. For instance, all store workers, from managers down to sales assistants, have the power to lower the price of any Wal-mart product if he/she spots it cheaper elsewhere. But rates of pay appear lower than for other retailers in the United States, like Safeway and Kroger. Yet it has a loyal work force. For example, in terms of distributing goods to its stores, turnover of drivers is only 5 per cent a year, compared with an industry average of 125 per cent.

It seeks to promote partnerships with trusted suppliers, while its pull on suppliers is so strong that 450 suppliers have opened offices near its headquarters. It is predicted that as many as 800 more such offices will be opened in five years. Its position as the world's biggest retailer means that it the biggest customer for most of the leading consumer-product companies. This makes those companies dependent on Wal-mart, providing the latter with enormous power to drive down the prices it pays suppliers. This buyer power is increasing further as it extends its own-label ranges.

Through its sheer scale and by maintaining rigorous control of costs it has unsurpassed efficiency and productivity as a retailer. For instance, the company shifts inventory twice as fast as the industry average. Combined with its buying power over suppliers it is able to offer its customers lower prices than most if not all its rivals. This it does through its aggressive 'every day low pricing' (EDLP) policy that applies across all its stores.

The result of all this is unmatched performance in the retail sector. In less than four decades it has come to account for nearly a quarter of US general merchandise sales and 8 per cent of total consumer spending (excluding cars and restaurants). Its same-store sales growth is running at five times the industry average and its pre-tax profits grew by 15 per cent a year over the 1990s. It operates in nine countries but has ambitious plans to extend into new ones. To retailers in those countries it may well seem that an unstoppable juggernaut is about to hit them.

Sources: 'Wal around the world', *Economist*, 8 December 2001; 'Wal-mart's influence grows', *USA Today*, 29 January 2003.

The strategy is likely to be most successful when demand is price-sensitive and the firms in the industry produce essentially standard products, with competition being mainly in terms of price. This could apply when buyers are not willing to pay the extra for differentiated products, or have common user requirements, or incur few switching costs in changing from one seller to another and are thus able to shop around for the best price.

There are attractive advantages in being the low-cost producer in an industry regarding defending oneself against the five competitive forces as defined by Porter (see chapter 2). In terms of industry rivalry, the low-cost company is in the best position to compete offensively on price. The low-cost company also has some protection over its profit margin when facing strong buyers, since prices will rarely be bargained below the survival level of the next-most-efficient firm. The low-cost firm's greater efficiency also protects it from upward pressure on input prices; in addition, its high volume will give it increased bargaining power against suppliers. Defending against potential entry is also made easier, since its low-cost position will make it difficult for new firms to compete effectively on price, and the (credible) threat of a price war will also act as a barrier to entry. Furthermore, the low-cost firm is in a favourable position, compared with its rivals, to use price cuts to defend against competition from attractively priced substitutes. There are, however, risks to following this strategy:

1 Technological changes can result in cost or process breakthroughs which nullify past investments and efficiency gains. Staying on top of cost-saving technological improvements can be expensive, especially if it involves scrapping existing equipment.
2 The advantage may be short-lived if rivals can easily imitate the leader's low-cost methods.
3 There may be a shift in the market, with consumers being less price-sensitive and willing to pay for added quality and service features. Commitment to this particular strategy can often lead to strategic inflexibility, such that the firm cannot easily respond to changes.
4 Strategic success in trying to be the low-cost producer requires the firm to be the overall cost leader, not just one of several firms vying for this position – for this would result in fierce competition and grim profit prospects until the leader was established and recognized.

By way of an example of what can go wrong, exhibit 3.2 considers the strategy of the Ford Motor Company in the early part of the twentieth century. Ford developed mass manufacturing based on being the low-cost leader, an extremely successful strategy for over a decade, but failed to take into account the changing nature of the market, with consumer preferences moving away from simply price to desiring more and different features. The problem arose because Ford's strategy of cost leadership necessarily entailed inflexibility, notably in production, but this spread right across the value chain into other activities, so much so that when the market changed Ford could not respond. Since this episode Ford has remained a long way behind General Motors in terms of worldwide market share.

EXHIBIT 3.2 COST LEADERSHIP BACKFIRING

In the early 1900s Henry Ford froze the design of the famous Model T and concentrated on mass production at low cost. Motor chassis parts were completely interchangeable for the entire period 1909–26. The Model T's price was cut from US$950 in 1909 to under US$300 in the early 1920s. As a result Ford's market share increased from 9 per cent in 1909 to a high of 55 per cent in 1921. Thereafter Ford failed to take into account the changing nature of consumer tastes and lost market share to General Motors. While the Model T was economical and dependable, for about US$100 more consumers could buy a Chevrolet which offered not only more modern styling but also greater speed, better transmission, cooling, lubrication, ignition and suspension. Consumers increasingly turned towards this car. Ford's market share fell to 41 per cent in 1925 and to 35 per cent in 1926.

Sources: Naylor *et al.* (1983); Lanzilloti (1961).

Differentiation strategies

Successful differentiation strategies are not simply based on giving a product additional or different attributes to those of its rivals. Key elements in success are that buyers can see the differences, customers are willing to pay extra for the differentiated product and rivals find it difficult to match the quality (attributes) of the product (either actual or as perceived by customers).

There are many ways in which products and services can be differentiated, for example:

- ease of use – Apple Mac user-friendly personal computer;
- consistent performance – Dyson vacuum cleaners;
- overall value to the consumer – McDonald's;
- reliability – Toyota cars;
- comprehensive range of products – Toys'r'us, B&Q, Decathlon;
- convenience/accessibility – Amazon;
- top-of-the-line image and reputation – Rolls Royce cars;
- different taste – Coca-cola;
- engineering design and performance – Mercedes Benz cars;
- unusual quality and distinctiveness – Rolex watches;
- technological leadership – Sony consumer electronics;
- rapid made-to-order service – Dell computers;
- late availability – Lastminute.com;
- safety – Volvo cars.

This list of approaches is not exhaustive. Successful differentiation strategies are numerous and can arise from any area or combination of areas in the value chain. For instance, the procurement of raw materials affects the performance and quality of the end product. Product-oriented R&D efforts lead to improved design, performance features, product variety and being the first to come out with new models. Process-oriented R&D efforts lead to improved quality, reliability and product appearance. Emphasis on the manufacturing process can give consistent product quality, maintenance-free use and long-term durability. The emphasis on the outbound logistics system can lead to improved delivery time and accurate order filling. Marketing, sales and customer service activities can result in quicker order processing, more and better training for end users, faster maintenance and greater customer convenience.

As with successful cost leadership, successful differentiation creates lines of defence for dealing with the five competitive forces. First, it raises the firm above intense price competition rivalry within the industry. Second, it acts as a barrier to entry in the form of customer loyalty and uniqueness that new entrants must overcome. Third, it puts the firm in a stronger position to ward off threats from substitutes, owing to its acquisition of a loyal clientele of customers. Fourth, it reduces the bargaining power of buyers, since the product alternatives are less attractive to them. Fifth, it puts the firm in a stronger position with regard to bargaining with its suppliers, based on the high selling prices and given its position of eminence in the market. Successful differentiation acting as a defence against the competitive forces puts the firm in a position whereby it can secure high levels of profits.

The extent to which a firm is able to differentiate, given the nature of the market, depends on the skills and competences available to it that competitors cannot easily match. Sustained competitive advantage is likely to come from four areas:

- technical superiority;
- quality;
- giving customers more support services;
- more value (for the same money).

Differentiation strategies are best suited to markets where there are many ways to differentiate the product or service and these differences are recognized by consumers to have value. This is especially so when buyers' needs and the uses of the item are diverse. Differentiation, as the word implies, means not following the crowd. In this sense it helps if few other firms are following a differentiation strategy.

Be warned – there are risks to following a differentiation strategy:

1 The additional cost of adding enough product attributes to achieve differentiation can result in a selling price so high that buyers opt for lower-priced brands.
2 Buyers may, over a period of time, decide that they do not need or want extra features, concluding that a basic model adequately serves their purposes, in which case emphasis is turned to low cost.
3 Rivals may imitate the product attributes of the leaders to such an extent that buyers cannot sufficiently distinguish between the products. In this case the

product developments of the firms cancel each other out and price becomes the main basis of competition.

4 Continual product innovation is expensive but may be necessary to sustain competitive advantage. Breaking new ground only for followers to follow quickly and more cheaply may not be attractive.

5 Broad-based differentiators may be outmanoeuvred by specialist firms focusing on one particular segment.

Focus strategies

A focus or specialization strategy aims at building a competitive edge and carving out a market niche position by concentrating on only a portion of the market, e.g. concentrating on a particular group of consumers or a limited geographical market, or certain uses for the product. Examples of firms employing a focus strategy include Rolls Royce (luxury cars), Land Rover (off-road vehicles), Ferrari (sports cars), Ryanair (low-cost flights to non-major airports), and Body Shop ('green' toiletries and cosmetics).

Competitive advantage via focusing is won either by cost leadership in the segment served or differentiation from meeting the needs of the target segment more effectively. This means either concentrating on cost-effectiveness for custom orders and short production runs, or providing unique and valued product features. The methods are very much the same as the broad-based cost leadership and differentiation strategies outlined above.

Focusing is particularly attractive when there are distinctly different market segments, no other rival is attempting to specialize in the same segment, the firm's resources do not permit it to operate right across the market, and when segments differ widely in the size, growth rate, profitability and intensity of the five competitive forces.

The successful focuser's specialized approach and unmatched skills in serving a limited market help it defend against the five competitive forces. Rivals do not have the same ability to serve the focused firm's clientele. Entry into the niche is made harder by the focuser's distinct competence. This also acts as a hurdle that substitutes must overcome. The unwillingness of customers to shift their business to firms with less capacity to serve their needs blunts their bargaining power.

As with the other generic strategies, there are risks involved in pursuing a focus strategy:

1 There is the possibility that broad-range competitors will find effective ways to match the focused firm in serving the target segment.

2 Unfavourable shifts in buyer preferences may leave the focuser without a viable market, or in the case where buyers start demanding additional attributes the segment may be taken over by a broad-based rival.

3 Competitors may find subsegments within the target segment and outfocus the focuser.

Being a focus operator can be difficult if what is being offered is fundamentally different from the existing offers and mode of operation in the market. As exhibit 3.3 illustrates, this can be particularly difficult for a focus cost leader that has to strike the right balance between keeping costs down but still be sufficiently attractive and accessible to consumers to ensure that demand is adequate.

EXHIBIT 3.3 SLATER MENSWEAR: IS BEING UPSTAIRS A SENSIBLE STRATEGIC POSITION?

Slater Menswear is a privately owned men's wear company that operates men's wear retail superstores. Launched in 1973, Slater's approach to men's wear retailing is markedly different from the norm. It aims to save on overhead costs by taking non-prime retail premises with very low visibility in town centres. This it achieves in a very distinctive way. All its stores are in tertiary retail positions on first or second floors, and most have no conventional ground-floor shop fascia or shop window. Being located 'upstairs', it can operate on a large scale at low cost. Its stores range in size from 16,000 sq. ft to 40,000 sq. ft. Indeed, it can proudly boast that its Glasgow store is the largest single men's wear store in the world.

The size of its stores allows it to stock very large ranges of clothes, mostly top brand names with the same or greater choice as in high-street retailers. Focusing on an up-market position, reflecting the designer-label clothes it sells, its showroom areas are laid out and equipped to a high specification, encouraging customers to browse around. While the location and positioning of its stores are poor, relative to those of its rivals, its lower cost base allows it to offer substantially discounted prices compared with those rivals (at around 30 per cent below recommended retail prices). Its pricing policy is to focus on offering continuous discounts across all ranges, and not to hold temporary sales or mark-downs, as these would undermine the strong value proposition that the company seeks to offer. Unusually for a discount retailer in the clothing sector, it is an official stockist for all its designer suppliers. This ensures that its merchandise is current, and styles are the same as can be found in other up-market men's wear retailers.

The company is rolling out its format across the United Kingdom. It has twelve stores, but more are planned. In order to make a success of its business proposition the company clearly needs to build up a strong customer base. However, in retailing the most important form of advertising is usually the store itself: the retail outlet acts as an advertisement for the store's wares to passing customers (e.g. through its shop windows). But in the case of Slater's passing consumer footfall is low (given its tertiary locations) and, of those passing, few might even notice its presence (given its upstairs locations). This means that Slater's must rely on other, expensive forms of advertising, like press advertising, to raise initial awareness and then hope that customers remain loyal and spread news of it by word of mouth – a notoriously unreliable mechanism for building custom in a fast-moving sector like fashion retailing. But, without it, Slater's may remain unknown to the great majority of the public and accordingly never become a major player in this market segment.

Sources: www.slatermenswear.com and *Menswear Discount Retailing*, Mintel report, 2001.

Key features of the generic competitive strategies

Each of the competitive strategies has its own distinctive features which lend themselves to particular management styles and points of emphasis as well as organizational culture. For convenience, these are summarized in the following list:

Overall low-cost leadership:

- production emphasis: 'nobody could do it cheaper';
- marketing/promotion emphasis: 'low, low prices' and 'outstanding value for money';
- operating culture: 'no frills' – reputation for being 'lean and mean';
- economies of scale from high volume: lower costs due to experience and bulk purchasing cost savings;
- process innovations to cut costs;
- high productivity per employee;
- price cutting as an offensive or defensive weapon;
- low profit margins in return for high volume – 'stack 'em high, sell 'em cheap'.

Broad differentiation:

- production emphasis: 'nobody could make it better';
- marketing/promotion emphasis: 'simply the best there is' and 'reassuringly expensive';
- operating culture: 'many frills' – 'the widest range of options/features' and 'something for every taste';
- create something different from competitors' products/services;
- product innovation to bring new products with new options to the market;
- premium pricing to cover added cost of differentiation;
- intensive advertising and sales efforts.

Focus:

- production emphasis: 'we tailor our product to meet your particular needs';
- marketing/promotion emphasis: 'just for you';

- specialization, e.g. buyer segments, geographical areas, final-use applications: 'we're *not* a Jack-of-all-trades, we're *master of one*';
- competitive advantage in the target segment depends on either (a) low-cost leadership (e.g. specialized experience/knowledge advantages); or (b) successful differentiation (e.g. offering something unique).

QUESTIONS

1 Which competitive strategy would work best for your company?
2 Would this involve a change from the present direction?
3 If yes, do you think the costs of repositioning the firm would outweigh the benefits?

EXERCISE

Consider the competitive positions of your rivals. Identify their strengths in terms of (a) their cost position (b) whether they have successfully differentiated their product(s) from the rest of the competition. Are there any lessons to be learned? Can you identify any unexplored but potentially profitable market niches?

Gaining Competitive Advantage

The message behind Porter's conceptualization of competitive strategies is that firms should select and commit to just one basis for competing and devote resources and attune the organization to this end. But is that the right way or even the only way to gain competitive advantage?

This section takes a critical look at Porter's prescription, examining the practical use of his concepts, the problems associated with putting theory into practice, and the ways in which it appears that many firms have managed to have the best (or at least the better part) of both worlds – differentiation advantages combined with low-cost positions. First, though, we begin with some observations on the undeniable economic logic behind Porter's concepts of competitive strategies, explaining why respectively cost leadership and differentiation can lead to superior performance.

Economic logic behind competitive strategies

In the case of being a successful cost leader, the firm is endowed with having lower operating (unit) costs than its rivals. Then (crucially) as long as the firm is not at a demand disadvantage relative to its rivals (say, due to inferior product/service quality) it will always earn more profit than its rivals no matter how intense competition becomes. We can see this through considering two cases. First, consider the situation where the firms compete under mild competitive conditions which lead to the establishment of a market price that allows most firms to earn positive profits. In that case, whatever the market price is, the cost leader will earn a higher profit margin than its rivals. Then, so long as the demand it receives is broadly equal to each of its rivals, it will earn greater overall profits. Second, the cost leader has the ability to win a price war in intensely competitive conditions. No matter how low a rival can price, the cost leader can still undercut the rival and make a profit. Indeed, it may even be a profitable strategy for it to drive competitors from the market and capture all their sales (and may be perfectly legal as long as it does not involve below-cost pricing as part of a predatory pricing campaign). This latter strategy becomes more profitable the greater the relative cost advantage.

A similar line of reasoning can explain why successful differentiation leads to superior performance. In this case, as long as the firm is not at a cost disadvantage to its rivals (say, owing to excessive expenditure on R&D and brand promotion) the firm will be able to earn superior profits compared with its rivals no matter how it chooses to react to competitors' positions. For instance, if it chooses to match rivals' prices, and thus earn broadly the same profit margin, then customers' stronger preference for its products will enable it to sell more than its rivals, and thus earn more profit overall. If, on the other hand, it wishes to match its rivals' level of sales, it will be able to command a higher price for that particular level, given the greater demand for its products, allowing it to earn a higher profit margin on that level of sales, and thus again higher total profits.

The message from this economic logic is that you cannot lose as a cost leader as long as you are not (significantly) demand-disadvantaged, and you cannot lose from being a successful differentiator as long as you are not (significantly) cost-disadvantaged. Clearly, though, these are important caveats to bear in mind if superior performance is to be guaranteed.

Factors influencing choice

So both strategies can offer superior performance compared with rivals, but which competitive strategy is the right one for you? There are no strict rules to follow here, as much depends on the firm's current position, the specifics of the market and existing competition within it, and the nature of products and services it provides. For instance, the current position is important because reorienting and consequently repositioning the firm may be no easy task and may involve substantial costs. For example, to pursue more rigorously a focused differentiation strategy may mean giving up existing customers if a move out of a market segment is required. Similarly, shifting emphasis towards low-cost leadership may mean giving up fairly successful differentiation advantages as the frills are dropped. But, more important, repositioning the firm towards a particular competitive strategy is likely to be very expensive if it involves major internal adjustments (changing and reorganizing resources), and there may be a long time lag before the firm is able to operate both efficiently and effectively.

The nature of the product, in terms of how easily consumers can evaluate quality, is likely to be a further important influence on the choice of strategy. 'Search' products, where consumers, and rivals, can easily evaluate the quality attributes of the product (prior to purchase), are typically best marketed by following a cost leadership strategy, unless the firm's product has a unique (or far superior) search attribute that rivals cannot immediately emulate (e.g. Coca-cola), in which case a differentiation strategy is appropriate (at least temporarily). On the other hand, 'experience' goods, where the product attributes are evaluated after purchase (e.g. food and modes of travel), offer more opportunities to pursue a successful differentiation strategy, since the attributes are less easily emulated by rivals. The same applies to 'credence' goods, where the attributes are only imperfectly evaluated even after purchase (e.g. the competence of services provided by solicitors or accountants, medical products and long-term financial service products like pensions), in which case the credibility of the seller, the brand name and the firm's reputation become very important. In this latter case differentiation strategies emphasize 'perceived' quality, rather than actual quality.

Thus market conditions and the nature of the product can have important external influence on choice, while the firm's resources and capabilities act as the internal drivers on choice of competitive strategy.

Hybrid strategies

But is it really essential to choose between the strategies? Is it not possible to pursue some hybrid strategy whereby the firm strives for both differentiation and cost leadership? Would this not lead to the best of all possible worlds? In response to such questions, Porter takes a very strict line:

> The worst strategic error is to be *stuck in the middle* or to try simultaneously to pursue all the strategies. This is a recipe for strategic mediocrity and below-average performance, because pursuing all strategies simultaneously means that a firm is not able to achieve any of them because of their inherent contradictions. (Porter, 1990: 40)

Thus, for Porter, the emphasis must be on the firm pursuing only one of these competitive strategies, since otherwise it will fall into the trap of being 'stuck in the middle'. In this case it will be unable to compete effectively either in terms of price competition (won by the low-cost firm) or in terms of non-price competition (won by successful differentiators). A classic example might be British Leyland, especially in the 1970s. The message is that highest profits are to be achieved by specializing (in the strategic sense), otherwise profit prospects will be poor. The point about 'inherent contradictions' has some basis in the very different management and organizational styles associated with each strategy (as shown in the list above). For instance, 'lean and mean' might be appropriate for cost leadership but not for differentiation, while 'providing the best' might be appropriate for differentiation but not for cost leadership.

Nevertheless, it is not always easy to attribute a firm's success to how well it has undertaken a particular (generic) competitive strategy. Think of a few really successful examples. Usually there are elements of differentiation that stand out, but this can sometimes be combined notable cost efficiency. Indeed a much discussed case in the early 1990s concerned the retail grocery chain J. Sainsbury. As discussed further in exhibit 3.4, Sainsbury's 'good food costs less' philosophy would seem

EXHIBIT 3.4 IS SAINSBURY'S (TERMINALLY) 'STUCK IN THE MIDDLE'?

To British consumers, Sainsbury's is a leading household name, a trusted company that has built up a loyal following among its shoppers. It has long been associated with the slogan 'Good food costs less at Sainsbury's'. This essentially characterizes the market positioning of the company, targeting cost-conscious customers who place a high value on good-quality food. As the diagram illustrates, the slogan is an assertive expression of a position that is 'stuck in the middle'. This figure represents Sainsbury's taking the middle ground of the market. For example, its prices are typically above those of stores like Asda, but quality is not as highly perceived as in stores like Marks & Spencer, where prices are higher.

	Unique value as perceived by customer	Lower cost
Broad	The best food is at Sainsbury's	The cheapest food is at Sainsbury's
	Good food costs less at Sainsbury's	
Narrow	Only organically grown produce is sold at Sainsbury's	Dairy produce is cheap at Sainsbury's

(Strategic scope)

From the late 1980s to the mid-1990s this position served Sainsbury's extremely well. It became the leading supermarket retailer in the United Kingdom, earning high profit margins in a sector traditionally associated with low profit margins. Group pre-tax profits grew at a staggering 20 per cent per annum over most of the period.

Much of this success was attributed to Sainsbury's strenuous efforts to keep costs down and at the same time maintain high quality. One of its primary corporate objectives was 'to provide unrivalled value to our customers in the quality of goods we sell, the competitiveness of our prices and in the range of choices we offer'. To this end it greatly extended its own-label products to up-market convenience foods, extended its fruit range to more exotic fare, and invested heavily in new technology, notably electronic scanning, to keep costs down and improve customer service.

In this period the company appears to have done remarkably well from blending the twin goals of low cost and high quality. Success, it would seem, came about through neither focusing on consumers who were purely price-conscious nor pursuing quality regardless of price.

Yet such stellar success did not continue. By 1995–6 Tesco had seized the leading position in the sector, on acquiring Wm Low. It has since increased its lead substantially and its group profits are nearly double those of Sainsbury's, whose profit performance has stagnated and whose second place looks increasingly vulnerable to the challenge from Asda/Wal-mart.

If Sainsbury's initial success was down to its market positioning, it might be considered that this also led to its relative decline, successfully challenged by more aggressive and more focused rivals. Certainly matching Sainsbury's perceived quality has been a major objective for many of its rivals, and then once achieved the fight has been about lowering prices to capture market share and exploit economies of scale. This is a game that appears to be much better suited to scale operators like Tesco and Asda than to Sainsbury's. But the game is far from over while there is still scope for further consolidation in the sector.

Sources: Cronshaw *et al.* (1994); authors' research.

to be a classic case of a firm falling between a cost leadership position and being a leading differentiator. Yet the company's success was substantial – it was the market leader in terms of market share and profit performance throughout the late 1980s and early 1990s. Subsequently it was overtaken by Tesco in terms of market share and profit performance, but it could be argued that Tesco is equally stuck in the middle – offering good but not exceptional food, at less cost than many but not necessarily all rivals. According to Porter's definition, both Sainsbury and Tesco in their respective heyday ought to be stuck in the middle, earning below-average performance rather than the stellar performance that they actually managed to achieve.

But Sainsbury and Tesco are not alone. A number of UK markets are dominated by such firms, e.g. Ford in cars, Cadbury's in chocolate, Marks & Spencer in retail clothing, and Boots in health and beauty retailing. One possible response to the accusation that they are stuck in the middle is that they are in fact successful differentiators, offering 'best overall value' in their respective markets, and this has led to them becoming market leaders and has helped them maintain that position and become established household names.

Table 3.1 Return on investment, by strategic position (%)

Relative quality	Cost relative to competitors		
	Low	Medium	High
Low	11.7	6.8	3.4
Medium	14.2	13.9	4.8
High	19.7	17.9	13.8

Source: Cronshaw *et al.* (1994).

Yet, on a more general level, there is broad empirical evidence to support the view that being stuck in the middle can be a profitable position. Table 3.1, based on US business-line data, relates return on investment to strategic position and shows that the stuck-in-the-middle position – medium cost, medium quality – offers slightly higher returns than the clearly focused choices of high cost/high quality or low cost/low quality:

So what can explain this result? One feature that many of the apparently stuck-in-the-middle firms have is a large market share. Market share only comes about if both the product and the price are right for customers. This in itself is nothing to do with profitability – a firm can 'buy' market share by selling an expensively produced quality product at a ridiculously low price. But empirically there is a strong statistical relationship between market share and profitability. This comes about by the two advantages that market share usually offers – economies of scale (lowering costs relative to rivals) and market power (allowing the firm to raise prices over costs when rivals' products are not perceived as identical). So that once high market share is acquired it could be self-sustaining, given the competitive advantages it offers over other firms. Indeed, having the highest market share can place a firm in a virtuous circle, whereby market share allows efficiency gains to be made through reaping economies of scale and increased buyer power which leads to high gross profits which can then be ploughed back into the business in the form of investments in product and process innovation to improve quality and so provide a differentiation advantage which in turns allows the firm to increase its market share, and so on, increasing market share and profits. This argument is illustrated diagrammatically in figure 3.2.

But even if we accept this virtuous-circle argument about why a firm that is stuck in the middle can carry on earning superior profits, a key question remains unanswered. How did the firm reach such a fortunate position in the first place? The answer would seem to be that it found a unique market position that had distinct appeal to consumers from its value proposition, which allowed it over time to build up both cost efficiency and improved product quality and delivery. In the context of retailing this appears to fit the origins of both Marks & Spencer and Boots from their market pioneering efforts over a century ago. With more recent cases, opportunism seems to have played an important role. In the case of Sainsbury it was about expanding a supermarket store network rapidly, while supporting this with

Figure 3.2 The virtuous circle

advanced logistical arrangements and tight supplier relations, and at the same time appealing broadly to the middle of the market, where the bulk of consumers lie, and so allowing significant market share gains, reinforcing its buying advantage compared with rivals. Economies of scale allowed a cost advantage while a combination of features (including emphasis on quality own-label goods and store quality and ambience) allowed it to develop a differentiation advantage over other mainstream grocery retailers. The combination allowed it superior performance.

However, Porter's criticism still remains an issue in view of the mixed fortunes that stuck-in-the-middle firms have enjoyed. In 1995 Sainsbury lost the crown of market leader along with its superior performance to Tesco, which went on to increase its market share and profits considerably, leaving Sainsbury in a distant second place. Similarly, while M&S and Boots are still market leaders in their respective markets they face major challenges to their position – the former by more fashion-oriented retailers and discounters, the latter by supermarkets.

The secret appears to be that once in the virtuous circle you must never stop using it. For if investment is not undertaken then differential and scale advantages can be lost to rivals, and once that happens the virtuous circle reverses, to become a vicious circle of declining (relative) market share and declining performance.

Demand-led strategy

Yet, at least in the context of retailing, there does appear to be a class of firms that seem to have real sustainable advantage from both differentiation and cost advantages. Specifically, so-called 'category killers' operate by providing the widest possible product range in their category (the differentiation advantage) at competitive prices, exploiting economies of scale at the store level and chain level (the cost advantage). Examples include B&Q, IKEA, Staples, Computer World, Toys'r'us, Hobby Craft and Decathlon.

To see why these firms are successful it is perhaps useful to consider their strategies not with the supply-oriented perspective of Porter but rather from the

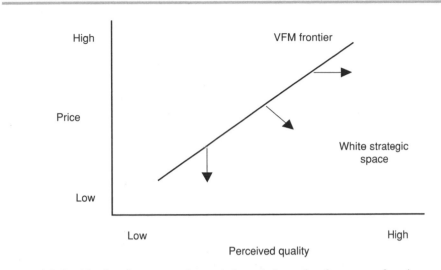

Figure 3.3 Positioning for success beyond the existing value-for-money frontier

perspective of the customers. Here customers' prime concerns will be price and their perception of quality, which together indicate overall value. With this perspective we can consider the choice and the trade-offs that firms will have to make when they position themselves. Ideally consumers would want both low price and high quality, but for firms to provide this would normally mean them earning low profits, as the two are normally incompatible. Thus we might normally see firms deciding to trade off one variable and accordingly we might observe low price/low quality and high price/high quality combinations, or alternatively trading off both for a mid-price/mid-quality position. This is indeed what we observe in many markets, where a value-for-money (VFM) frontier faces individual consumers from which they can choose a price–quality combination that best suits their needs when the ideal combination is unavailable.

We represent this VFM frontier diagrammatically in figure 3.3, with 'up-market' players at the top end and 'down-market' players at the bottom end, with 'mid-market' players in the middle. The challenge then for a firm wishing to stake out a new position in white strategic space, which allows a competitive advantage, is to devise a way of operating that allows it to lower price and/or raise (perceived) quality over and above existing price–quality levels (as indicated by the arrows) while maintaining its profit margins. Category killers appear to have achieved both aims, and have accordingly reaped the benefit of attracting additional demand at rivals' expense. But theirs has not been the only successful innovation in retailing. Hard discounting has taken off successfully in a number of markets, notably food (e.g. Aldi, Lidl and Netto), clothing (Matalan, TK Maxx and New Look) and car retailing (e.g. various car supermarkets), where efforts have been made to lower prices substantially while seeking to maintain a reasonable degree of quality.

Used together, this demand-side perspective and Porter's supply-side perspective give a more rounded viewpoint on strategic positioning – allowing the firm to consider not only what attributes it can add or processes it can use for differentiation or cost advantage, but also to see more clearly how it will stand in regard to gaining custom by increasing the value for money it ultimately offers its customers relative to its rivals.

QUESTIONS

1 What, in your opinion, was the reason for Sainsbury's initial success? On television Porter claimed that Sainsbury's success was derived from its attempt to be a low-cost firm; it did not try to compete on quality with other firms. Is that plausible?

2 In view of Sainsbury's losing its top position to Tesco, do you think that the other examples of successful stuck-in-the-middle firms are likely to sustain their positions without concentrating on one particular competitive strategy? Is it possible that success is more to do with the way the business is run than whether the firm has a low-cost position or its products are markedly different from its rivals?

Competitive Advantage through Resources and Capabilities

If competitive advantage is initially gained from distinct market positioning then it will be very temporary success unless there are reasons why other firms cannot take up similar or even identical positions. What underlies the success of any competitive strategy is ultimately to do with the firm itself: either what it possesses, i.e. 'resources', or what it can do, i.e. 'capabilities' – where both are intrinsically linked. Moreover, this is relative to what competitors do not have or are not capable of doing.

This becomes immediately apparent if we reflect for a moment on what is the actual source of a cost leadership or differentiation advantage. In the case of cost leadership it is often about resources that allow low cost (e.g. the most productive workers, the most efficient suppliers, the leanest production system and routines, the largest plant, the most efficient distribution network, a cost-cutting and process innovation culture, etc.). Similarly, in the case of differentiation it is often about resources that allow a distinct position on product or service attributes (e.g. the most skilful workers, the highest-quality suppliers, the most adaptable or intricate production system and routines, the highest-quality distributors, the strongest brand name or best reputation, a quality enhancement and product innovation culture, etc.).

With this in mind, and with the aim of securing long-term competitive advantage, the battle is not just about positioning but about competing on resources and capabilities. Here resources can be physical or intangible (e.g. brand names or technological know-how) while a capability might be an organizational one embedded in a company's routines, processes and culture. Competitive advantage ultimately can be attributed to the ownership of a valuable resource or capability that enables a company to perform activities better or more cheaply than competitors. Accordingly, superior performance is based on developing a competitively distinct set of resources and capabilities and then deploying them in a well conceived strategy.

Collis and Montgomery (1995) argue that, for a resource or capability to be competitively valuable and qualify as the basis for an effective strategy, it must pass a number of external market tests of its value:

1 *The test of inimitability.* Is the resource hard to copy? Inimitability may be due to (a) physical uniqueness (b) path dependence (i.e. history) (c) causal ambiguity (often organizational capabilities) and (d) economic deterrence.
2 *The test of durability.* How quickly does the resource depreciate?
3 *The test of appropriability.* Who captures the value that the resource creates?
4 *The test of substitutability.* Can a unique resource be trumped by a difference resource?
5 *The test of competitive superiority.* Whose resource is really better? Identify distinctive competence by disaggregating resources

In practice, firms will rarely be ideally positioned with competitively valuable resources. More likely, they will have a mixed bag of resources – some good, some mediocre and some outright liabilities. Even for those companies which have unusual assets or capabilities, these valuable resources will need to be joined with other resources and embedded in a set of functional policies and activities to distinguish the company's position in the market. Appropriate management of the resources and capabilities is therefore crucial and involves three activities:

1 *Investing in resources and capabilities*: continual investment to look after the crown jewels that distinguish the business.
2 *Upgrading resources and capabilities*: add new resources, upgrade to alternative resources or to move to another industry.
3 *Leveraging resources and capabilities*: continual reassessment of the company's scope for new markets in which to exploit current resources.

In respect of where distinctive capabilities are derived from, John Kay (1993) points to the 'architecture' of the organization as a key source. As he illustrates with examples, many of the most successful companies have built and maintained superior performance through their distinctive architecture. He distinguishes between three levels of architecture:

• *Internal*: between the firm and its employees and among employees.
• *External*: between the firm and its suppliers or customers.
• *Networks*: between a group of collaborating firms.

At each level, architecture can add value to individual contributions through the creation of organizational knowledge, through the establishment of a co-operative ethic, and by the implementation of organizational routines. Architecture may thereby lend itself either towards reinforcing cost leadership, such as external linkages allowing just-in-time production processes and efficient quality control, or differentiation advantages, such as selling through a network of high-quality dealers. More generally, an effective architecture can allow swift changes and responses to changing business environments that can suite either cost leaders or successful differentiators.

In situations where customers can learn about product characteristics only from long-term experience (i.e. over experience and credence products), *reputation* may be a critical resource. The reputation of a company in providing good-quality products can be a useful means of competitive advantage by allowing the firm to price higher than rivals and still make strong sales. Building reputation comes through building consumer trust. This may be facilitated by providing money-back assurances, free trials and long-term warranties, as well as making commitments to the market, e.g. by large advertising and promotion expenditures. Also staking a reputation from elsewhere may prove useful, such as Virgin's expansion into new, demand-unrelated markets.

In dynamic markets it can often be a firm's ability to innovate that keeps it one step ahead of competitors. Undertaking innovation and ensuring that returns are fully appropriated by the firm (and not by its rivals immediately copying the innovation) can lead to the generation of new products and/or process which respectively yield increased demand or increased cost savings, both aiding competitive advantage. An innovative product or process is clearly an important resource. Managing the process for repeated success is a distinct capability, which few companies can attain. Ensuring full appropriation can be difficult unless the innovation is legally protected (e.g. by patents or copyright), obscure/hidden (such as a secret process or formula) or sufficiently complex and/or expensive to put rivals off copying it.

Even in markets where product characteristics are immediately apparent, innovative activity is limited, and no distinctive capability is apparent, it can still be resources that allow for competitive advantage to be sustained. Kay (1993) points to three types of 'strategic assets' that can fill this role: (1) natural monopoly, (2) experience and commitment through sunk costs, (3) market restrictions providing exclusivity. In all three cases the strategic assets allow the firm to defend its market position and protect it from rivals invading its strategic space.

First, natural monopoly results from scale economies and narrow markets and can follow from compatibility standards or interdependence between customers. Here competition may be restricted owing to the market being able to support only a limited number of firms – possibly just one. This can apply to the natural monopoly elements of utility and transport industries such as the network infrastructure for gas pipelines, electricity transmission and rail track, but it can equally apply where the market is just narrow on a geographic or product basis.

Second, sunk costs as strategic assets arise through tangible capital investment as well as through reputation, advertising and market knowledge. These are irreversible investments made by the firm that provide advantage when rivals cannot match or beat the investment. Duration and experience in the market can provide similar benefits (e.g. through cost reduction and reputation building) when it is difficult or even impossible for rivals to match these benefits, which only come with time served in the market.

Third, exclusivity can result from licensing (e.g. to exploit a resource or an exclusive right to supply) and regulation. These can provide important first-mover advantages that can be reinforced through strategic action to establish and sustain incumbency advantages. For example, exhibit 3.5 considers the thorny issue of how much OfTel should intervene in the UK fixed-line telecoms market to promote

---

EXHIBIT 3.5 RETAINING MARKET SHARE BY 'SAVING' CUSTOMERS AT BRITISH TELECOM

Exhibit 2.1 in the last chapter detailed the potential for opening up the fixed-line telecoms market to greater competition with the introduction of carrier pre-selection (CPS) services. In principle, other telecoms operators and new entrants could be encouraged to compete against BT by the prospect of winning consumers over by offering lower prices. However, many of these competitors claim that even offering low prices may not be enough to weaken BT's dominant position in the market. In particular, BT has been accused of sharp practice to encourage disaffected customers to remain loyal to its service.

Specifically, nineteen telecoms companies, including leading firms such as Cable & Wireless, Centrica and Energis, made a joint protest to the industry regulator, OfTel, over its failure to stop attempts by BT to frustrate the introduction of competition. Their claim is that OfTel has not prohibited BT from attempting to 'save' customers who have already decided to defect. When BT is notified that customers wish to switch supplier, it is free to contact them and try to persuade them to change their minds. They argue that this is fundamentally anti-competitive when used by a dominant incumbent in an immature CPS market. They point out that 'save' activity is not permitted in any other EU country that has introduced CPS.

According to its rivals, BT is managing to hang on to about a quarter of the customers who initially opt for a cheaper alternative. This increases customer acquisition costs and consequently cuts profitability in an industry where BT's rivals earn very thin margins. In the absence of regulatory intervention, it looks as if BT will be able to use its strong position as incumbent to considerable effect, making it difficult for rivals to gain market share at its expense. This benefit, along with its others like experience and scale, means that BT's dominant position may yet last for quite some while.

Of course this could all change if OfTel did respond with tighter regulation on BT and/or there is a concerted attempt by rivals with deep pockets to wrestle market share from BT – in which case a bloodbath could ensue, with competition focused purely on price.

Source: 'Regulator asked to block BT ploy that stops customers defecting', *Sunday Times*, 25 May 2003.

competition, while at the same time BT seeks to defend its dominant market position from attack by other firms. Here a major advantage for BT would appear to be its *installed customer base* as a legacy of when it was the only provider in the market prior to deregulation in the early 1980s. In order for rivals to take customers away from BT they have to overcome consumer inertia (where consumers may be unwilling to change suppliers even if there are cost savings to be made), but even if they are successful in gaining some customer interest in switching away from BT, BT may still be able, through direct contact, to persuade such customers to remain loyal.

Market Turbulence and Hypercompetition

Can competitive advantage be sustained by only applying one competitive strategy supported by resources and capabilities that are difficult to imitate? Richard D'Aveni (1994) suggests not in *hypercompetitive* markets, that is, in situations where firms are forced by the intensity of competition to keep innovating and/or adapting their offer to keep one step ahead of competition. Reminiscent of Joseph Schumpeter's (1943) notion of 'creative destruction', firms are obliged to change their product offer or processes in order to sustain a strong market position by the fear of competitors overtaking them. This particularly applies in mature oligopolistic markets where competitive pressure comes less from the threat of entrants or substitutes than from the intensity of rivalry among existing players. In this setting, established firms can quickly learn to imitate strategies of market leaders, and it becomes harder to sustain any competitive advantage for long.

Classic examples are the strategies pursued by Intel and Microsoft. Both firms could have sat back on their dominant positions in computer processor chips and operating systems and business application software respectively. However, both firms have continued to release new versions of their products, making the old ones redundant but in the process raising the stakes in their respective industries, and so making it more difficult for competitors to gain market share or even a foothold.

Lessons come from where others fail to keep reinforcing their advantage, allowing rivals to catch up and overtake. Classic examples include IBM in personal computers, Philips in video-cassette recorders, Hoover in vacuum cleaners and Xerox in photocopiers. In all these cases a rival usurped their market-leading position and changed the rules of competition in its own favour. The loss of an apparently impregnable position only serves to spur on other firms in other markets to challenge and outmanoeuvre market leaders, to develop ways round the existing basis of competition and change the rules of the game in their favour.

In some cases, the failure to sustain competitive advantage arises from the firm 'taking its eye off the ball', through complacency and lack of appropriate investment in the source of its advantage (what essentially amounts to pressing the self-destruct button). In other cases, though, it is down to a smart rival finding a way round the existing basis of superior performance, even when it is fortified by differentiation, first-mover advantages, dominance in geographical areas or market segments, and by considerable financial and other resources (like scale economies).

The point is that building barriers to defend distinctiveness may not be sufficient to ensure competitive advantage. In fast-changing markets it becomes likely that the relative advantage diminishes as competitors learn how rapidly to imitate the leader or indeed find new ways of doing business which take away the leader's advantage entirely. An example that has changed the established order in many markets is e-business. Electronic commerce, in respect of B2B and B2C, has revolutionized business practice in many markets. Often the old guard have been caught off-guard by e-savvy new businesses. When a bricks-and-mortar store network once seemed like a critical resource for a retailer, Internet retailing has in several instances made this resource considerably less important, if not redundant. It has already had a considerable impact on the retailing of books, CDs, DVDs, flights and packaged holidays, and its share of sales looks set to increase in other areas, such as household appliances, hi-fi systems, computers and even food. Moreover, while there are many instances of calamitous failure as the Internet bubble burst (such as Boo.com), there are important success stories that have revolutionized the mode of exchange or character of competition in their respective markets, e.g. eBay, Amazon and Lastminute.

Yet it is not just e-business that has changed many markets. Finding alternative ways of reaching consumers such as through direct selling have fundamentally altered several markets (consider, for example, the success of Dell in computers and Direct Line in insurance). Sometimes it is about the development and promotion of a new product standard or technology that changes a market. For example, the triumph of VHS over Betamax favoured Japanese VCR producers, with Philips losing out. Similarly, Nokia and Ericsson gained considerably from the introduction of digital wireless and cellular technology, circumventing Motorola's dominance of analogue-based cellular phones. In other cases, it can be radically changing the scale of business activity. Consider the earlier example of category killers – dedicated specialists that dominate competition through the comprehensiveness of their product range and their low prices.

In respect of developing strategy either in regard to maintaining or challenging dominant positions much depends on the degree and nature of market turbulence. D'Aveni (1999) usefully distinguishes between four situations:

- *Equilibrium,* where the environment is characterized by long periods of little or no change with incumbents controlling the environment by creating barriers to entry for potential competitors and restraining rivalry within the industry allowing it to exploit a protected competitive space (e.g. De Beers' control of the diamond market).
- *Fluctuating equilibrium,* with rapid turbulence based on frequent competence-enhancing disruptions by industry leaders as they lay new competences on top of old ones. This, in turn, forces everyone else to catch up and allows the leader to leverage its core competences into new product markets while others are still catching up (e.g. Sony combining competences in electronic miniaturization and brand name to move into new digital electronic markets).

- *Punctuated equilibrium*, with brief dynamic periods based on discontinuous change or competence-destroying revolutions, each in turn followed by longer periods of convergence (where the market organizes around the new common standard established by the revolution) and greater stability. Where radical technological changes are followed by an emerging dominant design or standard a period of stability can ensue, until the next technological revolution, with the cycle repeating itself (e.g. the flat glass industry over the last century).
- *Disequilibrium*, a hypercompetitive environment characterized by frequent, discontinuous disruptions, as in many high-tech industries and newly deregulated markets. Here competence-destroying changes take place as successful incumbents constantly create new competences to replace obsolete ones, keeping rivals off balance, forcing them to spend even more energy catching up and reacting (e.g. Amazon targeting new product markets).

In regard to each of these four characterizations, the goal of incumbent leaders and challengers is to achieve strategic supremacy by controlling the degree and pattern of turbulence. Strategic supremacy in this context means not only control over the environment, but also the paradigm used for the creation of wealth. Different rules or norms of competition create profits differently in each environment. In an equilibrium environment, dominant firms can profit by shutting out rivals and using power over buyers and suppliers to extract monopoly profits. In environments of fluctuating equilibrium, dominant firms use core competences to profit from customers seeking to use these unique competences. In punctuated equilibrium, dominant firms make profits from the first-mover advantage of a revolution that sets a new industry standard and then positioning themselves to react to the next revolution. The dominant firm in disequilibrium profits by constantly improving and creating value through innovation.

In some cases, firms have turned around their own performance by fundamentally altering the nature of competition in their own favour. Exhibit 3.6 illustrates how Gillette transformed the basis of competition in the razor market – shifting it from a low-value, cost-focused market into a high value, innovation-led market through a series of product innovations that each time displaced the existing product standards.

EXHIBIT 3.6 RAZOR-EDGED INNOVATION: GILLETTE REWRITES THE RULES OF COMPETITION

Becoming a market leader is difficult; sustaining that position can be equally difficult. In the case of Gillette, it learned its lesson the hard way.

In the early 1970s Gillette's position in the razor market looked secure. It had been a pioneer in developing cartridge-based razors and was market leader in both North America and Europe. But Bic's disposable razors threatened to shift the dominant value proposition to low-cost convenience, in the process shaking up the established order in the industry. Bic successfully grew a small niche into a mass, worldwide market, cannibalizing Gillette's cartridge approach by continually lowering the cost and increasing the value of its razors to attract customers and stimulate new demand. For Bic, the move transformed the game to one that it knew how to play well, with its low-cost plastic manufacturing and efficient distribution for pens, lighters and other products. At the same time, the shift threatened to transform Gillette's heavy R&D investment from an advantage to a burden as the name of the game shifted away from differentiation to being all about cost leadership. Indeed, for Gillette, being forced to play by Bic's rules and offer its own disposable razors left it in the uncomfortable position of earning wafer-thin margins while still seeing market share being eroded.

Yet today Gillette reigns supreme in a market from which it earns high returns. How did it manage to achieve this? In a word: innovation. But not just one-off innovation, rather a series of major breakthrough innovations that each time raised the quality game and ensured that competitors were forced to catch up. And not just innovation on its own: each innovation was backed by massive promotion to establish instant brand recognition and appeal.

The launch and promotion of Mach 3 in 1998 is an illustration of these moves by Gillette. With an investment of more than US$1 billion in development and advertising, the product redefined the rules of competition by shifting the focus from established twin-blade razors to the novelty of triple-blade razors. The move allowed Gillette to continue dictating the rules in an industry in which it has created the world's No. 1 shaving system. It is also indicative of Gillette's intention to disrupt the market periodically by launching breakthrough products, which ratchet up the design specification and quality of razor products available to consumers. Indeed, Mach 3 is just one of a long line of product innovations launched and promoted by Gillette, allowing it to sustain leadership in defining the shaving game.

Indeed, the success of Gillette redefining the rules away from cost leadership and cheap product competition goes back many years before the launch of Mach 3. A key date appears to be 1989, with the introduction of the Sensor. With this product Gillette shifted the rules of winning to brand image and shaving quality. The muscular R&D that had slowed its profits in disposables became an asset. Bic could not compete in this environment. (Although disposables did not vanish completely, they no longer defined the market, with cartridge use growing at the expense of disposables.) Meanwhile Gillette continued to disrupt the environment and perfect its game of shaving closeness with the introduction of the Sensor Excel in 1993 and Mach 3 in 1998, establishing a pattern of stability punctuated by disruptions.

The pattern with each innovation is the same. After each disruption, Gillette consolidates its gains around the new standard. Each time the new overtakes the old in terms of sales. But, just as the market appears to settle again, Gillette seeks to launch another product to punctuate the equilibrium. Even Mach 3 has now been superseded. The release of Mach 3 Turbo in 2002 continued the trend of a disruptive Gillette innovation for the rest of the industry to respond to.

This series of innovations, along with others in the industry, has fundamentally changed the nature of competition. Prior to them, competition became focused primarily on outplaying competitors at a fixed game (like making a better or cheaper disposable razor than Bic). Now, though, the central focus of strategy is on understanding the relationship between an environment's turbulence and the company's choice of strategy. In an environment in which quality is defined by technological progress and branding Gillette wins and achieves strategic supremacy.

Sources: Richard A. D'Aveni, 'Strategic supremacy through disruption and dominance', *Sloan Management Review*, 40, 1999, pp. 127–35; gillette.com.

While the Gillette case illustrates how one firm took control and maintains control of the rules of the game, in other markets the battle continues for dominance, not in the usual context of market share and present performance, but in respect of determining the main basis for competition. This can be a bloody battle where firms try to mix strategies from all four of the above environments, often simultaneously striving for competence-enhancing changes in some dimensions and making competence-destroying changes in other dimensions. A current case in point is the personal computer market (exhibit 3.7), where two giants with

EXHIBIT 3.7 THE BATTLE FOR SUPREMACY IN THE PC INDUSTRY

The battle for top spot in the worldwide personal computer market has come down to Hewlett-Packard (HP) and Dell, two heavyweight rivals that have outlasted or vanquished a long list of contenders. Both companies, though, have very different business models – HP is geared to product innovation as its key basis for competition; Dell is geared to cost reduction in the provision of low-cost personal computers (PCs). For both firms, it is not just about gaining top spot in respect of market share but also about determining the very basis of competition in the market, to ensure that the game is played to their respective strengths. Clearly, in such a battle, with such disparate positions, there is going to be only one winner. But who will it be?

Dell holds the upper hand in respect of both market share and profitability. It has a lean, mean low-cost emphasis much suited to a market where PCs are made of standard components and where innovation is incremental and broadly predictable. Its low-cost direct sales approach has paid considerable dividends, allowing it to gain market share to the point where its controls 17.3 per cent of the world market. Moreover, with its low R&D costs, efficient supply chain management and direct sales model, Dell is widely expected to extend its lead.

In market share terms, HP, at 15.4 per cent of the world market, is not far behind Dell. Yet its profits are considerably smaller. It has been playing to Dell's rules, slashing costs by reducing staff, squeezing suppliers for annual savings of US$3.5 billion and substantially lowering its PC prices. But while this may have saved it losing market share, its margins are still very small – all this at a time when its US$19 billion take-over of Compaq should have projected it into a profitable No. 1 position.

HP recognizes that for it to stand any chance of gaining supremacy it needs to change the competition rules in its favour. This, it feels, may be possible if it can offer better value by out-engineering Dell to build sleeker machines with more features for high-end markets. It is a strategy that invites the question: does innovation pay in a market now almost entirely based on industry-standard components?

HP's chief executive, Carly Fiorina, thinks that the fight is far from over. Her prediction is that the two companies will trade rounds like two prize fighters. She argues HP will hold its own by keeping costs down even as it invests in cutting-edge products and focuses on the fastest-growing and most profitable segments of the market. This view is given some support with HP leading the way with new concepts and models such as the PC Tablet and the Media Center PC. HP has also teamed up with Microsoft to design a concept PC dubbed Athens, rich in design features. Out-innovating Dell in an array of different segments and new product areas is the clear intent.

However, sceptics remain unconvinced that PC innovation will pay off for HP. Observers point to real innovation taking place in Microsoft's software and Intel's microprocessors while PC makers such as Dell and HP have become little more than assembly shops. They also point to Dell's history of taking advantage of other companies' innovations and efforts to develop new markets. Concern has also been expressed that HP could trip up as it pursues innovation while trying to keep costs down – two conflicting goals. Innovation can win, as demonstrated by the success of Apple, and to a lesser degree by Sony, but whether it is possible to mix models that can be in conflict remains to be seen.

Source: Scott Morrison, 'Clash of the PC titans', *Financial Times*, 28 May 2003.

very different core competences are trying to ensure that the market follows the rules that they are best suited to. As a high-volume cost leader Dell would clearly benefit from a market fought on a price base where products are standardized. Hewlett-Packard/Compaq would clearly like competition to be centred on innovation, where they have comparative strengths. With such a clear divergence of interests, this battle has all the hallmarks of turning the environment into a distinctly disequilibrium, hypercompetitive market until a winner emerges.

Dealing with the Opposition

We complete this chapter on business-level strategy by considering specific tactics and strategies in waging competitive warfare. Throughout the chapter many examples of successful companies and their general strategies have been cited, but to gain a fuller appreciation of how success is achieved we need to consider the strategic actions ('tools' or 'weapons') that can be deployed and the market circumstances when each of them appears most appropriate.

From the previous section we have observed that different markets are characterized by different patterns and degrees of turbulence. Yet for firms in any environment there is generally a common set of tools that could be used with the specific purpose of tackling competition – either through undermining it (to 'beat rivals') or softening competition through co-operative moves (on the basis of 'if you can't beat them, join them'). Yet, while the tool set is common, the appropriateness will vary according to circumstances. This is an important aspect, sometimes overlooked in devising appropriate competitive strategy. Consideration of it helps in taking better account of actual and potential competitors and assessing their likely response to the organization's strategy. With better understanding of the competitive response and possible counter-responses, the strategist is better placed in devising a plan of campaign to beat or at least neutralize these competitors in order to enhance or at least protect its market position.

An important distinction is in regard to whether we are concerned with a *new* market or an *existing* market with several competitors. In the former case, if the firm is the sole operator, say through inventing a new product, and is the first firm in a newly created market, it will be in a monopoly position. We are then concerned with how to protect that position and prevent new entry by other organizations.

Being the first firm into a market may give the firm a 'first-mover advantage' over other firms. This advantage arises when the existing (i.e. incumbent) firm has natural advantages over other firms, say thanks to experience effects making its costs lower than rivals' and reputation and/or brand loyalty effects to make consumers unwilling to try another firm's product. These 'natural' barriers to entry can also be enhanced by 'strategic' barriers to entry, where the organization's deliberate actions seek to make entry difficult. Strategic actions may involve direct pre-emptive strategies, say by continued product innovation or by creating the industry standard (e.g. Microsoft operating system) and protecting it by patent to make further entry into the segment unprofitable. Alternatively, it may involve the organization taking a more aggressive action to convince a likely entrant that it is not in its best interests to enter the market by (credibly) threatening to use predatory behaviour. This may take the form of building extra plant capacity to fight a price war, tying up all available raw material suppliers with long-term contracts or tying up a distribution network to foreclose the market unless the entrant can enter as a vertically integrated firm making its own inputs and selling its own output to final consumers. A common element among each of these tactics is *strategic commitment,* using a first-mover advantage to commit (irreversibly) to an investment pattern and mode of behaviour which put other firms off entering the market or encourage them to compete less aggressively (see Ghemawat, 1997, for further examples).

In contrast, strategic actions in established markets are likely to be undertaken for a different purpose. While it is still important to prevent new entry, the organization is probably more likely to be concerned with existing rivals and the competitive pressures they pose. In established and especially mature markets, the organization may be faced with several competitors offering broadly similar products and operating with similar cost structures. This can lead to intense rivalry, and the firm may be concerned with developing and implementing policies aimed at changing its operating environment to make competition less fierce. Of course, differentiation strategies are directed towards this intense competition problem, but the firm also has the opportunity to alter the business environment by using either *aggressive* (a.k.a. *non-co-operative*) strategies to remove existing rivals from the scene. They may do this by forcing rivals out of the market through predatory behaviour, say by initiating and winning a price war and thus establishing a reputation for responding aggressively and so making other firms think carefully about moving onto their 'patch' in the market.

Alternatively, the firm could use *co-operative* strategies to induce the other firms to behave more co-operatively and lessen the intensity of competition through collusion, e.g. by price information sharing schemes, forming strategic alliances, or through non-compete arrangements (e.g. each manufacturer using exclusive supply agreements with its own suppliers and using exclusive dealing arrangements with its own retail customers). In this context, a little bit of game theory (e.g. Dixit and Nalebuff, 1991) helps us see that even apparently ultra-intense competitive strategies can serve to reduce competition. Consider for a moment price-matching promises made by different retailers in the same market. These sound distinctly pro-competitive. The consumer can search around and use the lowest price found in the market to obtain the goods from any retailer offering such a price-matching promise. However, looking at this from the perspective of the firms, such price promises offer the possibility of supporting a collusive agreement to maintain high prices. The reason is that if a high price exists in the market there will be no individual incentive to undercut it, for if a firm did so the move would in effect be automatically matched by its rivals, and thus would confer no benefit, not even a temporary one, in gaining any extra sales for the undercutting firm. Faced with this instant response mechanism, each firm would have no incentive to cut prices and thus price would remain high. Thus we have the paradoxical result that what appears to be ultra-competitive may in fact be an effective co-operative strategy, in theory at least!

Table 3.2 Importance of strategic tools

Policy	Chemicals/ pharma	Electricals	Food/drink	Financial services
Patenting	5/5	6/6	7/7	5/5
R&D	1/1	1/1	1/1	2/3
Advertising	6/6	5/5	4/5	4/4
Capacity creation	7/7	7/7	6/6	n.a.
Pricing policy	4/4	2/3	5/3	3/2
Assured supply of materials	2/3	4/4	3/3	n.a.
Selling network for products	3/2	3/2	2/2	1/1

The highest ranking is 1. The first figure is rank in existing firm competition, the second relates to new products.

Source: Singh *et al.* (1991a).

With such a range of possibilities, it might be instructive to see the extent to which they are used in different contexts. With this aim in mind, and more generally to throw some light on the degree to which firms in different markets use these tools, Singh *et al.* (1991a, b, 1998) conducted a questionnaire survey of 377 UK companies involved in manufacturing and (financial) services. Their study shows how the use of strategic policies by companies to deal with competitors varies between established markets and markets for new products, as well as across different sectors of industry. Table 3.2 shows the ranking that firms assign to a variety of strategic tools in four sectors of the economy both for competition with existing products and for dissuading entry of new products.

Table 3.2 reveals that the main tool used is research and development (R&D). This was found to be primarily attributable to firms giving high priority to continual improvement of the quality of the product launched (i.e. for product development) or to modifying products to sell overseas (i.e. for market extension). Other motives cited for using R&D included finding derivatives to plug gaps where competitors could enter (i.e. a strategy of 'brand proliferation', e.g. consider the product range of Procter & Gamble and Unilever in the household detergent market or Kellogg's in the ready-to-eat breakfast cereals market) and keeping pace with other firms' imitative products (especially in the electricals sector, where technological opportunity is high). However, even though R&D was seen as the main competitive weapon, protecting these innovations by patents was seen as having a low priority. This suggests that the nature of R&D is for incremental innovation rather than for fundamental innovation. Only in the chemicals and pharmaceutical sector (where, incidentally, the United Kingdom does have international market leaders) do patents assume some importance.

Advertising, somewhat surprisingly, was not ranked especially high. Its main purpose was to ensure sales of new products. Only in the food/drinks sector was advertising seen as being important over the product life cycle to build and maintain brand loyalty. Similarly, pricing policy was not viewed as being especially useful, possibly because of the recognized dangers to profitability of price wars. The chief exception was in the electricals market for established products. Competition here to establish market share can be cut-throat: life cycles are fairly short and heavy R&D and product launching costs must be recouped. In general, prices were determined by a standard cost-plus-mark-up procedure, with firms seemingly trying to 'meet' rather than 'beat' the competition.

Apart from R&D, the other chief policies appear to be concerned with the vertical linkage in the market, i.e. between suppliers and buyers. Both the use of long-term buying contracts with suppliers (giving assured supply for the firm while at the same time limiting the availability of raw materials to new entrants) and the creation of distribution networks through which the organization's products can be sold (preferably on an exclusive dealing basis) appear to be widely used in the manufacturing sector. Both tactics are important for long-run performance beyond the life cycle of the current product range. They make entry into the market difficult for new players, but make it relatively easy for the organization to bring new products to the market successfully by having the input suppliers lined up and 'guaranteed' outlets for the new products.

According to the survey, countering a competitor's move was viewed as the best way to react to entry. In the manufacturing sector this generally means altering the product range, by updating or providing additional features, or looking for new markets in which to sell the existing product. Copying the competitor's product was not a common reaction, nor was the use of price cutting or intensive advertising and other promotional activity.

A slightly different picture emerges in a similar type of questionnaire study by Smiley (1988) on strategies that US firms use to deter entry. Contrary to the above findings for the United Kingdom, Smiley's study found that advertising to build up brand loyalty was the most widely used and best regarded weapon to prevent entry and protect market share in markets for both new and existing products. R&D (including patenting) was found to be the second most used tactic, but seen as significantly less important than advertising in markets for established products. As in the UK study, attempting to foreclose markets through distribution channels or input purchases was also widely used, while price policy (e.g. keeping prices low to make the market appear unattractive to potential entrants) and excessive capacity creation (to show how aggressively the firm would respond to entry) were rarely used.

Conclusion

At the business level, having a clear, well-defined competitive strategy is fundamental to success. Possessing a distinct if not unique business formula and customer offer is critical to gaining meaningful competitive advantage. Yet to sustain that competitive advantage the company must build up its resources and capabilities and employ strategic actions to match and support this competitive strategy. The importance of ongoing investment cannot be overestimated. Complacency and sitting back on one's laurels will inevitably lead to loss of competitive advantage and allowing a rival to take control, driving its own agenda, based on how it is best positioned to dominate the market. Few firms are given a second chance – Gillette's story is an exception. Usually, once competitive advantage is lost it is lost for ever.

The point is that, in a market economy, competitive pressures never cease (e.g. Kay, 2003). You have to keep racing. You can never stop or even pause. To do so could put you out of the game – overtaken and replaced by ever-hungry competitors waiting for the opportunity to exploit any weaknesses or missed opportunities. This means that if risks for high reward are not taken then someone else will take them. If opportunities are not seized then someone else will seize them. The point is that nothing in business stands still. Markets change, competition changes, as products and processes change. Achieving success is one thing, sustaining it is quite another.

Taking a static view of markets and positions within them is not appropriate. While defending existing market positions can offer superior returns in the short to medium term, it is unlikely to be sustainable in the longer term unless competitive advantage is reinforced by considerable resource advantage *and* rivals can be constantly outmanoeuvred. In the face of never-ending competitive pressures, for many companies, the only way of securing long-term advantage is to keep on outdistancing competitors through constantly innovating, developing fundamentally new products and processes – in Hamel and Prahalad's (1994) terms, exploiting new, 'white' space where there is no existing competition.

This need to be constantly innovative is a tall challenge for any firm. But it is one that is widely recognized by businesses. For instance, the previously mentioned survey of UK managers by Singh *et al.* in revealing the importance of R&D for different industries also revealed that the most common policy employed in striving to achieve business success was the introduction of new products. As table 3.3 shows, this policy dominates others and reflects the concern to keep ahead of the market. But the table also reveals the perceived importance of taking competitive action against rivals (essentially strategic action to undermine their position), where clearly competitors' positions are viewed as being an important limitation on profit potential. In contrast, developing existing products or processes are used far more rarely compared with the more aggressive policies concerned with innovation and attacking competitors' positions.

Table 3.3 Policies to achieve business success

Policies	% of respondents
Development of existing products	3
Development of existing production processes	8
Introduction of new or improved products in the same area	53
Competitive actions taken against rivals' new products (or new rivals)	36

Source: adapted from Singh *et al.* (1991a).

Of course, these more aggressive policies not only have the benefit of keeping the organization one step ahead of the competition (by fair means or foul!) but also alter the business environment to the advantage of the firm by creating new demand (or even a new market with a fundamentally new product) or by changing the structure of the industry to a more comfortable situation, say by inducing existing rivals to exit the market (e.g. through predatory pricing) or by preventing (viable) new entry. Indeed, it is this mechanism to manipulate the industry environment that offers organizations the potential to operate in attractive industries. This, combined with resource and competence advantage, allows an organization the better chance to achieve long-run superior performance over other firms, all the better if new lucrative markets can be opened up through innovation.

As Gary Hamel (1996) has put it, strategic success can come from being a 'rule maker' but perhaps more likely from being a 'rule breaker', an industry revolutionary. The former creates and then protects the industrial orthodoxy (IBM, Coca-Cola, Marks & Spencer, British Airways, etc.). The latter are intent on overturning the industrial order, rewriting the rules of competition (Dell, IKEA, Matalan, easyJet, etc.). Being a 'rule taker', a second rate 'me too' operation, is by comparison an unenviable position, always struggling to catch up, always at a competitive disadvantage, ultimately doomed to failure when the disadvantage becomes too great or at best left in a situation of perpetual mediocrity.

REVIEW EXERCISE

1 Following on from your SWOT analysis from the review exercise in chapter 2, identify the competitive strategy that most suits your company's needs. State the reasons for your choice.
2 What particular actions do see the firm pursuing to obtain and maintain a position of dominance in its markets?
3 Who do you see as the most serious threat to the market position of your organization? Do you consider the most likely threat to be a firm already competing in the market, a firm in a related industry, a supplier or buyer, a foreign firm or a new arrival (possibly from an entirely unrelated industry)?
4 How would you deal with encroachment on your market position by an existing rival or new entrant?
5 So what is your company – a rule maker, a rule taker or a rule breaker? If not the latter, how could the company bring about radical change by reconceiving products or services in the market, redefining market space (breaking existing geographical and product bounds) or redrawing industry boundaries (e.g. compressing the supply chain)?

CHAPTER 4

CORPORATE-LEVEL STRATEGY

Strategic Considerations

This chapter extends the strategic analysis of the last chapter on business-level strategy to consider strategy at the corporate level – examining strategic choice for large organizations. Here our prime interests are with *directional strategies* concerned with routes to development and growth, along with the structural methods by which this can be achieved, *portfolio strategies* concerned with building and managing a diverse range of business units, and *parenting strategies* where the corporation seeks to exploit synergies and leverage core competences across the organization.

A critical issue, for general consideration, is whether the corporation can add value beyond the value of the individual business units of which they consist (i.e. the value of the corporation compared to the sum value of the individual business units as if they were instead independently owned and controlled businesses). This is very pertinent, given that many commentators and analysts argue that corporations more often than not destroy or trap value rather than create or liberate it. Indeed, while large, diversified corporations used to be seen as great value and wealth creators, they have fallen somewhat into disfavour. The emphasis of the modern corporation has more often than not been about focusing on 'core businesses', with the result than many conglomerates have undertaken large-scale restructuring, divesting their non-core businesses.

Today, more than ever, senior management teams are thus under considerable pressure to justify extending the boundaries of the business beyond what might be seen as the core or very essence of the organization as it stands. However, as this chapter illustrates, well planned developments can not only be individually profitable but may allow the corporation to maintain its overall success by serving to reinforce competitive advantage in the individual markets in which the firm competes. Such moves call for careful judgement with regard to overall corporate strategy in building up the corporation in respect of its development directions, managing capital flows across the portfolio of business units and ensuring that resource and competence links are fully exploited. This all necessarily implies the corporation be *dynamic*, evolving to the needs of the markets its serves. To be successful, it also necessitates that the corporation should be *innovative*, on a regular if not continuous basis, in respect of the processes it uses and the products/services it supplies.

As with the last chapter's analysis of business-level strategies, the consideration of corporate-level strategy is mainly in regard to identifying and discriminating between different strategic options. The final part of this chapter is devoted to evaluation of strategic options. Put simply, we consider evaluation with reference to the following criteria:

- *suitability*: 'strategic fit' in relation to developments in the internal and external environment (based on situation analysis) and opportunities to 'stretch' and exploit core competencies and strategic resources;
- *feasibility*: an assessment of how it might work in practice;
- *acceptability*: consequences in terms of the risk and return to interested parties (shareholders, management, employees, etc.).

The firm's resources and the market conditions will have a large part to play in determining which options are most appropriate. Yet how these criteria will ultimately be weighed may depend on the strength of voice of particular stakeholders. In recent years a number of corporations have based their strategic decisions entirely on achieving one overriding aim: maximize shareholder value. This approach, known as 'Value Based Management' (VBM), emphasizes choosing between options based on generated 'economic profit' (or 'economic value added'). While this approach is popular with a number of leading corporations, it remains contentious. Other corporations appear to favour a broader approach, acknowledging directly the expectations of different stakeholders, such as those implicit in the 'balanced scorecard' approach. Neither of these approaches, or possibly others, can be considered right or wrong. Rather, they reflect different beliefs about what needs to be achieved to make an option 'acceptable'. Of course, they are also indicative of the culture of the organization and how different stakeholders are viewed.

Directional Strategies

Devising a strategy for development involves making a decision, first, over which is the most appropriate direction for the company to move in and, second, on the most appropriate method. In this section we outline various strategic directions. The next section covers the methods.

The simplest way to depict the directions is in terms of the products made by the firm and the markets it operates in, as represented in figure 4.1 – which should be familiar to you from the introductory chapter (figure 1.2). The diagram illustrates four directions. First, continue to operate in the same market with the same product. Growth in this situation, especially in a mature market, comes about through

Product line \ Markets	M_0	M_1	M_2 — — — — — — — M_N		
PL_0	Market penetration	Market development			
PL_1					
PL_2	Product development		Diversification		
$\vdots$					
PL_N					

Figure 4.1 Alternative directions for strategic development

market penetration, whereby the firm increases its market share through improved quality or productivity or increasing its marketing activity. This is obviously an easier task if the market is growing. In static markets, the market leaders have advantageous cost structures (from economies of scale and the experience curve) over smaller firms, making market penetration more difficult. If market penetration is not feasible, then at least the firm may try for *consolidation*, where market share is maintained. Failing even this, *withdrawing* may be the only other option remaining.

The second route is *product development*. Here the firm develops new products while maintaining the security of operating in its present markets. This direction is typically adopted in consumer-oriented industries where tastes are continually changing. For example, the short life cycles of consumer electronics mean that product development needs to be a central part of company strategy. In retailing as well, we see firms continually introducing new product lines. This direction may be relatively easy to implement, particularly as it involves building on present knowledge and skills (especially in R&D). However, there are risks involved. Costs are likely to be high and new products may be unprofitable, in which case it may be better simply to modify existing lines and use new marketing approaches.

The third alternative is *market development*, where the firm maintains its present product lines but seeks to extend its market operations. This may come about through opening up new market segments, devising new uses for the products or extending into new geographical areas. Developing markets rather than products is a common feature of capital-intensive industries, where the firm's assets (money, plant and skilled labour) are tied to a particular product, such that the firm's distinctive competence lies with the product, not the market, in which case it makes sense to exploit the product further. The strategy also makes sense when old markets become saturated and the firm can develop overseas markets (e.g. cigarette manufacturers are increasingly targeting developing countries). This route has also been followed by service industries – e.g. banking, insurance and advertising – which have sought to 'globalize' their activities. This process is also beginning to emerge in retailing – see exhibit 4.1. 'Globalization', and the move towards being a multinational operator, has several attractions. First, it can be seen as a 'defensive' measure against tariff barriers and import controls. Second, it can be undertaken for logistical reasons over the costs of labour, transport and supplies. Third, in capital-intensive industries globalization may have the benefit of switching away from declining home-based demand.

The fourth direction, and the most complex in terms of both implementation and options, is *diversification*, where the firm moves away from present products and present markets. We can distinguish two broad types: *related* diversification and *unrelated* diversification.

EXHIBIT 4.1 THE INTERNATIONALIZATION OF RETAILING

Wal-mart is both the world's largest retailer and largest corporation measured by revenue. It has spread from the United States, its country of origin, to operate in a range of countries, across several continents. But Wal-mart's international moves are far from unique, as is demonstrated by the similar moves made by other large-format operators like Ahold, Carrefour and Tesco, and far from original. Indeed, pioneers of international retailing go back almost 100 years, such as the moves of the clothing chain C&A to operate in different European countries.

Yet it is only in the last decade or so that internationalization of retailing has really taken off. Much of it has been concerned with the development of 'global retailers' operating with replicated formats and identities, like IKEA, McDonald's, Toys'r'us, Virgin, Benetton, Gap and Body Shop. Yet others have chosen to internationalize as 'multinational retailers', using customized formats and mixed identities, such as Wal-mart, Carrefour, Tesco, Sainsbury, M&S and Metro. The former category have tended to build their businesses through internal expansion or franchising, while the latter category have tended to develop through acquisition or establishing joint ventures with existing domestic retailers.

The factors behind the internationalization of retailing are similar to those of other industries. 'Push' factors include market saturation and restrictions arising from public policy in the home country. 'Pull' factors include the market growth potential and higher profits available owing to differences in competitive or cost structures in the host country (such as Tesco's targeted move into eastern Europe and the Far East).

In addition, a key reason behind the spread of global retailers is often down to the opportunity to transfer a successful, novel store format or concept to different countries. This requires, though, cross-cultural acceptance of the retail concept, which is not always the case (as many retailers have found to their cost, such as Boots' failure in Asian markets). In the case of multinational retailers, it is often about the retail management skills and systems that can be exported, rather than the retail brand itself. Thus Wal-mart seeks to apply the same retailing philosophy and systems across all its international operations, but not necessarily its name (e.g. retaining the Asda retail brand in the United Kingdom).

But the race to internationalize has been far from straightforward for many retailers. Indeed, British retailers, with a few notable exceptions, have had disappointing experiences. Marks & Spencer admits that it grossly overpaid for the American men's wear chain Brooks Brothers and failed to make the business successful. It has subsequently retreated from all its international operations. Dixon's also overpaid in acquiring a US business, the electrical goods retailer Silo, and failed to turn it into a success. Boots has retrenched from its foray into Japan and South East Asian markets following disappointing sales levels. W. H. Smith is reportedly seeking to sell off its loss-making US newsagent/bookselling business. But British firms are not alone in their difficulties. Even the mighty Wal-mart has struggled with Wertkauf and InterSpar, its two German acquisitions. Similarly, Carrefour, the world's No. 2 retailer, has struggled in America.

There are few general lessons, but cross-border acquisitions in particular can often be difficult to integrate and improve performance unless the businesses are a close match in the first instance (such as Asda/Wal-mart). Organic growth, in contrast, can offer more security in this regard but can be a slow process, particularly in overcoming regulatory restrictions such as planning hurdles, as very large-format operators like IKEA and Costco have found to their cost.

Nevertheless, and despite all these difficulties, the internationalization of retailing appears set to continue, especially in segments amenable to global branding (like fast food and clothes) and where scale advantages are crucial (like food and general merchandise). For the time being, though, retailing is likely to remain a largely nationally, if not locally, based industry, finely tuned to satisfying local customer needs.

Sources: 'Why Britannia's shops fail to rule across the waves', *Sunday Times*, 3 February 2002; 'Tesco stays hungry for overseas growth', *Sunday Times*, 15 June 2003; 'City finds W. H. Smith lacking in magic', *Sunday Times*, 29 June 2003; Alexander (1997); Wileman and Jary (1997).

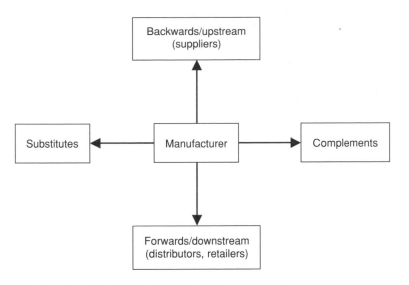

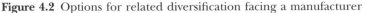

Figure 4.2 Options for related diversification facing a manufacturer

Related diversification

This involves increasing the range of activities in the value chain which the organization undertakes itself, essentially through building and extending links in or across the chain. By way of illustration of the different options, figure 4.2 shows the case of a manufacturer. The figure shows for the manufacturer, as there are generally for any type of firm, two routes for related diversification – vertical or horizontal – but each of these has two directions (i.e. up or down, left or right), providing four broad options. In the case of vertically related diversification, the firm may chose to vertically integrate 'backwards' (or 'upstream') towards its inputs, e.g. by producing its own raw materials or machinery, which may enable the firm to control better the quality, quantity and price of its inputs. Alternatively, the firm can vertically integrate 'forwards' (or 'downstream') towards its output markets, e.g. by moving into transport, distribution, retailing or services and maintenance, to have more control over the final product market. In both cases of vertical extension, the length of the value chain is extended.

In the case of horizontal integration, the move could be towards substitute activities (i.e. rival products/services). Alternatively, a horizontal move could be towards complementary activities in respect of demand (e.g. marketing different products to the same customers) and/or supply (e.g. marketing by-products arising from the same production process).

In each case there can be two types of advantage – efficiency gains and increased market power. Productive efficiency gains can arise through a better use of resources and a wider spread of risk as the range of activities is increased. Particular cost savings may be associated with each route. For example, with vertical integration 'economies of span' may be available where the integration of two sequential activities can offer cost savings over them being undertaken separately (e.g. operating an integrated steelworks as opposed to separate production of pig iron and steel). With integration towards substitute products, 'economies of scale' may be available where cost savings can arise from the greater size of the operation producing similar products (e.g. from building larger, more efficient plants). With integration towards complementary products, synergistic benefits may be generated through 'economies of scope' where cost savings result from the different activities being undertaken jointly rather than separately (e.g. from better utilization of resources, such as plant, machinery and labour).

While efficiency improvements may be a key way to achieve increased value from the move, there may also be benefits to the business through increased market power. Again, this can come in different forms associated with each route. For instance, vertical integration can offer market power through foreclosing supplies (with upstream integration) or foreclosing markets (with downstream integration) to rivals, putting them at a competitive disadvantage respectively in sourcing supplies and obtaining distribution. It can also increase bargaining leverage over suppliers or distributors by making more credible the threat of extending vertical integration to take business away from them. In the case of horizontal integration towards substitutes the firm may gain both increased buying and selling power from increased market share (in respect of both input and output markets). Finally, in the case of horizontal integration towards complements, when selling complementary products to the same customer they may be scope to increase sales through the exercise of 'portfolio power'. This could arise where the firm would be more attractive to customers because it could offer a wider range of products (e.g. combining beer, cider and soft drinks to sell to on-trade customers) or greater opportunities for tying and bundling products (e.g. full-line forcing where the customer is required to take the entire range of the firm).

However, while there may be advantages arising from both increased efficiency and market power, there may equally be disadvantages associated with related diversification. There may, for example, be disadvantages in the form of management overextending itself into unusual areas where it has no expertise or experience (e.g. from manufacturing into retailing). Furthermore, by vertically integrating, the firm is more exposed to, and dependent on, the market, and its extended chain of activities makes it less flexible: if the market should dramatically change it may find it difficult to respond and reposition. Similarly, with horizontal integration towards substitutes there may be concern that the firm has less strategic flexibility if the market starts to decline or fundamentally different and superior substitutes emerge using different technology. Indeed, if anything, the trend has been towards firms increasing their strategic flexibility by outsourcing different activities, letting others undertake roles that were previously undertaken internally to the organization, with contracts replacing ownership as the control mechanism. Efficiencies are then created through exploiting the greater specialization of external parties, relying on performance-based contracts to ensure quality and reliability of services and products.

Unrelated diversification

This covers options that lie beyond the boundaries of the industry within which the company presently operates. This route is most likely to be appropriate when the firm's markets are saturated and/or declining, or when significant growth is sought but the firm's existing markets are small and offer few development opportunities. Yet, unlike related diversification, the advantages of unrelated diversification are less immediatcly apparent. For instance, efficiency gains and/or enhancement of market power are less likely to be a feature. Yet there may be financial advantages in unrelated diversification. For example, a firm may undertake an activity designed to generate short-term positive cash flows because its main activity needs a source of cash. Also, the firm can spread its risks by not putting all its eggs in one basket. By having a portfolio of activities the firm can smooth out the effects of market and business cycles, even seasonal factors, to maintain constant cash/profit flows, which can be used to finance further growth.

Nevertheless, of all the directions for development this route may prove to be the most tortuous. The firm may have to be internally restructured to form a 'divisionalized' firm. This may itself lead to a large management bureaucracy, with poor communication and control mechanisms, compounded by senior management moving into unfamiliar areas. It is often this route that leads to the downfall of many organizations because they simply overextend themselves (both financially and in terms of resources).

Yet, as Richard Whittington (2000) has observed, rumours of the death of the diversified conglomerate are much exaggerated. While there have been notable break-ups in recent years, such as those at ITT and Hanson Trust, there are many others that continue to thrive. One of the world's most admired industrial companies for many years has been General Electric, with business interests ranging from aircraft engines to television. Warren Buffett has managed to build a highly successful conglomerate through his Berkshire Hathaway investment fund that spans insurance, executive jets, fast food and home furnishings. In the United Kingdom serial entrepreneurs like Sir Richard Branson of Virgin Group and Stelios Haji-Ioannou of easyGroup preside over highly diversified businesses.

So what accounts for the success of these conglomerates in the absence of the operating-level synergies associated with related diversification? One possibility is 'corporate relatedness', where the kinds of decisions top managers have to make across a range of businesses are very similar (e.g. similarity in project sizes, time spans, risk profiles, critical success factors, etc.). In particular, Whittington suggests that corporate similarities that conglomerates can exploit across otherwise unrelated businesses include:

- *marketing* skills: generating free publicity (e.g. Virgin) or pricing novelty (e.g. easyGroup's variable pricing policy);
- *investment* skills: spotting and backing undervalued investment opportunities;
- *relationship* skills: such as in dealing with government and regulators;
- *entrepreneurial* skills: as demonstrated by serial entrepreneurs;
- *turn-round* skills: sorting out underperforming businesses.

The more of these skills possessed, the greater the chance of success with unrelated diversification. Yet even being armed with a combination of these skills offers no guarantee of success. For example, exhibit 4.2 considers the development of easyGroup and its mixed fortunes in seeking to stretch the 'easy' brand into strikingly different markets. A further illustration of stretching a brand with otherwise unrelated diversification, developed in exhibit 4.3, is that of Virgin Group. The

EXHIBIT 4.2 DIVERSIFYING THE 'EASY' WAY

'My record is patchy at best. I have had a couple of successes, a couple of failures – the jury is still out on everything else,' claims Stelios Haji-Ioannou, founder of the easyGroup of businesses. But there can be few entrepreneurs who have achieved such notable success, making him a near billionaire, in such a short time frame. It was only in 1995 that the first and most successful business in the group, easyJet, was established. It is now the leading budget airline in Europe, and its success allowed it to acquire the former BA low-cost operator, Go, in 2002. From this airline business others have sprung up, all sharing the same bright orange colour of the 'easy' logo.

Yet it is not just the bright orange logo that the different businesses share. They also share the same no-frills, cost-minimizing approach with the added spice of a radical variable pricing policy. Specifically, unlike its main competitors, the companies run by Stelios Haji-Ioannou do not set single prices, but rather adjust prices to match demand conditions. The principle is remarkably simple: as demand goes up so do prices. In practice what this means is that people who buy early, or choose a slack time of day, obtain better deals. For example, charges at easyInternetCafe rise as the seats fill up. Similarly, the more people who hire cars from easyCar the greater the cost to the remaining customers. The first seats sold on easyJet flights are cheap, the last few the most expensive. The same rule applies to seats sold at easyCinema.

Although many businesses practise such 'yield management', few do it as effectively as the easyGroup businesses. If applied correctly, it can be a very effective means of raising revenue when such services are popular and likely to be otherwise oversubscribed. Conventional fixed-price operators, by contrast, simply turn customers away when, say, the cinema showing or the flight is full. They may even lose money at peak times when they buy in extra capacity to provide customers with the service they want at the promised price. In contrast the easyGroup model seeks to milk the demand curve for every penny possible and pocket the extra that the impatient and spendthrift are willing to pay to have just what they want when they want it.

The other key feature of the easyGroup model is the emphasis on stripping out costs wherever possible and being able to offer publicity-grabbing prices, like 20p cinema seats and £1 airline seats. To do this, extras, such as meals, flexibility or convenience, are dispensed with. The same basic service applies to all customers, and bookings usually need to be made on-line. For example, easyCinema customers are not issued tickets: rather they print out a bar-coded entry pass from their computer when making a booking. EasyCar offers one kind of car at each location and it is the responsibility of customers to bring their car back within a one-hour slot, clean and ready for the next user, or pay a penalty. EasyJet offers short-haul flights only, mostly from minor airports, with no food or drink. All these and other innovations make for a low-cost operation.

Yet, of all the ventures, only easyJet has proved to be clearly successful, with industry-leading load factors (on average filling 87 per cent of seats) and managing to generate profits at a time when most airlines are making considerable losses. Repeating the success of easyJet, though, is proving no easy task. EasyCar looks like it may break even soon but has so far not managed to dent the big rental firms' business. EasyCinema appears to be a one-off venture located in Milton Keynes and has found it difficult to obtain new releases from the major film distributors, who dislike its cut-price offerings. Moreover, easyInternetCafe has proved to be a big loss maker (with total losses estimated at £90 million), and easyMoney (credit cards) and easyValue (price comparison service) have also proved to be loss-making ventures.

Other ventures are still being considered, such as easyDorm (budget-price hostel accommodation), but, even with an apparently consistent and novel business model, successful diversification may still prove to be far from *easy*.

Sources: 'The big easy', *Economist*, 31 May 2003; 'Stelios shows there's an "easy" way to smart pricing strategy', *Marketing*, 10 April 2003; 'Stelios makes growth look easy', *Fast Company*, November 2002.

EXHIBIT 4.3 VIRGIN TERRITORY

There can be few business brands stretched as far as Virgin. As one of the United Kingdom's largest private companies Virgin Group has in its time spawned or lent its name to over 200 businesses. From a single record shop founded in 1970 the group, under the leadership of Sir Richard Branson, has moved into becoming a major music business both as a retailer (Virgin Records) and as a producer (Virgin Music), and subsequently diversified into airlines (Virgin Atlantic), financial services (Virgin Direct and Virgin Money), holidays (Virgin Holidays), passenger train services (Virgin Rail), radio (Virgin Radio), mobile telephony (Virgin Mobile), cinemas (Virgin Cinemas), drinks (Virgin Cola and Virgin Vodka), car retailing (Virgin Car) and cosmetics (Virgin Vie), to name but a few of its ventures.

The impression is that there is little business territory where Virgin does not operate in, or conceivably might not choose to operate in at some future point. However, a closer inspection of the businesses shows that a connection between them does indeed exist, beyond the name Virgin. The business model which has been applied across all the businesses is in reality tied to the portrayal of the Virgin brand: vibrant, innovative, challenging authority, good value and trustworthy. The group accordingly looks for opportunities where it can invigorate a relatively static market, successfully challenge incumbents, and create a new proposition for consumers, particularly for younger consumers, more desiring of something new and amenable to the appeal of the Virgin brand. Indeed, its brand strength is such that it can be used to overcome the key barriers usually discouraging entry: brand identity and recognition (to encourage consumer experimentation with its offer) and trustworthiness (to encourage repeat purchases and long-term consumer relations).

Yet, while brand strength can be a major asset in entering new markets, it needs to be backed up by the right skills and resources to ensure effective entry. In this respect, Virgin often recognizes that it cannot undertake ventures on its own. Accordingly, it looks for suitable partners that have the resources (often technical) it does not have, and vice versa. Indeed many of the Virgin businesses have been undertaken through joint ventures, e.g. Virgin Retail (joint with W. H. Smith), Virgin Mobile (with T-mobile in the United Kingdom and with Sprint in the United States), Virgin Direct (with Norwich Union/AMP), Virgin Rail (with Stagecoach) and Virgin Cola (made under licence by Cott Beverages).

As a corporate operation the group gives the appearance of a venture capital firm investing in a series of brands and ventures. Businesses are built up and then often partially or completely sold off, with the funds generated being ploughed back into the next generation of businesses to be built up, and so on. Thus whilst they carry the Virgin name the group seldom owns the businesses outright (e.g. Singapore Airlines owns 49 per cent of Virgin Atlantic) or even at all.

The benefit of this build–sell approach is that it offers the group quick returns on business ventures, and considerable strategic flexibility. The danger is that it exposes the brand to being in the control of external parties, and being diluted by over-exposure through operating in so many markets. Yet, perhaps, the main concern is that reliance on a single brand identity may be the group's ultimate undoing if a public relations disaster in one market (as conceivable with the ongoing problems with Virgin Rail) serves to undermine the brand more generally in the public's eye.

Source: 'Branson plans $1 bn US expansion', *Times*, 30 April 2002.

approaches taken by both companies are markedly different from an operational perspective, but share some obvious similarities in the attempt to shake up the markets they enter. The interesting feature is just how unrelated the activities are within each group, other than being consumer-oriented.

QUESTIONS

1 Virgin Group and easyGroup both appear to base their business development on stretching a brand in new directions but each using a consistent (and notably different) business model. What are the benefits and dangers of operating such an approach?
2 In your view, which of the two groups has the better long-term prospects? Why?
3 Consider the direction your firm is likely to move to next. What pitfalls do you think await the firm?
4 What actions do you propose to safeguard the firm?

Methods of Development

In addition to identifying directions for growth, consideration of the best method of achieving business development is also required. We can distinguish between three distinct categories of methods for extending and/or adapting an organization:

- internal development;
- mergers and acquisitions;
- hybrid arrangements: joint ventures, franchising, agency dealings, licensing, and minority stakes.

The choice between each method involves a trade-off between cost, speed and risk, while taking into consideration the strategies that rivals are following and how best to deal with the threat they pose. Previous experience in these activities is often telling, given that learning by doing is likely to be an important factor in determining the efficiency and effectiveness of the method. Indeed, corporations may even build up distinct competences in using a particular method – such as integrating new acquisitions into the organization.

In practice, much may rest on the firm's resources and the market conditions, as well as preferences based on management's own experience of each type. While cost and speed may be important considerations, the choice itself will determine the degree of ownership and control that the organization will possess. Here there are risks both ways. Internal development or acquisition allow full ownership and control, where new activities are integrated into the organization, yet require large commitments and entail a degree of lost strategic flexibility. On the other hand, a move towards partial ownership and control would be reflected in a minority shareholding or a joint venture, whereas licensing, franchising and long-term contracting offer partial control without ownership. These alternatives to full control and ownership may involve elements of risk about future relations with partners, but can allow greater strategic flexibility by not tying up so many resources.

Internal development

This method of development appears most appropriate when the activity requires a build-up of knowledge and skills – especially if they are highly technical in design or methods of manufacture. It may well be the only method for small companies to develop, since they have no other choice, owing to lack of resources. In addition, it is also the only method open to the firm when it is developing new products or new markets, since it is breaking new ground. Internal development necessarily involves a slower rate of change, which has the benefit of minimizing disruption within the organization. On the other hand its slowness may mean that opportunities are lost or not fully exploited.

Acquisition

Acquisition enables the firm to enter new product or market areas with greater speed than through internal development. The firm can acquire expertise, e.g. R&D, knowledge of markets and products, or a particular type of production system, all of which may have taken years to develop internally. Acquisitions also offer the firm the opportunity of a 'cheap buy'; if the target firm is going into liquidation, the acquirer can buy it cheaply and 'asset-strip' the firm (i.e. dispose of under-valued assets in a piecemeal fashion). This method also offers a quick and relatively painless way of entering static mature markets, since acquisition reduces the risk of competitor reaction. Cost efficiency may also be a key consideration if learning and experience curve effects are important in the industry, since the organization can overcome these problems by acquiring an experienced (cost-efficient) firm.

The major problem with acquisition (apart from paying too much!) is integration with other parts of the business. For example, business practices between the two organizations, such as the way activities are conducted, monitored and supported, may be fundamentally different and company cultures (and philosophies) incompatible.

Joint development

This method became increasingly popular over the 1980s and 1990s. In essence, it involves the firm entering into 'partnership' (via a contractual arrangement) with another party (a firm or even an individual) to undertake a business task. There are a variety of methods, each differing in their legal status, in terms of the balance of the partnership, and their purpose. The closeness of the relationship varies from almost complete arm's-length (where the ties and extent of contact are very limited) right through to almost full integration (where the parties are tied by part ownership into a long-term, exclusive relationship). In practice, we observe relationships right across this joint development spectrum.

A 'joint venture' represents a very close relationship, as it usually involves the setting up, by two or more companies, of a jointly owned, independent organization. The 'parent' companies share the costs and rewards (both profits and gained technologies/expertise). These arrangements offer flexibility, both strategically, since they generally do not tie up all the firm's resources, and because they can be dissolved relatively easily. The exception is with 'consortia', contractually obliged to finish a project, which are especially associated with large civil engineering projects (e.g. the Thames flood barrier). Joint ventures are generally undertaken for mutual interest. For instance, one side may gain technological expertise while the other gains access to different markets (e.g. telecoms moving into China), it could be that parties need to pull together different but complementary technological strengths (e.g. Sony Ericsson mobile phones), or because a project is so expensive that a number of companies decide to pool resources to share the risks (e.g. the European Airbus consortium). As a defensive ploy joint ventures can be used to reduce competition, or act as a 'poison pill' to thwart a take-over attempt. Alternatively they can be used as an offensive strategy, where two firms link up to put pressure on a common competitor.

Nevertheless, though there are many advantages to creating joint ventures, they tend not to last more than a few years, either because they complete their project (task) or because of difficulties encountered in running them. Difficulties can arise because of the influence exerted by the parent companies and the divided loyalties of management, which result in the joint venture losing its direction.

Another popular alternative is 'franchising', where the established firm sells the right to its product/brand name for another party to exploit, e.g. McDonald's, Body Shop, Kentucky Fried Chicken (KFC). This has advantages for both sides. The franchiser has the flexibility to change franchisees and can concentrate on its core business, while the franchisee can use an established brand name, backed up with mass consumer advertising and training, on a relatively small capital basis.

If the firm feels unable or is strategically unwilling to produce for all markets, it may have the option of 'licensing' its product or manufacturing process to another party. Licensing is more common in industries where patents and trade marks feature widely, e.g. in the pharmaceutical industry or the brewing industry. In this case the firm offers a licence to manufacturers, who pay a percentage of turnover to the firm. This route is useful for developing overseas markets.

Another alternative is to use 'agents' to conduct part (usually on the fringe) of the firm's business. For example, the company may prefer to use agents in small overseas markets. As well as being cost-efficient compared with the alternative of maintaining permanent staff, the advantage of using local agents is that they have local knowledge of the market, culture and customs. This is, for example, a common practice for universities in seeking to recruit overseas students.

QUESTIONS

1 What method has your company traditionally relied on for development? What have been the benefits and costs to the company?

2 What difficulties do you think would be encountered if your company acquired a vertically related business concern (e.g. a retailer, or input supplier)? How long in your view would it take to overcome these problems?

3 Assuming that there is some scope for your business to undertake a joint venture, what purpose would be best served by such a venture? What would you realistically expect to gain from this joint venture? What would be the costs to the firm?

Portfolio Strategies

In this section we consider the management of the diversified firm's portfolio of activities/products, where strategy is developed to cover the overall interests of the company rather than simply the component parts. Thus strategy may well be aimed at maintaining a balanced portfolio of activities where certain parts are generating profits and significant positive cash flow while other parts are growing towards this position. The firm is then viewed as a continuing process, whereas in contrast its products are seen as having only a limited life span.

The approaches we concentrate on are based on representing the portfolio in terms of its strengths and weakness. The first, and most influential, approach is the Boston Consulting Group (BCG) *growth–share matrix*. Other approaches are, in the main, extensions of this approach, such as the General Electric/McKinsey industry attractiveness–strengths matrix.

The growth–share matrix was developed by the BCG as a means of enhancing diversified companies' portfolio performance by identifying which 'strategic business units' (SBUs) to invest in, which to milk for funds and which to eliminate from the portfolio (e.g. Hedley, 1977). The BCG matrix, as depicted in figure 4.3, shows the position of the firm's business units in terms of their market share and the growth rate of their respective markets.

Market growth is measured, in real (i.e. inflation-adjusted) terms, as the growth rate per year of the overall market for the business unit (or product). The rate is calculated either as an absolute figure or relative to that of real GNP. Market share of the business unit in its own industry can also be measured in two ways: either as a straight percentage or as that percentage deflated by that of the leading firm (as a measure of 'market dominance'). The emphasis on the largest competitor is based on the relative cost implications of BCG's theory of experience effects, which claims that the firm with the largest market share will often have the greatest accumulated experience and thereby the lowest unit costs. The growth emphasis

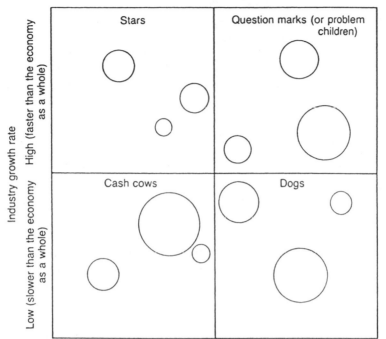

Figure 4.3 The BCG growth–share business portfolio matrix

is based on the product life cycle model, where growth is taken to be a measure of industry attractiveness.

Business units in each quadrant are assigned names based on their generation and use of cash, as well as their potential:

- *Stars.* High growth and high share. These are strongly placed in the growth phase of the product life cycle. Although cash generation is strong, it may not be sufficient to finance the rapid growth. As the market matures and slows, excess cash should be generated.
- *Question marks* (a.k.a. 'problem children'). Low share of a growing market suggests that considerable cash is required to maintain share. Investment to create a star is risky.
- *Cash cows.* Dominant products in a mature market produce excess cash that can be invested in stars and question marks.
- *Dogs.* Low-share products in low-growth markets. Cash flow is usually low and can be negative, owing to a weak competitive position. If investment is required to maintain the share of a dog, it may be better to divest it and reallocate funds to a star or a question mark.

The sizes of the circles in figure 4.3 indicate the size of revenues generated. The boundaries separating the quadrants in the matrix are to some extent arbitrary.

The market growth boundary is usually set at 10 per cent and the market share boundary at 1.0, i.e. parity with the market share of the largest competitor.

Viewed in terms of a business unit's development and life cycle, we see heavy investment at the question-mark stage, hopefully turning this into a star, from which, as the market matures, it turns into a cash cow which generates funds for investing in a new question mark or research and development, and so the process continues. The company should thus be careful to protect cash cows, since these supply the funds for future growth. The marketing tools to adopt for question marks and dogs range from identifying new target segments and exploiting them to cutting losses by divesting – either selling to another firm or via a management (a.k.a. leveraged) buy-out.

While being useful in terms of the analysis it provides for directing investment across the portfolio, the approach does have some drawbacks. It is mainly concerned with describing the uses of cash flows and relies too heavily on the notions of product life cycles and cost efficiency resulting from experience/market share. Furthermore, according to the matrix's boundaries most firms' business units or products would fall into the dog category! Only a very limited number of products would seem, by definition, to reside outside this quadrant. (There can only be one or possibly two products in the cash-cow or star category.) This raises the question of why firms retain these 'dog' products. It would seem highly unlikely that firms keep dogs simply because they are unable to divest, though 'barriers to exit' are possible, such as redundancy costs. A more plausible explanation is that they are in fact useful. Dogs do not cost much to feed and they may be useful in keeping predators at bay and stopping intruders. Indeed, dogs may even be profitable. While the BCG approach relies on the argument of cost efficiency for generating profits, it neglects the point that a small market share can still result in high profits if product quality is high or unique. Furthermore, simply following the BCG's rules of taking cash away from cash cows and discarding dogs is likely to have very adverse effects on management and employee motivation in such areas of the corporation.

The BCG approach's limitations are in part due to its measures of business strength ('market share') and market attractiveness ('growth rates'). A number of other approaches have been proposed which seek to generalize the BCG matrix. The General Electric/McKinsey (GE) attractiveness–strengths matrix approach has a more broadly defined measures of industry attractiveness and the business's competitive standing. Figure 4.4 illustrates the GE matrix. There are several internal and external environmental factors that need to be considered before determining the position of each product. Business strength is measured in terms of the organization's ability and relative competitive position and so takes into consideration relative market share, profit margins relative to competitors, ability to compete on price and quality, knowledge of customers and market, competitive strengths and weaknesses, technological capability, employee relations and goodwill, and the calibre of the management. On the other hand, long-term industry attractiveness is measured with reference to the operating and general environment and addresses market size and its growth rate, industry profit margins (both historical and

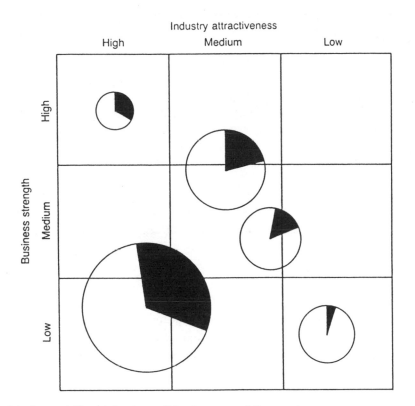

Figure 4.4 General Electric's nine-cell business portfolio matrix

projected), competitive intensity, economies of scale, the nature of demand (e.g. cyclicality), technology and capital requirements, barriers to entry and exit, social, environmental and legal impacts, and emerging opportunities and threats. As with the BCG matrix, the size of the circles indicates the amount of revenue generated, while the shaded pie area in each circle represents the product's market share. (The larger the black area, the larger the share the product has of its particular market.)

The GE matrix is certainly more complex, having nine cells compared with BCG's four. It is also harder to classify accurately each product into a cell, owing to the more ambiguous interpretation of 'strength' and 'attractiveness'. To determine each product's position, management needs to decide on the weight of importance it attaches to each feature making up business strength and market attractiveness. This in itself it is not an easy task, and will certainly be very time-consuming!

The general prescriptions for business policy are similar to those emanating from the BCG approach: maximize investment in strong businesses in highly attractive industries, undertake selective investment in activities which have market potential, specialize when business strengths are low but the industry is attractive, divest weak businesses in unattractive industries.

QUESTIONS

In arguing against a firm necessarily choosing to divest a 'dog' division John Seeger (1984) presents the following analogy. 'Divesting [such a] division would be analogous to a fire company's disposing of its Dalmatian hound. The dog does not contribute much to the direct function of putting out fires. But it looks good in photographs; it makes life more pleasant for the firefighters during their boring waits for alarms; and it keeps other dogs from pissing on the equipment.'

1 What points is the analogy trying to make?
2 Under what circumstances would you keep a 'dog'?

Parenting Strategies

The role of the corporate headquarters in the portfolio approaches associated with the BCG and GE matrices is implicitly one of acting as a surrogate for financial markets. The corporate centre is there essentially to dictate where capital should be moved in respect of the different business units under its control, following a few simple guidelines about business strength and market attractiveness. The entrepreneur's maxim 'buy cheap, sell dear' applies in this context, with the corporate centre seeking to acquire undervalued assets cheap and sell good performers at a premium, meanwhile ensuring that low-performing business units are divested quickly at the best possible price. The whole approach rests on a perspective that the business units have no real ties, that corporate management adds nothing beyond that created by the business unit managers with the appropriate capital allocation, and that there are no fundamental or 'core' businesses that really define why they belong within a particular corporate body as opposed to any other corporation. In essence, nothing dictates the composition of corporation beyond the need to generate capital and then spread capital around to ensure that future income and cash flow are generated.

In contrast, it is possible to see a much clearer role for the corporation when it has the purpose and ability to add value to individual business units which they would otherwise not be able to achieve under any other ownership arrangement. This is the perspective of *corporate parenting*. In this context, Goold *et al.* (1994) argue that corporate strategists must address how the corporation will bring about *parenting advantage*, being the best parent for each of the businesses in the corporate portfolio. This requires that corporate-level decisions relate to two primary questions:

1 In what businesses should the company invest its resources, either through ownership, minority holding, joint ventures and alliances?
2 How should the parent company influence and relate to the businesses under its control?

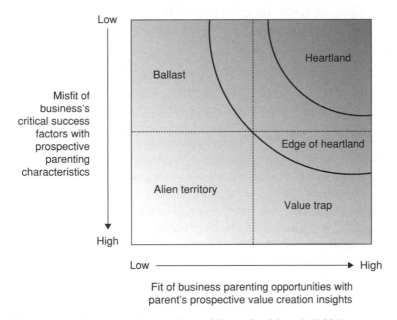

Figure 4.5 Parenting fit matrix. *Source*: adapted from Goold *et al.* (1994)

The first question relates to the ideal *composition* and *boundaries* of the corporation, i.e. what it owns and what it does not own. The second question is concerned with what the parent can bring to the business units that will foster superior performance. Jointly the two questions are about parent–SBU fit. If there is a good fit between the parent's skills and the needs and opportunities of the strategic business units then the corporation is likely to add value. If, however, the fit is poor, the corporation is likely to destroy value.

Goold *et al.* classify business units into five types – heartland, edge of heartland, ballast, alien territory and value trap. These are represented in the parenting fit matrix shown in figure 4.5. To identify and plot each business unit's position, two questions need to be addressed:

1 Do the parenting opportunities in the business *fit* with the value creation abilities and insights of the parent, allowing it potential to create a substantial amount of value?
2 Do the critical success factors in the business have any obvious *misfit* with the prospective parenting characteristics in such a way that the parent is likely to influence the business in ways that will destroy value?

In regard to the first question, when the *fit* is high then there is a high potential for the parent organization to add value (a so-called 'parenting opportunity'), to the extent that there is little or no room for any rival parent to develop superior value creation insights. For example, the parent could offer business skills to cut costs or improve marketing, or offer a network providing access to new markets (e.g. overseas) or better technology. However, when the fit is low, say owing to the parent's skills, resources and characteristics not bringing much benefit to the business unit, then it is possible that rival parents may have more to offer the business unit.

For the second question, *misfit* can occur for many reasons, though the most common cause may be the parent's lack of 'feel' for a business where its failure to appreciate the critical success factors in the business mean that it inadvertently influences the business in ways that destroy value. For example, if a critical success factor for a particular business is about producing quality tailor-made products for clients but the parent's skills lie in delivering mass-produced, commoditized, no-frills products at rock-bottom prices, then pushing the business unit to conform to this corporate model to take advantage of scale advantages will likely undermine the business and destroy value. The point is that if there a high degree of misfit between the nature of the parent organization and the critical success factors underlying a business the risk of problems arising is high.

In terms of guidance in developing corporate strategy, the framework suggests that corporations should focus on developing a portfolio of *heartland* businesses, the 'core' of the corporation, where the parent can add value without the danger of doing harm. In practice, assembling such a portfolio is likely to be difficult and some experimentation will likely be needed, perhaps giving rise to businesses that lie in the *edge of heartland* area, where added value generated is slightly lower and the risk of problems arising slightly higher than with heartland businesses.

As to the other types, *ballast* businesses are ones that the parent understands well but can do little for (e.g. where they could be equally successful as independent companies). While they offer scope for feeding into the corporation useful resources and cash flow, they equally take up corporate management time and effort that could be better spent elsewhere. Overall, though, they pose few risks by their presence in the portfolio. In contrast, *value trap* businesses are ones where they appear on the surface attractive, as there are opportunities for the parent to add value, but this is deceptive because of the high risk of the parent's attentions doing more harm than good. The rule is to avoid these value trap businesses unless the parent can learn, over time, to gain sufficient feel to make them ultimately heartland businesses. Indeed, it is not unknown for a corporation to take on such businesses and then over time change the entire character of the parent organization to tie in with these businesses rather than its traditional ones. A good example is given in exhibit 4.4 on the reinvention of Unipart as a logistics company from being a car parts manufacturer.

Businesses that do not fit with the prospective corporate strategy are designated as being part of *alien territory*. The corporate parent has little opportunity to add value and its characteristics misfit with the businesses'. For example, these could be businesses in markets unfamiliar to the parent (e.g. in high technology where the parent's traditional strengths lie in low-technology industries). In such cases, exit is usually the best strategy, selling on to a very different parent that is more attuned to the business needs and has the resources and skills to add value.

In practice, it is not just the parent in its own right that determines the category that different businesses fall into but the composition of the portfolio itself and specifically the nature of synergies that can be generated within it. At the very least,

EXHIBIT 4.4 UNIPART REBORN

Unipart began in 1974 as the parts division of State-owned British Leyland. Following a management buy-out in 1987, for £50 million, Unipart is now one of the United Kingdom's largest private companies, with sales of £1.5 billion and profits of £13 million in 2002. Since the buy-out the company has been reinvented as a delivery and logistics group servicing the automotive, telecoms, IT, health and defence industries. It supplies more than 80 million parts a year to customers including Jaguar, Vodaphone and Railtrack. Only a small part of the firm's sales come from making car parts; the vast majority come from distribution. This move into distribution is set to increase further following the announcement that Boots is likely, for the first time, to outsource the management of some of its warehousing needs to Unipart.

Sources: 'Boots makes move into warehouse outsourcing', *Times*, 25 April 2003; 'Top track 100', *Sunday Times*, 29 June 2003.

the assembled portfolio of businesses should yield benefits greater than the sum of its individual parts. To achieve this, the corporation must add something by way of its capabilities, resources or competences across the portfolio. This in part must be down to the relationship between the business units, what features they share, and where synergies can be developed. Here a high degree of *relatedness* may be expected to offer tangible benefits in the form of economies of scale and scope from using common resources (sharing suppliers, distributors, plant, equipment, warehousing, specialist personnel, training, marketing skills, R&D facilities, etc.) as well as potential for revenue synergies from cross-selling opportunities to the different customer bases or offering product bundles of complementary products (e.g. combined hardware and software product offerings).

Apart from the relatedness of the business units, another key aspect of whether the corporate parent will be able to bring additional value to the businesses is the extent of *manageability* by the parent. To ensure that value creation reaches its full potential the parent must be able to manage the interaction of the businesses, allowing cost and revenue synergies to be realised by ensuring that resources, capabilities and competences are shared appropriately across the businesses. It will also be important for the managers of the different businesses to co-operate in sharing activities and learn from each other. Much may depend on the compatibility between the systems and culture of the business units. Also, when the parent has built up specific resources and capabilities that can enhance the potential of business units (such as brand management, innovation management, internationalization) it must have the ability to implement and manage these across its business units.

As exhibits 4.2–3 on easyGroup and Virgin illustrate, added value can come about from operating a very diverse range of businesses as long as they share some degree of relatedness (through brand image, marketing approach, customer base, etc.) and they are manageable, which for both groups has not been straightforward for all the business units.

Yet, even where the degree of relatedness appears strong and manageability appears high by operating in similar markets, requiring similar management skills and resources, it is not always straightforward to create value from assembling a collection of supposedly heartland businesses. A good illustration of this is in retailing, where conglomerate retail corporations have generally performed poorly in respect of pulling together different retail businesses under a common umbrella, with the purpose of exploiting synergies and creating added value in the process. See exhibit 4.5 for some illustrations. Perhaps it is because of the apparent

---

EXHIBIT 4.5 WHATEVER HAPPENED TO RETAIL CONGLOMERATES?

In April 1999 Kingfisher was on the brink of becoming a true retail conglomerate. Already the owner of Woolworth (general merchandise), Superdrug (health and beauty), Comet (electrical goods) and B&Q (DIY products), it announced it was merging with Asda, the third largest food retailer in the United Kingdom. It had already expanded abroad by acquiring Darty, a French electrical goods retailer, and taking a minority stake in Castorama, a French DIY chain, but the acquisition of Asda was intended to project Kingfisher into becoming not only the United Kingdom's largest retailer but also one of the world's leading retailers by both size and scope. It was claimed that the key focus and connection for all its businesses was that they were 'value-led', concentrating on low prices.

However, questions were raised at the time whether this was a sufficiently strong reason for bringing such diverse retail businesses together. Ten year's earlier, a similar argument was used when Asda merged with MFI, the United Kingdom's leading furniture retailer. That merger had proved disastrous and had had to be unwound at huge cost, nearly sinking both businesses in the process.

Whether Kingfisher would have made a success of integrating Asda into its retail empire will never be known. Unfortunately for Kingfisher, it was outbid for Asda by the world's largest retailer, Wal-mart. This seems to have been a turning point for Kingfisher. With its failure to capture Asda, pressure was put on it by investors to determine its core business and divest the remaining ones. In response, it demerged Woolworth's and Superdrug in 2001. In early 2003 it signalled a commitment to focus only on DIY, building its stake in Castorama and announcing the sale of ProMarkt in Germany as well as signalling its intention to sell Darty and BUT in France, followed by plans to demerge Comet in the United Kingdom, through floating KESA Electricals.

Kingfisher's story is not unique. From operating as a conglomerate retailer after paying £900 million for Ward White in 1989, Boots also retrenched. Selling off its Do-it-all (DIY chain), Fads (decorating goods), Children's World (children's goods), A. G. Stanley (hardware) and Halford's (car parts and bikes) businesses, it concentrated on its core retail businesses of Boots the Chemist, along with Boots Optician (while retaining its manufacturing operation, Boots Healthcare International). Moreover, like Kingfisher, international expansion has not proved entirely successful. The company has been forced to retreat or cut back from its ventures in the Netherlands, Thailand, Taiwan and Japan.

Even where retail conglomerates still exist, they appear to be continually changing and evolving, suggesting that it is not always clear what parenting advantage they bring to the individual businesses, nor what is core or the essence of the corporation. For example, GUS (formerly Great Universal Stores) is a conglomerate business owning Argos (the catalogue shop operator acquired for £1.9 billion in 1998), Experian (financial information services, acquired for £1.04 billion in 1996), Homebase (DIY retailer, acquired for £900 million in 2002) and Burberry (luxury goods, partly floated in 2002), along with a number of other businesses. Yet the origins of the company lie with retailing general merchandise and its name is synonymous with mail order home shopping. After 103 years of operation, GUS sold its home shopping business to the Barclay brothers, owners of the Littlewood's home shopping operation, in May 2003, thus breaking decisively with its past.

What is sold by one party is bought by another. In the case of businesses, sometimes this is through management buy-outs or buy-ins (e.g. backed by private equity investors), but is often through sale to another existing or emerging conglomerate. The latter leaves the impression of a merry-go-round, where retail businesses are traded around the leading corporations, with history, core values and identity mattering less than individual business performance. In this process, some conglomerates refocus their activities, like Kingfisher and Boots, some increase them, like the Barclay brothers, and still others are in a metamorphic phase, both buying and selling businesses, like GUS. Yet while focused conglomerates (like Philip Green's Arcadia/BhS clothes retailing empire) may continue to perform well, it remains to be seen whether any truly wide-ranging retail conglomerates will ever emerge to challenge, in value creation terms, the largest integrated groups like Wal-mart, Tesco, Marks & Spencer, etc.

Sources: 'Shopping maul', *Sunday Times*, 25 April 1999; 'Kingfisher sells electrical business in Germany', *Financial Times*, 20 January 2003; 'Kingfisher downgraded on demerger costs', *Financial Times*, 15 April 2003; 'The secret of staying power in retail', *Times*, 30 April 2003, 'Goodbye to a little bit of history', *Financial Times*, 28 May 2003; 'GUS up 6 per cent after sale of catalogues for £590 million', *Times*, 28 May 2003.

similarity between retailing in different product and geographical markets that companies are so easily lulled into thinking that success in one market can be replicated readily in others and hence they embark on a diversification programme only to find that this is not in fact the case. In practice the degree of relatedness can be lower than expected meaning that additional value is not realized (as Kingfisher found). And particularly with acquisitions rather than start-ups, often the inherited culture and systems of the businesses are highly incompatible, making managing different businesses unduly difficult (as Boots found on acquiring Ward White).

QUESTIONS

Conglomerate businesses seem to perform well in other sectors, like manufacturing, but apparently not so well in retailing.

1 Is there something inherent about retailing that corporations, as multiple-business owners, appear to add little value (and may even destroy it) beyond that created at the business unit level?
2 Are there any exceptions?

With regard to ensuring close relatedness between businesses and a common culture facilitating manageability, the approach advocated by Gary Hamel and C. K. Prahalad is the development then leveraging of *core competences*. Thus, in their view, the corporate parent has the responsibility to ensure that the different businesses are connected through core competences, which they define as 'the collective learning in the organization, especially how to co-ordinate diverse production skills and integrate multiple streams of technologies' (Prahalad and Hamel, 1990: 82). The criteria for a core competence are threefold: it must provide unique differentiation, it must transcend businesses and it must be difficult to imitate.

Hamel and Prahalad argue that exploitation of these core competences can allow organizations to enter successfully seemingly diverse markets and build a portfolio of related businesses. They cite examples such as Sony for its core competence in 'miniaturization' (compactness and ease of use) which allows the company to make everything from a Walkman to video-cameras and notebook computers. Canon's core competences cover optics, imaging and microprocessor controls that have allowed it to enter markets as diverse as copiers, laser printers, cameras and image scanners. Honda's underlying competence is alleged to lie in engine design and manufacturing, allowing it to move successfully from motor cycles into other businesses, including lawnmowers, outboard motors and cars.

However, it is clear that core competences alone do not account for the success of these businesses. The core competences allow the technical possibility of new product development, but broader capabilities of the organization must also be in place. Often these are less visible, such as Honda's distinct capability in dealer management, offering specialist training to its dealers, providing new management systems and in the process raising service standards. Another capability central to Honda's success has been its skill in new product development in regard to minimizing cycle times from initial conception to product launch.

Nevertheless while the focus of their approach is centred on the mega-corporation, the Hamel and Prahalad concept is important in understanding where a corporation has the prospects of leveraging its strengths into new businesses, and push for development of new markets, what they term as 'competing for the future', going for 'white space', and 'mega-opportunities' (Hamel and Prahalad, 1994). Their approach also offers an alternative perspective on the corporation not as a collection of SBUs but rather as a portfolio of core competences and core products (as the components or subassemblies that contribute to the value of the end products) and that the task of the corporate parent is to build these up and ensure that these provide the source of new product development and continued competitive advantage.

Selecting Appropriate Strategies

Now that you have some idea of the range of options facing you, there remains the 'slight' problem of choosing between them! In our view there are three key criteria on which to make a basis for a decision: (1) suitability, (2) feasibility, (3) acceptability. We briefly outline the issues surrounding each aspect in turn.

Suitability

To be 'suitable' the strategy should match the needs of the firm in terms of exploiting strengths and grasping opportunities while defending against weaknesses and threats. The appropriateness of a strategy will be judged on the basis of how well it tackles the issues in the external environment and how effectively it can use and develop the firm's resources and core competences. The strategist must then relate back plausible options to situation analysis, say via the SWOT procedure outlined in chapter 2, to see how well the strategy deals with the internal and external environmental conditions. While simple techniques like SWOT are useful, a fuller analysis will be required, taking into consideration how well objectives are likely to be met, e.g. competitive advantage, synergy, life-cycle development and product portfolio development. It is also important for a firm embarking on acquisition and/or joint ventures to consider cultural fit between the organizations. Finally, tensions will need to be resolved between strategic options that suit 'environmental fit', which may be more short-term-oriented, against options that may suit 'competence stretch', which are likely to be oriented to a longer-term perspective. Preferably, options should be pursued that satisfy both 'fit' and 'stretch' aspects – but this may not be possible.

Feasibility

This concerns whether or not a strategy can be implemented successfully. To implement a strategy the firm must have or be able to obtain the necessary funds, along with the necessary materials, services, technology and managerial, marketing and operative skills. Management must also be sure that the organization is capable of performing to the required level (overall and in the specific areas of the value chain). It should also take into consideration whether the desired or target market position can be achieved.

In terms of *resource planning* the firm should use various finance techniques to assess feasibility, e.g. study the implications for funds (cash) flow and consider the 'break-even' situation and how attainable it is. In respect of *resource deployment*, consideration should be given to a resource audit to identify whether the (non-financial) resources are available in the required time frame on the right scale and of the right quality. Clearly, some resources can be acquired (materials, technology and skills), but others may be available only if they are already embedded in the organization, giving rise to distinct capabilities unavailable elsewhere. Feasibility needs to consider how quickly resource deficiencies can be overcome and how core competences can be developed or enhanced in order to create and then sustain competitive advantage.

Acceptability

There seems little point in undertaking a strategy if the end result is likely to be unacceptable to senior management, shareholders and other interested parties (e.g. employees, government, customers and suppliers). Strategies should therefore be assessed in terms of likely returns, e.g. profitability and growth rates, the risks attached to each strategy (especially financial risks, e.g. to liquidity), their effects on the firm's environment and whether it 'fits existing systems' within the organization (i.e. keeping internal changes to the necessary minimum, keeping activities in balance).

Management should be quite clear on expected profitability rates, such as anticipated 'return on capital employed' (ROCE), 'return on investment' (ROI) or 'economic profit' (accounting profit less the real cost of capital) and pay-back rates (i.e. time taken to pay back the invested capital by estimating net cash flows or discounted cash flows). The effect of the strategy on the firm's 'capital structure' (i.e. balance of debt and equity) will be a key measure of financial risk. Scenarios should also be used to examine worst, best and most-likely outcomes.

It goes without saying that the best route to follow is the one that is most suitable, feasible and acceptable. Unfortunately life is not so easy and management will be faced with choosing between strategies that are not unambiguously ranked. In this case they will have to decide on which strategy offers the best overall compromise to best meet their corporate objectives.

Corporate Objectives

The criteria used to determine the appropriate strategy and the means or tools for implementing it are as likely to depend on the make-up of the organization (and the preferences of key individuals) as the industry and culture in which it operates. Certainly, it appears that there are national differences in the key goals

Table 4.1 Ranking of business goals: a comparison between US and Japanese managers

Goal	American managers	Japanese managers
Return on investment	1	3
Higher stock prices	2	8
Increased market share	3	2
Improving products and introducing new products	4	1
Streamlining production and distribution systems	5	4
High net worth ratio	6	5
Improvement of social image	7	6
Improving working conditions	8	7

Source: Scherer and Ross (1989).

of business leaders which suggest that in different countries particular strategies may be more common than in other countries. Similarly, industry norms may dictate the kind of strategies that are followed, or at least limit the number of viable options.

By way of illustration of national differences, table 4.1 summarizes the findings of a comparative survey of top managers in 1,031 Japanese and 1,000 US industrial corporations in the early 1980s. The managers were asked how important eight diverse goals were to their organizations. The table shows the average rankings for the two panels. In the United States the managers seem to go for traditional profit-maximizing targets – return on investment and higher stock prices. In Japan, however, companies appear to go for future earning potential – in particular forsaking short-term profits in favour of introducing new products that enhance long-run profit performance. This could be attributable to a number of factors. For instance, in the United States (as well as in the United Kingdom) the stock market acts as a market for 'corporate control', where take-overs displace senior management teams: the incentive is to keep the share price high to maintain one's job!

In Japan the stock market is not so effective at disciplining management teams in this way and the more important characteristic is the link between banks and companies, which allows the latter to go for long-term investment. This link is further supported by managers' long length of service – Japanese managers often have contracts for lifetime tenure. Alternatively, cultural differences may also explain the ranking of the goals. US managers have been concerned with short-term cost reduction; the Japanese have concentrated on the long-term develop-ment of technological competitiveness. Japanese businesses have striven since the Second World War to become internationally dominant in high-technology and high-value-added industries where the scope for product and process innovation (including the reorganization of methods of operation) is high (see Best, 1990).

Further evidence of the differences between the United States and Japan is presented by Yoshimori (1995), where the stark contrast is drawn between the US position, where shareholder interest should be given first priority in managing a company, compared with the Japanese position, where firms exist for the interest of all stakeholders. Interestingly, the UK position is shown to be almost identical

Table 4.2 Business objectives in the United Kingdom

Primary objective	% of respondents
To earn as large a return on capital as possible	37
To earn as large a return on sales as possible	22
To maintain the firm's market share	15
To maintain the firm's ranking in the market	5
To make as great an absolute amount of profit as possible	22

Source: adapted from Singh *et al.* (1991a).

to the US one, whereas the two other countries in the study, France and Germany, appear somewhat closer to the Japanese position.

As for individual business objectives in the United Kingdom, these also seem to be in line with the US picture. A survey by Singh *et al.* (1991a, b) of senior managers across 293 firms in manufacturing and financial services, illustrated in table 4.2, shows the primary objective to be based on a measure of immediate profit maximization – either return on capital or sales or absolute profits. The firm's position in the market is not generally seen as the chief business objective.

At the corporate level, though, one objective, above all others, has emerged as the dominant one in recent years in the United Kingdom, and as indeed it has in the United States, where equity markets play a key role. This dominant objective is to maximize shareholder value, essentially the total value of the corporation. An extreme view on this is that it is the *only* corporate objective that matters. It is this perspective that essentially underlies Value Based Management (VBM), which has been avidly seized upon by many corporations in recent years – see exhibit 4.6 for details.

EXHIBIT 4.6 VALUE BASED MANAGEMENT

Value Based Management (VBM) has at its core the aim of maximizing shareholder value. It is an approach that has been popularized by a number of consultancies, including McKinsey, Marakon and Stern Stewart, and has been taken up wholeheartedly by a number of major corporations, including Coca-Cola, AT&T, Quaker Oats, Briggs & Stratton, Lloyds-TSB, Boots, Cadbury Schweppes, Lufthansa and Reuter's. The governing objective is to maximize corporate value and the wealth of its shareholders. This entails, under VBM, evaluating every business and opportunity simply against the potential for long-term shareholder returns.

Its proponents claim that VBM offers a management mind set and philosophy (a set of principles for managing value to guide decision making at all levels of the company), a process for strategy development and approval (using value creation principles to guide business analysis) and a set of tools (taking a rigorous, fact-based approach to understanding and exploiting drivers of value creation). The alleged benefits of VBM are that it:

- identifies which businesses or business segments really make a profit and generate cash;
- enables the allocation of resources to enhance better performance;
- helps to select strategies that maximise the value of each business.

The key measure of value creation is in relation to the 'economic profit' generated. Here, economic profit (also termed 'economic value added' or 'economic rent') is a single period measure of the profitability of a business unit, taking account of all the costs, including the cost of capital in the business. In essence, it is the net operating profit after tax, less a charge for the capital employed in the business. As such, it provides an indication of whether an activity creates value (when economic profit is positive) or destroys value (when economic profit is negative). Taken over the expected lifetime of a project or activity, value is created only when the net present value of the generated economic profits is positive. At the business level, value is created over time only when the value of a business exceeds the capital invested in it. The critical aspect in evaluating a strategic option is thus to consider the levels of economic profit that it will generate over time.

Following the line of Michael Porter, the VBM approach recognizes two ways to sustain value creation: (1) participate in economically attractive markets, (2) gain and hold a competitive advantage (in respect of differentiation and/or cost). An attractive market is defined where the average level of economic profit per competitor is greater than zero. Similarly, a business is advantaged if its level of economic profit is higher than the average for competitors participating in the same market. Taking each of the corporation's businesses, this allows for a mapping, somewhat akin to the GE matrix approach but with 'strength' and 'attractiveness' measured by a single variable – economic profit. Such mapping allows the corporation to chart the broad areas where economic value is created or destroyed and where appropriate investment might best be directed.

For all its apparent virtues, the VBM approach has been criticized as open to short-termism, with its focus on looking at economic profit on a year-by-year basis rather than looking to the long term. This criticism is particularly telling if management play up to any short-termism in the stock market, for example by hiking up short-term profits at the expense of longer-term profits if this raises the share price (by sending a false signal that future profits will also be high).

There are also practical issues about the measurement of economic profit. These largely revolve around measuring the real cost of capital. Here debate continues about how to treat unrecorded intangibles, the treatment of gross relative to net assets, and how to handle fluctuating cycles of working capital – matters which could fundamentally alter the perception of whether a project is likely to yield positive or negative discounted economic profits.

Yet, to many organizations, the most telling deficit of the VBM approach is not so much its guidance on assessing individual projects as its overall business ethos that amounts to holding that only share-holders matter, in the process disenfranchising other stakeholders. The VBM proponents counter this claim by arguing that only by maximiz-ing shareholder value can the corporation guarantee that the interests of all other stakeholders are served, by ensuring long-term survival (and thus job and work security) and sharing in the rewards (such as through profit-related pay). However, motivating interested parties, like workers, by asking them to increase their efforts in order to increase the wealth of shareholders may be a tall challenge for any VBM corporation!

Sources: Kay (1996); Milburn (2001); authors' own research.

QUESTION

1 If VBM is the right corporate approach to take, why have VBM com-panies like Reuter's and Lufthansa performed so poorly in recent years and destroyed shareholder value?

A benefit to arise from the VBM approach has been greater understanding and appreciation of what creates and underlies value – essentially competitive advant-age in attractive markets – and how to measure it at the business or project level – through the 'economic profit' generated. This assists strategists in determining where and how value can be created (as opposed to destroyed) in the corporation, providing guidance on where investment is most needed and where it is not desir-able. It also encourages senior management to review and reconsider the current portfolio of activities and assess which elements of the company might usefully be disposed of, cutting through sentimental attachment to businesses and projects which may actually be destroying corporate value.

Senior managers have seized on VBM, notably when their own remuneration is related to corporate performance. With remuneration based on stock-market performance, profit-related pay, and backed up with shares and share options, the incentives of senior managers are much more closely aligned with those of share-holders. In these circumstances, senior managers will be motivated to push for maximizing value. But will they go so far as to weaken their empire by reducing the size of the organization if it creates shareholder value? In theory, if senior managers truly buy into VBM, then yes, they should. Here there is evidence of this through the trend in corporate divestments, spin-offs and downsizing. In addition, Boots and other corporations have simply returned money to shareholders, either directly in increased dividends or indirectly through share buy-backs, when they feel that they cannot add value through investing the money in the corporation. That is, rather than sit on a cash mountain or sit on assets that could be translated directly into cash, they have given the money back to shareholders, allowing them to determine where it is best invested (such as in other businesses).

Such examples show an element of management self-sacrifice for the greater good of the corporation. But there may be natural reluctance to undertake such moves when senior management is concerned that this will be seen as a sign of its own weakness (failing to come up with good investment ideas) rather than a sign of strength (undertaking its 'duty' to shareholders). Senior managers may also be blinded by their own convictions and genuinely believe that it is only a matter of time before businesses and projects 'turn the corner', rather than accept the truth that poorly conceived or operated businesses destroy value. In both cases, the realization that value is being destroyed or at least trapped by their actions will never be easy for managers to accept. But the issue is not easy for shareholders (as outsiders) to see when it is management (the insiders) that controls the necessary financial information. Consider this issue in relation to exhibit 4.7 on whether McDonald's should be returning capital to investors in view of its recent poor corporate performance.

EXHIBIT 4.7 MCDONALD'S: TIME TO RETURN CAPITAL TO SHAREHOLDERS?

'The world has changed. Our customers have changed. We have to change, too,' claimed Jim Cantalupo, chairman and chief executive of McDonald's, 7 April 2003. The world's biggest fast-food chain announced that it no longer wanted to be simply bigger than everyone else, just better. After decades of phenomenal growth driven by new store openings, e.g. averaging 1,700 a year in the 1990s, and annual group sales reaching US$41 billion, sales at store level have begun falling. In 2003 the company announced its first quarterly loss (US$344 million) since going public in 1965. The group's share price slumped from more than US$48 in 1999 to a ten-year low of US$12.

Having gorged itself on vast amounts of capital to fund its restaurant opening binge over previous decades, the group plans to close 700 underperforming restaurants and concentrate on getting more customers into existing ones. Even so, it still planned to open over 1,000 new restaurants worldwide in 2003. In the face of deteriorating performance, and questions over its restaurant expansion policy and brand management, there is growing clamour among investors for McDonald's to return more of its capital to shareholders in the way of dividends.

Critics claim that McDonald's is no longer as relevant in today's market as it used to be, given the trend towards healthier eating. The response from the company is the promise to offer 'champagne taste on a beer budget' with healthier, premium-priced products such as salads, yoghurts and sliced fruit, in addition to improving advertising and restaurant ambience.

However, doubts remain over whether McDonald's can really turn its performance round. The company's detractors point to its poor record on service and product innovation, increasing competition and mounting external pressures:

- Once a byword for good service, McDonald's has been ranked the worst company for customer satisfaction in America for nearly a decade – below all health insurers, airlines and banks. It even ranks below the taxman (Internal Revenue Service) for customer satisfaction!
- Recent attempts at innovations like 'bacon butty', pizza or chicken sandwiches have not turned into big hits. Indeed, the last really successful innovation was the Chicken McNugget, launched in 1983 – a product recently described by a judge as 'a McFrankenstein creation'.
- Competition with rival burger chains has increasingly focused on price, resulting in incessant price wars.
- Alternative food outlets appear increasingly popular. There are now more subway sandwich shops in America than McDonald's restaurants.
- The rise of 'fast casual' restaurants such as gourmet sandwich shops appears to make the McDonald's offering look increasingly outdated.
- McDonald's appears particularly poorly positioned in regard to the looming prospect of obesity legislation in the United States and a general backlash against marketing 'unhealthy' food to children.

Investors may take the view that, with such a deteriorating position, now would be a good time for the company to give cash back to shareholders. The company clearly has the scope to do this. The group owns 75 per cent of the buildings and 40 per cent of the land at its 30,000 locations in 118 countries, making it the largest owner of retail property in the world. The land alone is estimated to be worth US$12 billion (before tax), the value of which could be exploited through a sale-and-lease-back programme. In addition, it could sell a stake in its non-core businesses, which it terms 'partner brands', including such chains as Boston Market chicken, Chipotle burritos and Pret-á-manger sandwiches. It is estimated that this portfolio is worth around US$1 billion.

Along with cuts in capital spending, it appears that the company could easily hand back several billion dollars to its investors. At present, though, it shows no signs of doing this.

Sources: 'Is the world fed up with McDonald's?' *Sunday Times*, 6 April 2003; 'Did somebody say a loss?' *Economist*, 12 April 2003.

> ## QUESTIONS
>
> 1 Is the feast over for McDonald's?
> 2 Should the company return cash to its shareholders or should it invest the cash in the business?
> 3 If the latter, what specific investments and strategic changes do you suggest in order to turn around its fortunes?

While using VBM performance measures like economic profit may be useful in making judgements about investment decisions, and certainly useful in satisfying shareholders, as external parties, that senior management is pursuing the corporate objective of maximizing shareholder value, they are unlikely to provide full guidance on the real health of a business. Indeed, as something of a counter to VBM, taking a more balanced view of the business by a range of measures beyond financial ones has become popular. The leading proponents of this move, Robert Kaplan and David Norton (1992, 1993, 1996), argue companies' tendency to fixate on a few measurements blinkers assessment of how the business is performing overall. Their concept of the 'balanced scorecard' is intended to focus management attention on a range of key indicators to provide a balanced view of the business.

As Kaplan and Norton point out, the problem with relying just on financial measures is that they tend to tell only the results of actions already taken. Operational measures on customer satisfaction, internal processes and innovation and improvement activities are useful counterpoints, as these measures can be indicative of future financial performance. Taken together, the measures (both quantitative and qualitative ones) may offer managers a more rounded view of how corporate performance is likely to develop and better ensure that the company is driven by its mission rather than by short-term financial performance.

More generally, and in contrast to the VBM approach, the balanced scorecard approach acknowledges the expectations of different stakeholders and seeks to relate an assessment of performance to choice of strategy. Here, four key perspectives require to be considered:

1 *Financial perspective.* How do we look to shareholders?
2 *Customer perspective.* How do customers view us?
3 *Internal business perspective.* What must we excel at?
4 *Innovation and learning perspective.* Can we continue to improve and create value?

The idea is that each goal in each area (e.g. financial survival) is assigned one or more measures, as well as a target (e.g. positive economic profit) and an initiative (e.g. move to JIT manufacturing). These can then be viewed as 'key performance measures', essential for achieving desired strategic objectives. In addition, measures of success in the financial area might include cash flow, sales growth and ROCE. Under the customer perspective, measures might be market share (reflecting a competitive position goal), growth of repeat sales (as a customer acceptance goal), delivery and maintenance response times (customer service leadership goal) and a price comparison index (competitive pricing goal). Under the internal business perspective, measures could be cycle time, unit cost and wastage rates (as a manufacturing excellence goal) or project performance index and project close-out cycle (superior project management goal). Under the innovation and learning perspective, measures might relate to a rate of improvement index (continuous improvement goal), the development time of next-generation products (technology leadership goal), staff attitude survey and number of employee suggestions (workforce empowerment goal).

The attraction of this approach is that it ties down more explicitly the specific strategic objectives and measures to be targeted while pursuing the ultimate aim of the organization, such as creating value for the whole corporation. It also has the attraction of giving specific recognition to the interests of different stakeholders, something that might encourage greater overall co-operation both within the organization and with key external parties (customers, suppliers, government, etc.).

REVIEW EXERCISE

1 Identify the key criteria for your company in respect of evaluating strategic options. Is there any overriding business objective aimed at satisfying one particular group of stakeholders (e.g. shareholders)? If so, to what extent is this likely to be in conflict with other objectives and the interests of other stakeholders?

2 In view of these evaluation criteria, what direction and method do you think would allow the company to develop most appropriately? Explain your reasons for this combination in terms of how feasible this option is. Is this the best option in terms of a balance between risk and return? If not, which option offers the most acceptable rewards?

3 As a corporate parent, what core competences and resources does your company possess? Are these core competences spread across the entire organization? If not, what opportunities are there for creating additional value by better exploiting core competences within the existing business operations?

4 Are there business units in the company where value is trapped or being undermined by the present organizational set-up? How should this be resolved?

5 To what extent would it be feasible for the company to exploit its core competences and strategic resources as a means of diversifying into new product lines and/or new markets?

6 List and rank-order the key acceptability criteria the company, in your opinion, should use in assessing strategic options. To what extent are they likely to be in accordance or conflict? How should they be weighed in conflicting situations?

CHAPTER 5

ORGANIZATION AND STRATEGY

Organizational Issues and Strategy

In chapters 1–4 we have been concerned with what strategy is, how firms define their strategic goals and the nature of the business environment. In this chapter we look at the organizational factors that impact on strategic management. First of all we address the issue of how we should think about the nature of *organization* – what are the important factors that make up an organization and what it means to be well organized. We then turn to the question of organization *culture* and *human resources* – the values that hold organizations together. To clarify the relationship between organization, culture and strategy we look at the work of Peters and Waterman, the success of Japanese management and work on organizations that survive over the long term. The latter is *not*, of course, the norm! Finally we look at the issue of organization *design* and *structure* – how organizations are designed and run to enhance strategic responsiveness – in the context of growth and internationalization, paying particular attention to the role of the corporate parent.

The key point we want to communicate is that the notion of organization subsumes a variety of variables, all of which impact on strategy. Traditionally, organization structure has been the factor most emphasized in the strategic management literature. The argument was that you decided upon your strategy and then designed an organization structure to support that strategy. Strategy, in this traditional view, determined structure. We now know that this is not always the case. Existing structures have important implications for strategy. They can facilitate strategy or impede it. And there are a range of other factors besides strategy that are important in strategic management.

Two key events were important in bringing the importance of organizational issues to the fore in considerations of strategic management: (1) Peters and Waterman's best-selling book *In Search of Excellence* and (2) the success of Japanese firms in the West.

Peters and Waterman's Excellent Organizations

According to Peters and Waterman, excellence in organizations is equated with the ability to change. Excellent organizations are continuously innovative, geared to quick action and regular experimentation:

> innovative companies are especially adroit at continually responding to change of any sort in their environments. . . . As the needs of their customers shift, the skills of their competitors improve, the mood of the public perturbates, the forces of international trade realign, and government regulations shift, these companies tack, revamp, adjust, transform, and adapt. In short, as a whole culture, they innovate. (1982: 12)

Excellent companies are characterized by 'quick action, service to customers, practical innovation'. These are not possible without the commitment of the staff to company philosophy. Structures and systems that inhibit quick communication and action are anathema. The customer is the key element in the organization's environment. There are three 'pillars' necessary for excellence:

1 the *stability* pillar: a simple, basic underlying form that generally corresponds to the old divisional product-based structure;
2 the *entrepreneurial* pillar: entrepreneurial 'small is beautiful' units, which are problem-solving, and implementation groups and measurement systems based on the amount of entrepreneurship and implementation;
3 the '*habit-breaking*' pillar: the willingness and ability to reorganize regularly on a temporary basis to create experimental project teams to attack specific problems. Regular reorganizing is a way to meet shifting pressures without putting in place huge, permanent integrating committee devices.

The three pillars represent a response to three prime needs: a need for efficiency around the basics; a need for regular innovation; and a need to avoid 'calcification' by ensuring responsiveness to major threats.

Hickman and Silva (1984), in an extension of Peters and Waterman's work, argue the need for managers to combine strategy and culture in seeking change by analysing customers and employers:

> While strategic thinking aims at getting and keeping customers, culture building attracts, develops, motivates, and unifies the right kind of employees . . . no matter how strongly an organization's culture motivates and develops employees, if customers do not perceive better products and services as a result, the culture has been wasted. The intertwined relationship between customers and employees requires watchful management, by well-trained executives. (Hickman and Silva, 1984: 85–6)

Excellent organizations need to build and sustain excellent cultures by selecting, motivating, rewarding, retaining and unifying good employees. The goal is an organization of many hands but of one mind devoted to building the best product possible, fully satisfying customers and taking care of one's own people. Key data for assessing an organization's culture are:

- *The organization's history*: the events, people and decisions that have shaped this history; how the organization has and is performing;
- *The dreams, ambitions and values of key personnel*. These key personnel are the 'opinion leaders', who can be both managers and employees;
- *Organizational stories* (often called organizational myths) that contain key information relating to beliefs, values, concerns, rules (the do's and don'ts) and general ways of getting things done. There is a strong 'people' emphasis in excellent organizations – successful relationships grow from kindness, empathy and commitment. Motivation is important because people want to be stretched and relish challenges to their competence.

A key argument of Peters and Waterman is that there is more to organization than just structure. They demonstrate that the skilful management of seven factors is important for excellence. This argument leads to their 'seven Ss' framework, depicted in figure 5.1. They define their seven Ss as follows:

- *Strategy*: those actions that a company plans in response to or in anticipation of changes in its competitive environment and the way a company aims to sustain or improve its competitive position.
- *Structure*: the organization chart and related information that show how the work of the organization is divided up and then co-ordinated.

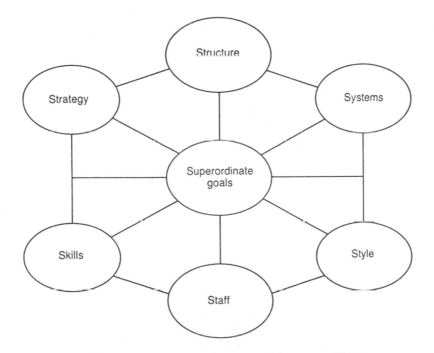

Figure 5.1 The seven Ss framework. *Source*: Peters and Waterman (1982)

- *Systems*: all the procedures and processes that enable the organization to run from day by day, year by year, such as capital budgeting systems, employee relation systems, information systems.
- *Style*: tangible evidence of what management considers important as demonstrated by how it spends its time and how it uses symbolic behaviour. Peters and Waterman point out that it is not what management say that is important but the way they behave. There can, in short, be a discrepancy between stated attitudes and actual behaviours. For example, most managers will say they are democratic. People reporting to them judge them as far more autocratic than the managers themselves think.
- *Staff*: the people in the organization. Peters and Waterman argue that we should think about 'corporate demographics' both in its hard, quantitative sense – appraisal systems, pay scales, formal training, etc. – and in the soft, qualitative sense of morale, attitudes, motivation and behaviours.
- *Superordinate goals*: the shared values and guiding concepts that underpin the formal statement of corporate objectives. Compelling superordinate goals pull an organization together and provide stability over the long term. Peters and Waterman suggest that, unlike the other six Ss, superordinate goals seem not to be present in most organizations but were a major feature of the excellent companies they studied. It is one of the main functions of leadership to articulate these goals and, thereby, create a sense of meaning for employees.
- *Skills*: the capabilities possessed by the organization. These are more than just the sum of individual skills and require skilful management. Some organizations with highly skilled individuals do not possess the ability actually to harness those skills to get things done, while other organizations are able to perform extraordinary feats with apparently ordinary people.

The '7S' framework illustrates two important facts. Firstly, the seven Ss cannot be treated in isolation from one another. The notion that if you get the structure right the people will automatically fit is simply wrong, as is the notion that if you get the right people then success is guaranteed. Structure and staff are important but so are the other five factors. Second, we need to take the 'soft' variables – style, systems, skills and superordinate goals – very seriously. They are at least as important as strategy and structure in achieving excellence. Take the problem of strategic change. It is very easy to state different strategic objectives, such as new target customers or new levels of product or service quality. It is relatively easy and quick to reorganize in the sense of changing one's structure, altering reporting relationships and so on. Hence the old managerial adage 'If you don't know what to do, reorganize.' But carrying these changes through is a far more difficult and lengthy process. A major change in systems to support a new strategy, a major retraining programme to change the skills base of an organization or the generation of commitment throughout the organization to a new superordinate goal can take years. Peters and Waterman's final important point is that you need to think of the seven Ss as seven compass points. It is only when they are all aligned and pointing in the same direction that you can truly call yourself well organized.

QUESTIONS

1 How would you assess your organization or an organization you know using the 7S framework?
2 What do these factors tell you about the organization's key values and beliefs?
3 What does the use of the framework tell you that you didn't know before?

Japanese Organizations and Strategic Management

> Culture arrived on the management scene in the 1980s like a typhoon blowing in from the Far East. (Quinn *et al.*, 1988: 344)

More specifically, the importance attributed to culture was due to the success of Japanese firms in markets such as consumer electronics and automobiles that had been traditionally dominated by Western firms. Culture is also a key issue in Peters and Waterman's work, discussed in the last section. Excellent organizations are 'rich in culture', i.e. they are characterized by strong, shared systems of beliefs about where they are going and what kind of organization they are. Culture constitutes a deeply entrenched perspective which conditions the ways in which an organization sees the world, develops new ideas and responds to changes in the environment.

Culture has a crucial role to play in strategic management. An existing management culture helps determine ways of thinking about strategy, as exhibit 5.1 demonstrates. A change in strategic direction will often necessitate a change in culture. Perhaps its most crucial role is in determining the way in which people are selected, trained, developed and rewarded. Organizational culture determines the kind of people who will be attracted to a firm and the way they will interact within the firm. Peters and Waterman's ideal image is of a shared culture based on a feeling of collective interest and a shared system of beliefs, habits and traditions. Of course, this is not always the case. Indeed, some would say that such an organization is the exception rather than the norm and that organizations are fundamentally political entities built on self-interest, not common interest, in which individuals and factions, like Machiavellian princes, are looking to build their own power bases at the expense of the common good.

The major examples of strong, shared, common cultures have been drawn from Japan. Akio Morita, the chairman of Sony, compares Japanese firms (*kaisha*) to families:

> There is no secret or hidden formula responsible for the success of the best Japanese companies. No theory or plan or government policy will make a business a success; that can only be done by people. The most important mission for a Japanese manager

EXHIBIT 5.1 CHANGING THE CULTURE OF ICI

One of the hardest parts of Sir John Harvey-Jones's task in turning ICI round in the 1980s was to change the culture of the organization. The choice of a new strategic direction for the company was relatively easy, i.e. the decision to de-emphasize its European business, to diversify into other geographical areas, particularly the United States, and to change the balance of its portfolio of products in favour of higher value added chemicals with greater margins than the bulk commodity chemical business. There was also a series of acquisitions, over 100 in the 1980s. The difficult problem was to implement the new strategy, to make it happen. This necessitated culture change. To change the culture meant getting rid of people and teaching those that remained to think in a different way. A key aspect of the latter was to persuade people to stop thinking as scientists and technologists ('This is an interesting product or technology') and to start thinking as business people ('This is a more profitable line of business'). This constituted a major new skills emphasis and a major task of rethinking the nature of the company and its values.

is to develop a healthy relationship with his employees, to create a family-like feeling within the corporation, a feeling that employees and managers share the same fate. Those companies that are most successful in Japan are those that have managed to create a shared sense of fate among all employees, what Americans call labor and management, and the shareholders. (1987: 130)

Morita's words are echoed by Konosuke Matsushita, the founder of Matsushita Electrical Industrial Company, who compares Japan with the West in chilling tones:

We will win and you will lose. You cannot do anything about it because your failure is an internal disease. Your companies are based on Taylor's principles. Worse, your heads are Taylorized too. You firmly believe that sound management means executives on the one side and workers on the other, on the one side men who think and on the other side men who can only work. For you, management is the art of smoothly transferring the executives' ideas to the workers' hands. We have passed the Taylor stage. We are aware that business has become terribly complex. Survival is very uncertain in an environment filled with risk, the unexpected, and competition. . . . We know that the intelligence of a few technocrats – even very bright ones – has become totally inadequate to face these challenges. Only the intellects of all employees can permit a company to live with the ups and downs and the requirements of the new environment. Yes, we will win and you will lose. For you are not able to rid your minds of the obsolete Taylorisms that we never had. (Best, 1990: 1)

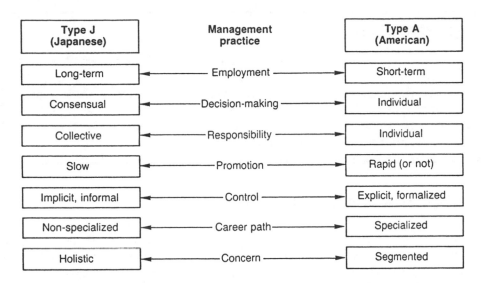

Type J (Japanese)	Management practice	Type A (American)
Long-term	Employment	Short-term
Consensual	Decision-making	Individual
Collective	Responsibility	Individual
Slow	Promotion	Rapid (or not)
Implicit, informal	Control	Explicit, formalized
Non-specialized	Career path	Specialized
Holistic	Concern	Segmented

Figure 5.2 Type J versus Type A organizations. *Source*: adapted from Ouchi (1981)

William Ouchi, a noted US management scholar, has studied the contrast in management practice between Japanese and American firms. Figure 5.2 sets out his findings in terms of the differences he observed. The Japanese (type J) firm looks to create, through its management practices, a sense of 'holistic' concern. That is, it looks to generate in each individual a sense of commitment to the good of the whole organization.

Since the successes of Japanese firms in the West, and Western firms' interest in Japanese management techniques, we have seen global economic changes that have impacted upon Japan. The Japanese economy has struggled to combat deflation and stagnation but in certain industries, most notably in automobiles, Japanese firms remain world leaders. Toyota remains the world's most profitable auto company, announcing twice as much profit for the current fiscal year as any auto company ever (*Financial Times*, 3 March 2003). Toyota, Honda and Nissan have operating profit margins above 10 per cent. The Japanese manufacturers are making all these profits from the United States, where the home manufacturers struggle with cost reduction exercises. Japanese cars remain more attractive – on price and quality – than their local competitors. In Europe too we are seeing a rise in the performance of the Japanese, although the European companies such as Renault and Volkswagen seem better placed to compete on the grounds of price and innovatory design, especially Renault. Visit the Renault and the other car company design studios on the Champs Elysées in Paris on a weekend afternoon to witness how consumers are excited by the strategy Renault and others have developed. Interestingly, the Japanese government has set up a think-tank to study its economic failure, the *shippai-gaku* or 'Failure-ology' Institute.

QUESTIONS

1 Would you describe British firms in general as more like type A or type J?
2 Will the Japanese auto firms be able to replicate their North American success in Europe?
3 Why did Britain fail in the automobile industry when other European countries have survived and even prospered?

Strategic Human Resource Management

Studies of Japanese success have suggested a variety of reasons for Japan's competitive advantage over the West. These reasons are summarized in figure 5.3. Some claim it is government fiscal and monetary policy that has given Japan its edge. Similarly the role of the government in targeting research and development in particular industries as part of its industrial policy has been mentioned. Others suggest it is due to technology, that Japan has had access to advanced manufacturing systems while Western firms make do with outdated machinery. Others argue that the differences are due to Japanese national culture, which very strongly values an ethic of hard work, commitment to the organization you work for and an education system that delivers highly skilled and motivated school leavers

	Macro	Micro
Hardware	**Government fiscal and monetary policies** Taxation Capital markets Savings	**Production capability** Plant Equipment
Software	**Socio-economic environment** Work ethic Regulation Education	**Corporate management** Organization Administration Production system

Figure 5.3 Key elements in manufacturing competitiveness. *Source*: adapted from Abernathy *et al.* (1981)

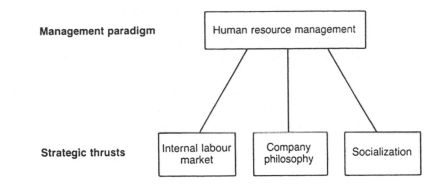

Figure 5.4 The Japanese management system. *Source:* adapted from Pucik and Hatvany (1983)

and graduates. But it is the fourth factor, 'corporate management' and the Japanese approach to human resource management, that have been given most attention in the West as the source of their success.

Japanese advantage, the argument goes, rests not on new technology or education or government policy, though these all play a minor role. It depends primarily on management's capacity to produce a nearly fault-free product cheaply through the diligent and skilful control of the system of production and the human factor. What, then, is the link between the Japanese system of human resource management and strategic management? Let us look at Japanese management practices in more detail. The elements of the Japanese system are set out in figure 5.4.

A paradigm is a shared set of rules and intuitions about the way things can and should be done. The Japanese system has as its core a set of shared rules and beliefs about how to deal with human resources. This focus on human resources reflects the belief that a key source of strategic success is the maximum utilization of available human assets. It has three main strategic thrusts. First, the emphasis is on creating an internal labour market made up of employees with the desired skills, both technical and social. The goal of the management of the internal labour market is to induce employees to stay with the firm over the long term, hence an emphasis on lifetime employment. Second comes the unique company philosophy to give employees a sense of meaning from their employment and a sense of where the organization is going in the future and what their role is in that future. Third, new employees undergo an intensive period of induction into the company to test that they possess the required characteristics and to teach them what it means to be part of the company.

The general strategic thrusts of the Japanese management system are operationalized through specific management techniques. Open communication is encouraged and supported. Employees' skills are developed continuously through job rotation, which focuses on a broad range of skills and ongoing training throughout their career. Employees are appraised on a variety of criteria, including contribution to team achievement, rather than just in terms of individual results. Work is structured so that it can be carried out by teams which are given the maximum autonomy possible. In return for this autonomy, teams are expected to exercise responsibility in the pursuit of agreed organizational goals. Decision making is preceded by extensive consultation. Again, the return for being involved in the decision-making process is the expectation that individuals and groups will assume responsibility for implementing the decision. Concern between management and managed is seen as mutual. Employees are expected to become involved and managers are expected to foster employee participation in pursuit of the welfare of all.

This management style has a strong effect on business strategy. Long-term socialization linked with the commitment to a unique company philosophy fosters a competitive spirit in employees. The mission of the organization is to survive as a group by defeating the competition. Japanese industry in those sectors where it is a world leader is characterized by intense levels of competition and Japanese managers are developed in an atmosphere of fierce competitive rivalry. This emphasis on competitiveness is reflected in the concern of Japanese firms with market share as a key business goal. The concern also reflects, in part, the goal of retaining core staff during periods of downturn, when Japanese firms tend to cut prices to maintain market share rather than protect their margins by reducing output and employment. The management approach is based on a long-term perspective because employment is for the long term and the firm exists to maximize all its members' interests. The emphasis is strongly on internal growth as a means of ensuring the survival of the corporation. Divestitures, mergers and acquisitions are unusual in Japan and strategy is based on continuous product and process innovation and improving quality while reducing costs.

The implications of the Japanese management system for business strategy can thus be summarized as follows:

- the generation of competitive spirit;
- emphasis on market share;
- a long-term perspective;
- emphasis on internal growth;
- the constant search for innovation, quality improvement and cost reduction.

One final point. It has been claimed that there is one major feature of the Japanese approach to strategy that distinguishes it from that of most Western firms: *strategic intent* (Hamel and Prahalad, 1989). The Japanese firms that have risen to global leadership over the decades invariably began with ambitions that were out of all proportion to their resources. One has only to look at how small firms like Canon ('Beat Xerox') and Komatsu ('Encircle Caterpillar') set their sights, not on the immediate competition, but on beating the industry leaders to illustrate this point. They achieved great things by creating an obsession with winning at all levels of the organization. This obsession creates strategic intent. The key focus is on winning, defined in terms of the hardest possible targets. The firms motivate employees by the value of this target. They use the target to develop a long attention span. They are clear about the end point (their strategic 'mission') but flexible as to means, leaving room for individual and team contributions and constantly emphasizing improving competences/skills. They look to develop layers of competitive advantage and do not just focus on one target. For example, they might combine cost reduction measures with differentiation strategies, expansion of markets and diversification. Their goal is to create new rules of competition. They refuse to play by the existing rules, which are set by industry leaders, because they realize they cannot hope to compete on the leaders' terms. They innovate by leveraging resources to achieve unattainable ends.

In comparison, the emphasis in most Western firms has been on strategic fit. Rather than 'leveraging resources to achieve the impossible', Western firms tend to trim ambition to match available resources. Strategy means positioning according to others' rules, i.e. the rules of dominant firms. All one can hope to achieve by doing this is to project the future forward. With strategic intent, the emphasis is on 'folding the future back', making a future vision a reality by evaluating present actions in terms of how they contribute to the realization of the vision. By playing to the same rules as everybody else, Western firms become very predictable and seriously limit their options. Their strategies tend to emphasize buying and selling businesses rather than developing them.

QUESTIONS

1 How does your firm or a firm you know welcome and develop its new members?

2 If you had to write a speech to welcome new recruits what would you put in it? Woody Allen's 'My speech to the graduates' begins: 'More than any other time in history, mankind faces a crossroads. One path leads to despair and utter hopelessness. The other, to total extinction. Let us pray we have the wisdom to choose correctly'! It ends: 'We are a people who lack defined goals. We have never learned to love. We lack leaders and coherent programs. We have no spiritual centre. We are adrift alone in the cosmos, wreaking monstrous violence on one another out of frustration and pain. Fortunately, we have not lost our sense of proportion. Summing up, it is clear the future holds great opportunities. It also holds pitfalls. The trick will be to avoid pitfalls, seize the opportunities, and get back home by six o'clock. It is interesting to compare this with Akio Morita's speech to Sony graduates: 'We did not draft you. This is not the army, so that means you have voluntarily chosen Sony. This is your responsibility, and normally if you join this company we expect that you will stay for the next twenty or thirty years. Nobody can live twice, and the next twenty or thirty years is the brightest period of your life. You only get it once. When you leave this company thirty years from now, or when your life is finished, I do not want you to regret that you spent all those years here. That would be a tragedy. I cannot stress the point too much that this is your responsibility to yourself. So I say to you, the most important thing in the next few months is for you to decide whether you will be happy or unhappy here' [Morita, 1987: 131–2].

3 Would you say that firms you know demonstrate 'strategic intent'? If *yes*, how? If *no*, what would it need to do to develop it?

CASE STUDY

Strategic human resource management:
Ford Motor Company

'Strategic intent' is not the sole preserve of Far Eastern companies. Leading Western companies such as Ford and IBM have set hard competitive challenges to their employees in the pursuit of new competitive advantage based on quality. Ford is synonymous with the creation of a particular management style – Fordism – based on bureaucratic organization, hierarchical decision making with strict functional specialization and tightly defined job design and specialized machinery to mass-produce a standard product for mass markets. A conjunction of market and technological factors in the 1980s forced Ford to rethink its organization, to redesign jobs and to radically change its culture. The organizational model for its rethinking of its approach to personnel management was, in part, Japanese-inspired. Indeed, the major change initiative of Ford of Europe in the early 1980s was called 'After Japan'. The primary impetus to change arose from growing recognition of the magnitude of the Japanese threat, actual in the United States and imminent in the United Kingdom with the establishment of the Nissan plant in the north-east of England. The new competition posed the threat of radically new standards of efficiency, quality and design. The company had its close links with Mazda, in which it owned a 25 per cent stake, to serve as a source of competitive benchmarking. This benchmarking formed the basis of its long-term strategy.

The major challenge Ford management has set itself is to develop a co-operative employee relations environment to improve its capacity for strategic change. The move is towards co-operative employee relations policies and practices in a firm and industry that has been synonymous with conflictual relations between management and employees. Company strategy is embodied in the 1984 mission statement (see figure 1.4). Ford's mission is to be a worldwide leader in automotive and related products and services, and in newer industries such as financial services. The human resource emphasis is reinforced by the company's value statement, 'Ford's basic values are people, products, and profits,' and guiding principles that include 'Employee involvement is our way of life.' The process was facilitated in the United States by the active co-operation of the United Automobile Workers union, a form of co-operation that was not forthcoming in the United Kingdom.

A key focus of employee and management development at Ford is the 'human resources issue'. All the company's strategic issues such as quality improvement, customer satisfaction, innovation and cost reduction have one common denominator. They all depend on the capacities, competences and commitment of Ford employees. The key strategic issue, now and into the future, is how to create and sustain a flexible work force with the capacities, competences and commitment (including the technical and managerial leadership) that will give the company a competitive edge in a turbulent, uncertain world market place.

At the core of Ford's new human resource management system lie participative management and employee involvement. Participative management is defined as 'the techniques and skills that managers use to provide employees with opportunities to participate actively in key managerial processes affecting job related matters'. Techniques include job redesign, team building, task forces and problem-solving groups. Skills include contracting (establishing clear expectations), rewarding and modelling participative skills. Employee involvement is defined as 'the processes by which employees at all levels have the opportunities to participate actively in the key managerial processes affecting job-related matters'. The processes offering opportunities for participation include consultation (to maximize information and commitment), collaboration (based on a norm of consensus) and delegation (the manager assigns responsibility for an agreed outcome to an individual or group). The joint aim of management and unions is, in the United States at least, to make work a more satisfying experience, improve the overall work environment, enhance creativity, contribute to improvements in the workplace, help to achieve quality and efficiency, and reduce absenteeism.

QUESTIONS

1 What are the links between strategy and organizational issues in this case?
2 The strategic change initiative described in this case was more successful in the United States than in the United Kingdom. What reasons can you think of to explain this?
3 Does the United Kingdom have particular problems of human resource management that are likely to impact on strategy? If *yes*, what are these problems and how should they be addressed?
4 Is human resource management in your company supportive of strategy? If *yes*, how? If *no*, why not?

EXERCISE

Peters and Waterman identified eight successful management practices that led to excellence. These are set out in figure 5.5.

1 Think of an organization that you would class as 'excellent'. List those features that you consider contribute to this excellence. Are these the same features that are emphasized in the Peters and Waterman approach or in the Japanese management system?

2 Think of another organization that you would class as excellent. List those features that you consider contribute to this excellence. Are these the same features that are emphasized in the Peters and Waterman approach or in the Japanese management system?

3 Are the features you found in the first organization the same features that you picked out in the second? If yes, you are well on the way to developing your own model of excellence. You will, of course, need a few more examples to complete the picture. If no, then you need to consider other organizations until the features start to repeat themselves to form your model.

4 Is your conclusion radically different from Peters and Waterman's and the Japanese model? If yes, write a book. You are well on the way to becoming rich and famous!

Magic Kingdoms?

Two examples illustrate the lengths to which management must go to establish excellence. These are two firms commonly acknowledged to provide an unparalleled level of service that many others would love to emulate – the Walt Disney Organization, which opened Euro-Disney in France, and Marks & Spencer, acclaimed by many as the United Kingdom's best-managed company.

Walt Disney

Walt Disney is one of Peters and Waterman's leading excellent companies and Disney World in Florida provides a model of excellent provision of service to the customer with outstanding value for money. The Magic Kingdom serves over 25 million customers a year, which requires over 25,000 people doing 1,100 different jobs. The quality of service depends on elaborate training to develop employees (though Disney does not use the term) who are committed to their jobs and the organization and deliver consistently high levels of work performance.

New employees receive extensive training in the way Disney is managed and the Disney way of doing things – the Disney philosophy. Individuals are socialized into

A bias for action
- Project teams that tend to be small, fluid, *ad hoc* and problem/action-focused.
- Communications are of the essence, and there is an important commitment to learning and experimentation.
- Complex problems are tackled through a willingness to shift resources to where they are needed to encourage fluidity and action (chunking).

Close to the customer
- The market-driven principle of commitment to service, reliability, and quality, based on an appreciation of 'nichemanship' and the ability to custom-tailor a product or service to a client's needs.

Autonomy and entrepreneurship
- A principle which champions innovation, decentralization, the delegation of power and action to the level where they are needed, and a healthy tolerance of failure.

Productivity through people
- The principle that employees are people and a major resource, and should be trusted, respected, inspired, and made 'winners'.
- Organizational units should be small-scale to preserve and develop a people-oriented quality.

Hands-on, value-driven
- Organization guided by a clear sense of shared values, mission, and identity, relying on inspirational leadership rather than bureaucratic control.

Stick to the knitting
- The principle of building on strengths and knowledge of one's niche.

Simple form, lean staff
- Avoid bureaucracy; build main commitments to projects or product division rather than to the dual lines of responsibility found in formal matrix organizations; use small organizational units.

Simultaneous loose–tight properties
- The principle that reconciles the need for overall control with a commitment to autonomy and entrepreneurship.

Figure 5.5 Eight excellent-management skills. *Source*: Morgan (1986)

the Disney tradition. They become 'cast members', *not* employees, whose work is to perform in a show. They wear costumes rather than uniforms. In public – 'on stage' – they perform according to carefully constructed scripts. Visitors to Disney World are 'guests'. Management's main employee relations objectives are to share company goals with employees, to give them a clear, consistent picture of the nature of the work required of them, and to make sure they share and live Disney values (in public, at least). The key strategic focus is on quality of service provided by committed and competent staff.

The arrival of Disney in Europe with the opening of Euro-Disney raised many interesting questions. The strategic focus is the same – the provision of a high-quality, value-for-money entertainment experience in a world of make-believe and fun. The major question is whether this American service idea is transferable to Europe. Will Europeans take to the 'Have a nice day' culture and, perhaps more important, will Euro-Disney staff be up to providing service with a smile? (The Magic Kingdom concept has, it should be noted, already been transferred successfully to Japan.)

The president of Euro-Disney argues strongly that Europe presents no special problems and that the levels of service provided by Euro-Disney are already excellent. His view is that it is not national culture that is important as the determinant of organizational behaviour, but rather the values of the company and how successfully it teaches these values to its employees. Press reports on Euro-Disney, however, suggest problems. The *Financial Times* (23 April 1992) suggested that the fair reward for some of the service that it had witnessed was 'confinement in Sleeping Beauty's casket with only Goofy for company'! Disney dismissed these criticisms as teething problems, inevitable in any start-up of this size and complexity. They did not, the company insists, mark a major 'culture shock' issue.

Competitive advantage in retailing: Marks & Spencer and IKEA

Marks & Spencer (M&S) was for a long period lauded as one of the United Kingdom's most admired and successful companies. In the 1990s this all turned round and M&S plunged into crisis. Marks & Spencer's spectacular success was built upon a strong sense of its values and the fundamental principles it expected its staff to adhere to. These principles included:

1 to offer our customers a selective range of high-quality, well-designed and attractive merchandise at reasonable prices under the brand name St Michael;
2 to encourage suppliers to use the most modern and efficient production techniques;
3 to work with suppliers to ensure highest standards of quality control;
4 to provide friendly, helpful service and greater shopping comfort and convenience to our customers;
5 to improve the efficiency of the business, by simplifying operating procedures; and
6 to foster good human relations with customers, suppliers and staff and in the communities in which we trade. (Tse, 1985: 9)

QUESTIONS

1 What went wrong at M&S?
2 How did it lose touch with its customers?

As M&S has declined other retailers have flourished. One of the great business success stories has been the international expansion of IKEA, the Swedish furniture retailing company. IKEA started in 1943 as a one-man mail order company. In the 1960s it pioneered its warehouse principle, huge out-of-town stores where customers view the products then pick the flat-packs up from the shelves themselves to assemble at home. Today IKEA group employs some 70,000 workers, has over 150 stores in more than twenty countries and a turnover of about US$11 billion. IKEA competes on the basis of its location and buying system and on the functionality, quality and low price of its products, a unique configuration of strengths that was established as a basic corporate principle in the 1970s and has remained relatively unchanged since. Its strategy is to be a low-price company. It designs its own furniture and cultivates close relations with its suppliers. It has a strong sense of its cultural heritage and values.

QUESTION

1 Why has IKEA flourished while M&S has struggled?

Critical Voices

Peters and Waterman's work met with huge success and stimulated great excitement in managerial circles, as did the lessons learnt from the Japanese approach to management. Both approaches, however, have had their critics. Two-thirds of Peters and Waterman's forty-three excellent companies lost their excellence rating five years after the book's publication (Pascale, 1990).

In Search of Excellence has been criticized for sloppy research methodology, for poor quality of data and for failing to consider important non-managerial variables such as technology or financial markets. It has been argued that the very variables that made the companies excellent in the first place planted the seeds of their subsequent decline, that their values were actually myopic and that they were overdependent on unusually charismatic leaders who must eventually burn out. It has also been pointed out that survey evidence suggests that, for people-centred organizations, they were not actually very popular organizations to work for. Some see their management style as manipulative, arguing that people are viewed as instruments of productivity and not valued as individuals in their own right.

In an amusing Fastcompany article, 'Tom Peter's true confessions', Peters himself admits that the research was done on the basis of 'travelling the world, meeting smart people and recording the meetings'. And the eight principles? Peters describes being faced with a presentation to Pepsico, which would be too impatient to listen to his 700 slide two-day presentation, so:

> One morning at about six, I sat down at my desk overlooking the San Francisco Bay from the forty-eighth floor of the Bank of America Tower, and I closed my eyes. Then I leaned forward, and I wrote down eight things on a pad of paper. Those eight things haven't changed since that moment. They were the eight basic principles of *Search*.

In a retrospective on *In Search of Excellence* in the *Academy of Management Executive* John Newstrom commends the book's simplicity, its readability, its upbeat message and the impact of Tom Peters as a 'gadfly' – but argues that the book 'neither stimulated widespread testing of their eight attributes nor spawned new theoretical frameworks for future generations of business leaders'. And concludes:

> it helped spark a twenty-year conversation in which readers began searching in both the academic and practitioner literature for practical answers to important questions – but only if they were based on substantive, careful research, as guided by solid theory. In fact it might be the *deficiencies* identified in the *Search* book that have allowed it to become a focus of long-term conversation and controversy, much of which still continue today.

Or, as Peters puts it somewhat differently, '*Search* said, It's not all about the numbers. Profits are cool. They give you room to invest in cool stuff. But somebody has to bleed. Somebody has to show some passion. *Search*, I like to think, put the blood back into business.'

Criticism has also been levelled at Japanese companies, which are accused of driving their employees unmercifully – employees tolerate the pressure imposed on them because they fear losing their jobs and having to leave the core internal labour market with its long-term employment. Japanese firms are also accused of exploiting those who are not part of the internal labour market, their temporary staff and women, who never make it to senior positions. Marks & Spencer has been criticized by some for an 'exploitative' attitude to its suppliers, using its power and their relative weakness to negotiate contracts that work very much in M&S's favour.

QUESTION

1 Do you agree or disagree with these criticisms? Give your reasons for agreement or disagreement.

New Perspectives on Excellence: *Built to Last* and *Good to Great*

Jim Collins and Jerry Porras took the excellence debate further in their two influential books *Built to Last* (1994) and *Good to Great* (2001). In both they have tried to overcome the methodological criticisms aimed at Peters and Waterman by carefully specifying the criteria by which they selected their companies and especially by choosing comparator companies.

Built to Last was based on a study of the eighteen companies most frequently identified in a thorough survey of chief executives as being 'highly visionary', which were contrasted with a comparison group of companies, founded in the same era, in similar products and markets, which, while still successful, had fewer mentions in the same CEO survey. The authors found that, in terms of shareholder value, while the comparison companies outperformed the market by a factor of 3 : 1, the visionary companies outperformed the market by 15 : 1 – a substantial and significant difference.

Jim Collins calls *Good to Great* a 'prequel' to the previous book. He and his research team identified eleven companies that had made the leap from good results to great results and sustained those results for at least fifteen years. Great results were defined as fifteen years' cumulative stock returns at or below the general stock market, punctuated by a transition point, then cumulative stock returns at least three times the market over the next fifteen years. Again, the most successful companies were compared with companies which had similar resources and opportunities but which had not made the same transition and with others which had made but not sustained such a shift in performance.

While *Built to Last* aimed to find the successful habits of visionary companies, *Good to Great* aimed to answer the question about how to turn a good organization into one that produces sustained great results. A number of the findings are worth studying.

All the visionary companies (such as 3M, Boeing, GE, Procter & Gamble, Wal-mart) preserved a core ideology while still having a passion for change. In fact they tended to overcome a number of paradoxes and apparently contradictory tensions by escaping what Collins and Porras call 'the tyranny of the "or" and embracing the genius of the "and" '. So while they all pursued profit successfully they also had a purpose beyond profit. They had 'big hairy audacious goals' *and* pursued continuous improvement; they had 'cult-like cultures' *and* retained the ability to change, move and adapt. Collins and Porras give some classic examples of their precepts:

- *Purpose beyond profit.* Merck elected to develop and give away Mectizan, a drug to cure 'river blindness'. 'Not to do so would have demoralized their scientists.'
- *Big hairy audacious goals (BHAGs)*: GE – 'become No. 1 or No. 2 in every market that we serve and revolutionize this company to have the speed and agility of a small enterprise'.
- Disney's *'cult-like culture'* where nobody's been hired for a job. 'Everyone's been cast for a role in our show.'
- *Trying a lot of stuff and keeping what works.* Wal-mart's 'greeters' originated from one store manager trying to reduce shoplifting.
- *Home-grown management.* 'P&G understood the importance of constantly developing managerial talent so as never to face gaps in succession at any level and therefore to preserve its core throughout the company.'
- *Continuous improvement* has been commonplace in P&G since the 1850s, in 3M since the 1910s, in Marriott's since 1927 and in H&P since the 1940s.
- '*It's the whole ball of wax that counts.*' Ford's statistical quality control methods were reinforced by participative management programmes reinforced by promotion criteria based on participative management skills. 'In hundreds of ways – big and small – Ford translated the MVGP (Mission, Vision, Goals, Programme) into daily practice, into reality.'

The issue of leadership is also central to the 'good to great' companies. Here the central finding was that the leaders in all eleven companies had a combination of will and humility that enabled them to put the company first. And rather than start with their own vision they first put together a strong top management team to generate what Collins calls the 'hedgehog concept', i.e. the central idea of the firm. The term is based on a distinction drawn by the philosopher Isaiah Berlin and based on the parable of the 'fox who knows many things and the hedgehog who knows one big thing. . . . Hedgehogs simplify a complex world into a single organising idea, a basic principle or concept that unifies and guides everything.'

Collins pictures the concept as the intersection of the following three circles: 'what you can be the best in the world at' (not just competent), 'what drives your economic engine' (signified by a single key performance measure) and 'what you are deeply passionately about' (a process of discovery rather than invention). For example, the people at Fannie Mae 'were terrifically motivated by the whole idea of helping people of all classes, backgrounds and races realize the dream of owning their own homes'. They realized they could become 'the best capital markets player in anything that pertains to mortgages' and shifted their key measure from profit per mortgage to profit per mortgage risk level, reflecting the 'fundamental insight that managing interest risk reduces the dependence on the direction of interest rates'.

Similarly Nucor could become the best at harnessing culture and technology to produce low-cost steel. The key measure was dollars per ton of finished steel. Gillette was passionate about shaving systems, and became the best at 'building premier global brands of daily necessities that require sophisticated manufacturing technology' using a key measure of profit per customer based on repeatable purchase of high-margin systems.

Collins and Porras's work, like Peters and Waterman's, is unashamedly normative: they are intended to inspire mangers both to higher goals (purpose beyond profit – an enduring company rather than one that is simply there to be sold) and to recognize the importance of attitudes to people (customers and staff). They also share a taste for colourful language (bias for action, big hairy audacious goal, hedgehog concept). As such they may oversimplify the world but they spark debate and are not too far from the current resource-based view of the firm (see chapter 6).

Organization Design: Strategy and Structure

We have already mentioned the link between strategy and structure. This is an important link and we will finish this section by looking at it in more detail. The classic example of how strategy influences structure is the way in which the strategy of diversification led to the development of the multi-divisional firm. Changes in strategy led to changes in structure. As we said earlier, the relationship can work in the opposite way. Just as culture can help determine strategic thinking, so an existing structure can affect thinking about strategic options.

Perhaps the most familiar form of organization structure is the *bureaucratic organization*, made up of rigid functional divisions and clearly defined roles and rules with a hierarchical chain of command and control. The multi-divisional firm is often made up of a number of bureaucratic subunits dealing with its different markets.

The bureaucratic form of organization has been much criticized. Management gurus such as Peter Drucker and Tom Peters have warned that it must radically change if firms are to survive into the twenty-first century. The bureaucracy is criticized for being:

- too hierarchical, thus stifling creativity lower down the organization;
- costly to run, e.g. because of the many managers it needs to try to put into effect its elaborate rules;
- too slow to adapt to increasingly complex and fast-changing environments;
- out of touch with customers – this applies particularly to the strategic apex of senior managers at the top of the hierarchy;
- demotivating to its employees, who are stifled by the rules and denied the freedom to exercise their creative potential.

Proponents of matrix organizations have tried to balance the functional orientation of the bureaucracy with the priorities of key product and project areas. In the matrix organization, functions are aligned with and balanced by project needs. Rather than abandoning the functional structure, project groups are set up alongside functional departments in a grid or matrix. The matrix structure is thus, in theory, responsive to two managerial needs: the need for strong, specialist functional departments and the need to be more responsive to the customer whose demands the project is aimed at satisfying, e.g. the need to fine-tune products or services for specific, narrowly defined markets, or the need for products for specific geographical areas.

Initially, in the late 1960s and the 1970s, the matrix was seen as the model for the organization of the future. Later it was increasingly criticized as expensive and over-elaborate. Critics pointed out that it meant that each individual was answerable to two bosses – thus violating the classical management principle of unity of command – and was a member of at least two potentially competing groups. This can create conflict and confusion. Among the most vociferous critics of the matrix were Peters and Waterman, who argued that the matrix violated one of their cardinal excellent management principles – 'simple form, lean staff'. For Peters and Waterman the major weakness of the matrix is its lack of responsiveness to the need for change. They argue that the matrix virtually always ceases to be innovative, often after just a short while; that it has particular difficulty in executing the basics because the authority structure is weak; and that it also regularly degenerates into anarchy and rapidly becomes bureaucratic and non-creative. The long-term direction of the matrixed organization is usually not clear.

The ideal organization of the future, critics of the bureaucracy and the matrix argue, will be flat, non-hierarchical, 'knowledge-based' and flexible, with highly skilled employees. It will be essentially *project-based*. There may be functional departments but the key organizational unit will be the project team upon whose innovativeness the organization's future depends. In this form of organization, project teams are given the maximum freedom to search for new ideas. Senior management's major role is liaison with the external environment in search of opportunities, contacts and contracts and to publicize the capabilities of its organization.

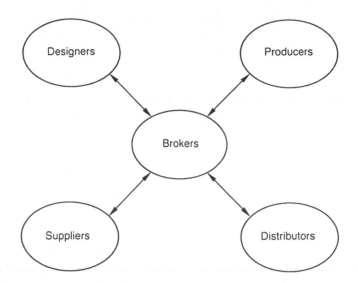

Figure 5.6 The dynamic network. *Source*: Miles and Snow (1986)

More radical critics of the large, inflexible organization argue that internal reform will never save it and that the organizational form of the future will be the *organic network* operating on a 'small is beautiful' principle with a very small core of staff subcontracting in other skills as and when necessary. The large bureaucratic organization is the result of vertical integration. The organic network is the outcome of vertical disintegration as large firms split themselves up and 'return to basics', concentrating only on their core competence. The fashion industry provides good examples of the network form. A firm like Benetton has created a name and an image, but has a core staff of only around 1,500 people, contracts out its production to a range of small firms and sells through some 2,000 sales points, none of which it owns. One of the roots of IKEA's success has been its elaborate and dynamic network of suppliers.

Figure 5.6 represents a variant on the organization network theme, the dynamic network, as an illustration of how key tasks can be contracted out. Figure 5.7 shows one such network, in the film and television industry, where one-off projects such as film production are performed by a network of independent firms co-ordinated by a broker, in this case the producer.

If the network form becomes more widespread, it is the broker who is going to play an increasingly important role. If we think back to the value chain and its importance in strategic analysis, we can see how firms choose to contract out some elements of the value chain in network relationships. For example, in the computer industry IBM subcontracted out work on the development of its personal computer to a network of designers, suppliers and producers. The important issue to be considered in subcontracting is the nature of the firm's core competence. Work on that core, be it in research and development; manufacture or marketing, should not be contracted out.

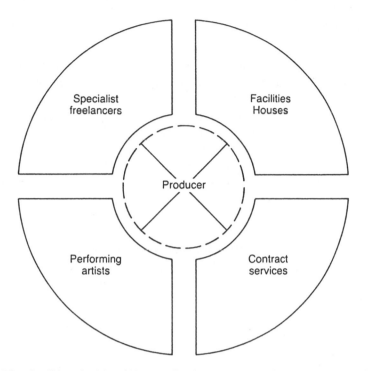

Figure 5.7 The flexible television/film production company. *Source*: Barnatt and Starkey (1991)

EXERCISE

In which industries is subcontracting likely to provide an attractive strategic option? Illustrate your answers with models of the networks that might evolve in these industries.

QUESTIONS

1 What is the structure of the firm you work for and of the firms you have worked for?
2 What were the strengths and weaknesses of this/these structure/s?
3 Which do you think was the best structure?
4 If the firm/s you are thinking about was/were not designed as project organizations or organic networks, could they have been? If yes, could this have improved their performance? If no, why not?

Structuring for Complexity

Analysis such as that by Peters and Waterman has emphasized that structure is not the only organizational variable that is important in strategic analysis. Structure and structuring – a broader term that covers the organizational structure issue and how it meshes with the overall management process – are nevertheless still of great importance. Structure and structuring are particularly important as firms grow, and they become of crucial strategic concern when firms compete on international grounds.

A central managerial issue that the international firm, the multinational corporation (MNC) must resolve is the tension between central control and local autonomy. Take the example of Cadbury Schweppes. Schweppes tonic water must taste the same, look the same and meet the same quality standards wherever in the world you order it. This requires the centre to lay down strict quality and presentational guidelines to which the operating units must adhere. But in Britain tonic is drunk mainly to make alcohol potable, while next door, in France, it is an adult soft drink. The same product is, therefore, consumed for different reasons in the two countries, which in turn means different packaging, different channels of distribution and different customers. The managers on the spot, in charge of each market, have to have the freedom to meet the needs of their particular market place. All large enterprises wrestle with the balance between control from the centre and the ability to respond speedily in the market place. The aim in a branded business is to combine the maximum operating freedom with maintaining a clear worldwide identity for international brands (Cadbury, 1991: 10).

The most important single organizational question for the MNC is, therefore, the degree of decentralization that is most appropriate to its strategic concerns. There have historically been three answers to this question, according to the 'state of the art' study of the issue, Bartlett and Ghoshal's *Managing across Borders* (1989). They describe them as multinational companies (the typical European structure and management approach developed before World War II), international companies (the approach developed by American MNCs after World War II) and global companies (the Japanese response of the 1970s and 1980s). (Bartlett and Ghoshal's use of the term 'multinational' is rather confusing unless you remember that they use it to describe one particular strategic response, whereas others use it as a generic term to describe the full range of companies competing internationally regardless of their structure and management approach.)

The key strategic strength of the *multinational*, according to Bartlett and Ghoshal, is its ability to build strong local presence through sensitivity and responsiveness to national differences in demand. Many key assets, responsibilities and decisions are decentralized in this approach. Each national subsidiary is given a high degree of independence for strategic and operational decisions. Management regards overseas operations as a portfolio of independent businesses. The *international* organization adopts a different approach. Its key strength is its ability to exploit parent-company knowledge and capabilities through worldwide diffusion and modest adaptation. The US base acts as the source of new product and process knowledge. Management regards overseas operations as appendages to a central, domestic operation. Many assets, resources, responsibilities and decisions are decentralized but decision making has to be ratified by, and is therefore still controlled by, the centre. A key source of competitive advantage is technology transfer (product or process) from the centre to subsidiaries. The *global* company, again, is very different from the other two. Its main strength is the ability to build cost advantages through centralized, global-scale operations. Most strategic assets, resources, responsibilities and decisions are centralized, with tight central control of decisions, resources and information. Management treats overseas operations as merely delivery pipelines to a unified global market. Hence the criticism of Japanese investment in the United Kingdom: that it is only in manufacture, in 'screwdriver' assembly plants; the strategic and product development work is all done in Japan.

Each of these forms of organization has its own strengths. Each thrives in particular market conditions: the *multinational* form in markets that demand local sensitivity and responsiveness to a variety of demand at the local level; the *international* when the key source of competitive advantage is the transfer of knowledge with broad applications; the global when the key industry issue is global efficiency. Changing conditions of global competition, however, demand a new form of organization, according to Bartlett and Ghoshal – the *transnational*. The key strategic issues now encompass both global efficiency and responsiveness to the increasing variety of local conditions. The transnational demonstrates global competitiveness, multinational flexibility and worldwide learning. Its assets, resources, responsibilities and decisions are dispersed *and* interdependent, subsidiaries are given specific roles according to their special competences, and there is joint development and worldwide sharing of learning. The key management tasks include the legitimization and balancing of diverse perspectives, the development of multiple and flexible co-ordinating processes and the building of individual commitment in pursuit of a shared vision. The transnational provides:

- global integration;
- local differentiation;
- worldwide innovation.

To enable it to do this it has a range of novel features:

- Each national unit is a source of ideas, skills and capabilities that can be harnessed for the benefit of the total organization.
- National units achieve global scale by making them the company's world source for a particular product, component or activity.
- The centre [establishes] a new, highly complex managing role which co-ordinates relations between units but does so in a highly flexible way. The key is to focus less on managing activities directly and more upon creating an organizational context which is conducive to the co-ordination and the resolution of differences (Grant, 1991: 298).
- Creating the right organizational context involves 'establishing clear corporate objectives, developing managers with broadly based perspectives and relationships, and fostering supportive organizational norms and values' (Bartlett and Ghoshal, 1989: 388).

**Dominant strategic
requirements of
industry**

	Responsiveness (multinational)	Efficiency (global)	Transfer of knowledge and competencies (international)
Responsiveness (branded packaged products)	Unilever	Kao	Procter & Gamble
Efficiency (consumer electronics)	Philips	Matsushita	General Electric
Transfer of knowledge (telecommunications switching)	ITT	NEC	Ericsson

Dominant strategic capability of company

Figure 5.8 Industry requirements and company capabilities. *Source*: Bartlett and Ghoshal (1989)

Figure 5.8 gives examples of very successful multinational (Unilever), global (Matsushita) and international (Ericsson) firms, together with the characteristics of their industries. The other firms in figure 5.8 are less successful because there is a lack of fit between their dominant strategic capability and the dominant strategic requirements of their industry. For example, Kao, a Japanese consumer goods company similar to Proctor & Gamble, has failed, as yet, to develop on the international stage, despite being very successful in Japan. Kao's strength is global efficiency, based on standardized products, but its market demands local responsiveness. In this industry the multinational, Unilever, has been better suited to this strategic requirement.

EXERCISE

It has been suggested that Sony and BOC are excellent examples of the transnational. Do you agree? Can you think of other firms that fit the bill?

Parenting

A major recent debate in strategy has been about the role of the centre in the large diversified company. At the corporate strategy level, Michael Goold and

Andrew Campbell of the Ashridge Strategic Management Centre have focused on the role of the corporate centre in managing diversified corporations. To the two key strategic questions – 'Are you in an attractive market?' and 'Are you competitively advantaged?' they have added a third: 'Do you have the right parent?'

Their starting point is that 'primary wealth takes place only at the business level and the parent must work through its businesses to create value'. And its not enough for the centre to avoid destroying value or just to create value – 'the appropriate benchmark for value creation is not what would happen without a parent, but what the best available parent would achieve' (Goold *et al.*, 1994) This can be accomplished by a range of means such as improving planning disciplines, making better senior management appointments or exerting more powerful financial controls.

In their first book on the topic (Goold and Campbell, 1987) they describe three different styles of parenting based on the distinction between the centre's planning role (involvement in strategic planning) and control role (holding businesses to account). The three roles are:

1 Strategic planning. This involves a significant measure of direct planning influence from the centre with a degree of flexibility on actual controls. Examples cited are BOC, BP, Cadbury Schweppes, Lex, STC and United Biscuits.
2 Strategic control. Here the centre exercises tight strategic control but engages in little direct planning. Examples are Courtauld's, ICI, Imperial, Plessey and Vickers.
3 Financial control. In these instances the centre leaves the strategy formulation and business planning function to the diversified business, but exercises tight financial control. BTR, Ferranti, GEC, Hanson Trust and Tarmac are given as examples of this third type.

Their original research showed that successful companies enjoyed a fit between their parenting style and the needs of their businesses.

In *Corporate Level Strategy* Goold *et al.* (1994) focus on 'much finer grained aspects of fit' and build a framework for analysing corporate strategy. The model begins with the concept of fit between parenting style and the needs of the business units and then analyses the main characteristics the parent comprising:

• The mental maps that shape the parent's perception of business improvement opportunities.
• The quality of the structures, systems and processes through which the parent creates value.
• The functions, central services and resources that support the management's efforts to create value.
• The people and skills – whether the chief executive, the top management team – or a particularly skilled function head (e.g. treasurer).
• The nature of the performance contract (and the contracting process) between the centre and its business units.

Parents use these characteristics in order to identify parenting opportunities (e.g. to strengthen the management team or to leverage unidentified linkages between businesses) and critical success factors (e.g. the need to tightly control costs or to attract and motivate exceptionally creative individuals).

To create value, and avoid value destruction, the parent's characteristics must be compatible with the opportunities and critical success: but the most successful corporate strategies go beyond this because the parent:

- Brings 'value creating insights' about how they can create value from their businesses.
- Possesses 'distinctive parenting characteristics' that are unusually helpful in exploiting those opportunities.
- Understands its 'heartland business' – where its insights are particularly valuable and where its feel for the critical success factors will minimize the risk of serious damage.

These elements make up a 'parenting advantage statement'. (See exhibit 5.2 for Canon's parenting advantage statement.) Goold *et al.* discuss, for example, the parenting advantages brought by Lords Hanson and White to the Hanson Trust, a phenomenally successful UK-led conglomerate of the 1980s. These included identifying and screening low-performing and mature companies, deal making, systematic and fast integration, emphasis on financial control processes and culture. They then note how these advantages were later eroded as other predators moved into the market and other 'parents' became more aware of the need to create shareholder value.

Overall Goold and Campbell are gloomy about a parent's ability to add rather than destroy value – this is because they see only four ways to add value and each involves a paradox. They are:

- To add 'stand alone' value by advising on strategy and performance. But why should a parent which spends only part of its time on a particular business be able to outguess a full-time executive team?
- To create 'linkage' value by building closer links between the business units. But why wouldn't the businesses themselves spot these and co-operate themselves in a spirit of mutual advantage?
- To offer superior central functions and services. But why shouldn't the business be able to purchase superior specialist services on the open market?
- To manage the portfolio by identifying and purchasing businesses that add value. But why should the parent be able to 'buck the trend' of value-destroying acquisitions?

Goold and Campbell analyse fifteen companies which at the time were seen to be offering parenting advantages – but most (e.g. BTR) would not now be considered exemplar companies. And the trend continues to encourage more rather than less focus (e.g. Kingfisher and Bass have both demerged into smaller components). Nevertheless Canon and Unilever still create value through managing linkages, and 3M still offers a functional and service influence. Perhaps the overall lesson that

EXHIBIT 5.2 CANON PARENTING ADVANTAGE STATEMENT

Value Creation Insights
Individual businesses have resourcing difficulties in pursuing a range of technologies in depth and can benefit from shared resource within the parent.

Businesses find it difficult to create linkages and cross-fertilization between different areas of technology, between technologists and market needs, and between different markets, and there is a role for a parent in facilitating these linkages.

An inspiring corporate vision can help businesses to stretch for growth beyond the confines of each business.

Distinctive Parenting Characteristics
Ability to manage cross-fertilization:

- across different technologies;
- between technical and market specialists;
- across different markets.

A high level of corporate commitment to technology and learning. Company vision that energizes staff towards growth and stretch without prompting inappropriate risks.

Heartland Businesses
Businesses in which overall performance depends heavily on product performance and new product development, which in turn are driven by superior understanding and linking of three core technology areas: precision mechanics, fine optics and micro-electronics; where technology advantage is embodied in certain key components; where international presence and ability to manage multiple channels to market provide a major advantage; selling business machines, cameras and specialist optical products.

chimes with the work by Collins and Porras is that excellence is rare – not because the principles are difficult to understand but because the practice requires discipline and outstanding leadership.

Competition and Co-operation

Traditionally, the emphasis in strategy has tended to fall on competition. In an increasing number of industries – such as automobiles and computers – there is a new emphasis on co-operation and various forms of joint venturing between erst-while head-on competitors. Having suffered a major setback in the video-cassette recorder (VCR) market with its attempt to develop its Betamax format as an indus-try standard, in later R&D activity Sony has focused on joint ventures with appar-ent competitors. One such joint venture was with Philips in the development of the compact disc (CD). Like Sony, Philips had suffered in the VCR format battle. The logic of the joint venture was to safeguard both parties against the risks of another such failure. The strategic goal of such ventures is to develop jointly a stand-ard of product specification that dominates a particular television market. When the standard is accepted the development partners can again become competitors, but only in manufacturing, using the same industry standard. Both thus safeguard their R&D investment. In this way the two firms guard against the certainty of one losing heavily if both had pursued individual developments.

The other way of thinking about co-operation and competition is in terms of how strategy is often a complex of both. Brandenburger and Nalebuff (1995) coined the term 'co-opetition' to describe the interdependence that exists in business. They argue that if you call a player in an industry a competitor then you tend to focus on competing rather than looking for opportunities for co-operation. Key here is their concept of complementarity. Complementors are players from whom customers buy complementary products or to whom suppliers sell complementary resources. In the computer industry hardware and software companies are classic comple-mentors. Companies that develop more powerful chip technologies impact upon buyers' demands for more sophisticated software and thus increase opportunities for firms in this business, and vice versa. Industries are increasingly made up of complex networks of competition and co-operation – co-opetition. In telecommun-ications, for example, firms function as competitors, as suppliers, as buyers and as partners of other firms in the same industry – at the same time. This makes the management of these relationships crucial. In chapter 7 we look at Linux's evolv-ing role in the computer industry. Linux has become a key partner of IBM. In devel-oping its new e-business on demand strategy, IBM is entering into a network of complementor relations in hardware and in software which is helping to bring the high-tech industry out of recession (see 'Remaking IBM', *Business Week*, 17 March 2003; 'Is Big Blue the next big thing?' *Economist*, 21–27 June 2003).

However, some analysts suggest that co-operation is usually at the expense of one of the partners and that in a competitive business environment truly co-operative relations are the exception. We return to this issue in chapter 7.

CHAPTER 6

THE MANAGEMENT OF STRATEGIC CHANGE

The reality of life is that while staying put is without doubt the most comfortable for the short haul, it is in fact the highest risk strategy of all. Sadly, one can see example after example where the company or the individual who was leading the race believed that they had found the ultimate solution and stayed with it too long, while somebody else was stimulated to greater effort and overtook. . . . The world of industry is one of perpetual change not only technologically, but also as a part of the continuous ferment of the developing universe in which we live. . . . By and large in an industrial organization one's people should be asking not whether you are going to change, but how long it will be before you do. Wait too long and you have lost control, move too soon and you will lack the commitment which is vital to success. (Harvey-Jones, 1989: 127–8)

Triggers for Change

Strategic management is concerned with the long-term health of a business. In many ways it is about creating predictability in the firm's relationship to its environment – an environment that is increasingly in flux – and stability in the organization in terms of its goals, policies and programmes. (Remember the strategy hierarchy in chapter 1.) But strategic management is also about monitoring one's present way of proceeding and deciding when it is no longer adequate. Strategic management is, therefore, often concerned with the management of change. Managers need to be aware of when change is necessary. Indeed, a major aspect of the techniques and concepts we have been addressing in the previous chapters has been an attempt to sensitize the reader to the need for constant strategic vigilance and evaluation. When this vigilance and evaluation suggest that the objectives of the business or the major plans and policies are no longer appropriate, or that the results of implementing the strategy do not confirm their critical assumptions, then is the time to change. The strategy may have become inconsistent (objectives and policies might no longer complement each other), it may have lost consonance (it is no longer responsive to important environmental changes), it may no longer generate advantage (the firm is losing its competitive advantage) or it may no longer be feasible (there are no longer the resources to implement it).

Triggers for change are many and various. The environment might become more complex and less predictable. Market change as consumers demand different products or services may render your offerings less attractive. The effect of Japanese products on consumer demands in the automobile, motorcycle and audio-visual consumer products industries are good examples of such a change. Competitors may come up with a radical innovation in technology that demands a total rethink of your technological base, in terms of both new product technologies and new production process. Pilkington's breakthrough in making float glass is a good example. It set the standards of competition for decades to come in the glass industry and meant that competitors had to get their production know-how under licence from Pilkington. Pilkington thus managed to dominate its industry. Change in the politics of the organization can occur when there is disagreement about the future mission of the organization or the way in which the organization is structured or about best modes of manufacture. The arrival of new top management can lead to change as the balance of power over decision making shifts. We have already referred to the effect of John Harvey-Jones's new vision at ICI when he turned this slumbering giant round. One can also think of the effect of Lee Iacocca at Chrysler. Such new arrivals lead to a political problem in the sense that the organization has to determine who has the power to decide on what course of action. This can lead to major changes in the culture of the organization and fundamental changes in its core beliefs and values. Top management has to determine what values need to be held by which people.

Radical Change

Figure 6.1 sets out a model of the strategic change process. There are two views of how successful strategic change needs to be managed. One argues in favour of radical revolutionary change, the need to sweep away the past to leave the stage clear for the new and radically different. The second view argues that change should be managed incrementally as a series of small gradual steps. We will consider the radical view first.

Radical change comes about as a result of the development of concern about the firm's current situation on the part of a subgroup of people in the organization. There may be a precipitating critical event. The subgroup with its new vision of the organization needs to assume a position of power to get its understanding of the problems facing the organization accepted. In this process the old guard of top managers moves aside or is replaced. New objectives are set and new plans devised. The new strategy is then implemented and the changes are stabilized. Change, according to this approach, tends to be dramatic, occurring in quantum leaps. If managed well, its supporters argue, radical change is more effective than a piecemeal approach in which change is introduced gradually in an incremental fashion. The radical approach leads to quantum leaps in strategy, which means that organizations

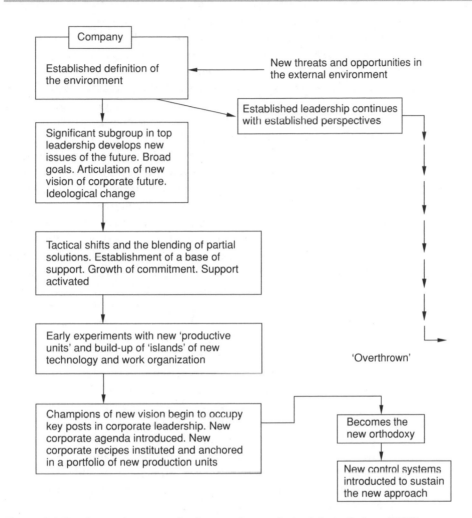

Figure 6.1 Implementing strategic change. *Source*: derived from Quinn (1980)

make clean, clear breaks with the past and move from one strategy to another without a long transition through a variety of interim stages where future direction is not clear. Customers and employees thus know exactly where they stand.

The Incremental Approach to Change

The alternative view of change is that it should be managed in a far more gradual, incremental way. Supporters of this approach argue that the strategy process is extremely complex. Managers need, therefore, to proceed cautiously. They also need time to explore the complexities facing their organization, to experiment with different strategies and to judge between a range of options. According to Quinn (1980), a leading proponent of theories of incrementalism, the processes used to arrive at a strategy are typically fragmented, evolutionary and largely intuitive. Their roots lie deep in top managers' minds and their rationality is, thus, difficult to assess. Pieces of formal strategic analysis do contribute to the final strategy – but only pieces. In the final analysis strategy tends to *evolve* as internal decisions and external events come together in the minds of managers, whose task is then to create a new, widely shared consensus for action. Far from being an abrogation of good management practice, Quinn argues, the rationale behind this kind of strategy formulation is so powerful that it perhaps provides the normative model for strategic decision making – rather than the step-by-step 'formal systems planning' approach so often espoused.

Incrementalism makes good strategic sense. Early commitments are kept relatively open and subject to review. Change programmes and their planning develop in phases or stages with concrete decisions to proceed further taken only at the end of each phase, say of new product development. Final commitments are postponed until the last possible moment. The rationale for proceeding in this way is that the full implications of alternative actions need to be explored. The organization's capability for alternative actions also needs to be explored. Top management needs to sense what their employees are capable of. Top management also needs to be sensitive to the politics of the organization, to create awareness of the need for change and to involve everybody in mobilizing the organization's resources for change. Top management also needs to test the inputs of various groups into the strategy process and to give people the opportunity to learn from and to adapt to the responses of others. Well managed interaction between opposing alternatives improves the quality of the final decision and builds commitment to that decision, even among groups whose initiatives are finally unsuccessful. The environment also needs to be explored in the sense that managers need to be as sure as possible of the direction of external change. New products are never justified by analysis. In the final analysis major changes are a matter of faith.

Incrementalism, therefore, should be conscious. Managers should accept the cognitive and process limits on each major change decision, while at the same time striving to build a logical analytical framework in which to take decisions. The success of incrementalism also depends upon top management's ability to create the awareness, understanding, acceptance and commitment needed to implement strategies effectively.

Radical and Incremental Change Compared

The alert reader will by now be asking whether or not the radical and the incremental approaches to change contradict each other. The answer is: not necessarily. It depends what you focus on. The incremental view focuses on the processes going on in the strategists' minds and the interactive way in which they manage their organizations to generate information and commitment. The radical change view focuses not on processes but on the actual content of strategic change, the realized strategies of the organization. These generally seem to change in a kind of quantum leap, particularly when viewed 'objectively' from the outside. But to achieve this apparent speed of transition that can so bedazzle competitors and business analysts when it is effective, managers might well have had to pursue the long, slow path of incrementalism to change people's minds within their organization, to sell the new ideas and to harness the effort to make the 'quantum leap' possible.

QUESTIONS

1 Have you had experience of a major change in an organization you have worked for or know? Was this change managed in a radical or incremental manner?
2 Which do you consider more effective, radical change or incremental change?

Strategy Subsystems

The management of strategic change is improved by applying incremental logic to the various elements of the change decision. Quinn (1980) suggests that we think of these elements as subsystems (figure 6.2). The successful management of change depends upon management's ability to focus strategic thinking by making the subsystems the object of ongoing analysis.

Figure 6.2 Strategic subsystems. *Source:* adapted from Quinn (1980)

If we analyse the workings of some of these subsystems we can appreciate better why they benefit from incremental management. The *acquisition/diversification* subsystem, as the name suggests, is concerned with strategic decisions concerning diversification through either internal development or external acquisition. An incremental approach is necessary to investigate options and prepare the way for internal or external diversification. Top management needs to manage skilfully the politics of such major changes, to create consensus concerning the need for change, and to develop commitment to new programmes of action. A 'comfort factor for risk taking' needs to be established, which may necessitate changing the value system of the organization and various subsystems, e.g. the capital subsystem centred on the finance department if (!) its attitudes are anti-risk. The organization has to be prepared to move opportunistically to take advantage of opportunities. The other side of the coin of diversification is divestment, and the same preparatory work is necessary to manage this successfully. The psychological effects of pulling out of what may have been core businesses should not be underestimated and they certainly have to be prepared for if they are not to prove disruptive, e.g. by demotivating people who feel their area may be next to go.

Diversification might require major reorganization and thus impact on the *organizational structure* subsystem. Diversification may be accompanied by decentralization, in which case staff manning the decentralized units will have to be prepared for this responsibility and staff at the centre will have to come to terms with a consequent loss of power. New roles thus created have to be carefully thought through in all their detail, e.g. in terms of how they affect individual career goals and the timing of individual career moves. While decentralized participative structures encourage new ideas, they can also make it difficult actually to implement any of them. The actual implementation of the change idea fostered by devolving more responsibility for ideas might need more centralized, more tightly controlled structures.

Logical incrementalism links together information gathering, analysis, testing of options, and the behavioural and political aspects of the strategic subsystems. Firms will explore a variety of options in the technology subsystem before deciding upon one product or process technology. They will also explore a variety of product positioning options before deciding upon one strategy for the marketing subsystem. By organizing its approach to strategic decision making using subsystems, top management can:

- generate better communications by bringing together representatives of the subsystems for interactive discussion;
- involve lower levels of the organization to the benefit of maximizing relevant information gathering;
- help generate commitment by disseminating information about the strategic issues facing the firm and how they impact upon the subsystems and the people in them;
- keep the future to the forefront of managers' attention so that they do not become buried under the day-to-day hue-and-cry.

Of crucial importance in the strategy process is the recognition that the various subsystems interact: the ramifications of decisions in one area for other areas have to be explored. For example, a major change in product technology is likely to require changes in production technology. This will affect marketing, and is likely to affect the organization structure. Capital will obviously be an important issue in the new investment required. And so on. For example, IBM's decision to invest in the production of a new family of computers using a new technology made obsolete a number of existing products manufactured in different divisions whose product lines were anyway beginning to overlap. Rationalization of the activities of these other divisions in one new division was considered appropriate. This also focused the whole organization's effort on making the new 'make or break' initiative work.

One ignores the interaction of subsystems at one's peril. One way of thinking about the decline of the British car industry is to consider the possibility that too much management time and effort was concentrated on one subsystem – employee relations – at the expense of marketing and technology. Thus, while the legacy of poor industrial relations problems that had bedevilled the company was much improved, research and development activity failed to generate innovative new products. The best employees in the world cannot perform competitively if they do not have a good product to make and if they have the wrong production system. Subsystems need to balance and complement each other.

QUESTIONS

1 What are the key subsystems in your organization or in an organization that you know or have studied?
2 How do subsystems interact, both positively and negatively?
3 Trace through the ramifications of decisions in one subsystem on others. What is the major subsystem at the moment? Why?

Managing Change

Typically you start with a general concern, vaguely felt. Next, you roll an issue around in your mind until you think you have a conclusion that makes sense for the company. Then you go out and sort of post the idea without being too wedded to its details. You then start hearing the arguments pro and con, and some very good refinements of the idea usually emerge. Then you pull the idea in and put some resources together to study it so it can be put forward as more of a formal presentation. You wait for 'stimuli occurrences' or 'crises', launch pieces of the idea to help in these situations. But they lead toward your ultimate aim. You know where you want to get. You'd like to get there in six months. But it may take three years, or you may not get there at all. And when you do get there, you don't know whether it was originally your own idea – or somebody else had reached the same conclusion before you and you just got on board for it. You never know. (Senior executive, quoted by Quinn *et al.*, 1988: 671)

Change tends to be easier in small, innovative organizations than larger, complex ones. Small entrepreneurial companies possess the following characteristics:

- *Need orientation.* Entrepreneurs have a strong need to achieve. They tend to be fanatical in their desire to succeed and to establish their companies as going concerns.
- *Flexibility and quickness.* Their simple structures and a management process dominated by founder figures make them quick to react to market signals and to adapt their product accordingly.
- *Strong incentives.* Entrepreneurs are clear that there are significant rewards available if they are successful in getting their ideas to market.

In the United States, more than in the United Kingdom, entrepreneurs also have ready access to capital through a variety of sources such as venture capitalists ready and willing to finance likely ideas.

Large companies, in contrast, experience major barriers to innovation. Top management tends to become remote from both the market place and those people lower down the company with good ideas (the 'intrapreneurs'). Indeed, they often see people who have new ideas as 'troublemakers', ready to rock the boat. They do not promote incentives to foster innovation. They also tend to become risk-averse as they proceed up the career ladder. Their decisions are dominated by short time horizons, linked with the constraints of accounting practices and the workings of the financial markets. Bureaucratic rules tend to dominate and these, by their very definition, are meant to safeguard the *status quo.*

Yet some large companies have found the secret of innovation. These companies are characterized by the following:

- *Atmosphere and vision.* Top management value innovation and manage their company culture to support it. Sony's policy on this is a shining example – the company goal is for motivated individuals to exercise their technological skills to the highest level.
- *Orientation to the market.* There is a strong focus on the customer, exemplified in the case of Sony by technical people having to spend time on learning marketing skills.
- *Small, flat organizations* with fewer management levels between the innovators ('intrapreneurs') and top management and a minimum of bureaucratic constraints on project teams. There are only short decision lines between the champions of new ideas and the top-level decision makers, thus reducing response time.
- *Concentrating on a few key thrusts.* Top managers focus attention and effort on a limited range of options (six to ten) that integrate the firm's existing and newly emerging concerns.
- *Developmental 'shootouts'.* A variety of groups may work on solutions to different problems. The groups are pitted against each other to ensure that the best solution to the problem emerges from the multiple approaches. Such interactions between different teams encourage learning from each other. Top management has to foster a spirit of 'win–win' competition rather than 'zero sum' games where one team wins at the expense of another. (Quinn, 1980.)

In these innovating organizations the emphasis is on 'means strategies' rather than 'ends strategies'. Strategic leadership is less concerned with formulating and implementing strategy in the traditional sense than with establishing the behavioural processes within the organization that will ensure new strategies emerge. The strategist is responsible for managing the process rather than the content. To manage this process is not to preconceive strategy but to recognize when a viable strategy has emerged, and then to step in and ensure that it is taken up by others in the organization to ensure its success. The strategy then becomes deliberate. During the course of its life cycle, top management must be looking to the processes that will encourage the emergence of the strategies of the future that will replace the current strategy, thus creating a virtuous circle of strategy renewal.

Quinn (1980) argues that the value of a strategy lies not in its clarity or in the rigid adherence to its plan. Rather a strategy is valuable to the extent that it succeeds in 'capturing the initiative' in the sense of helping the organization to deal with essentially unpredictable events, to redeploy and concentrate resources as new opportunities and thrusts emerge, and thus to use resources most effectively towards selected goals. The strategy sets clear goals but is flexible as to means. Successful managers who operate logically and proactively in an incremental mode become successful by building understanding, identity and commitment through the actual processes through which the strategies are created. Incrementalism allows them to improve the quality of information used in decisions, generated through the incremental management of subsystems, and to deal with the politics of change – i.e. the sensitive management of differences among interested parties – while they build, step by step, the organization's momentum toward the new strategy and generate the psychological motivation to carry it through.

The Innovating Organization

Some organizations exist in industries where survival depends on innovation – the fashion or film industries, with their constant search for the new, are good examples. Most businesses, however, do not have this total preoccupation with fickle fashion and with novelty. All organizations nevertheless do need to be aware of innovation as a strategic weapon. Many successful firms have run into difficulties because they refused to consider the possibility of change. It was said of Henry Ford, for example – one of the most influential inventors and businessmen in history – that 'the old master failed to master change'. He developed an incredibly successful product – the Model T motor car, any colour so long as it was black – and the organization to ensure its smooth production. But he lacked the strategic vision to see that, in time, consumer taste would change and a one-dimensional product would no longer satisfy it.

It is possible to design an organization for innovation. Such an innovating organization's design characteristics are depicted in figure 6.3. The task of the organization or subunit of the organization – innovation – is defined by the strategic concerns at its particular stage of development. Innovation needs key roles. You need the people with ideas, the idea generators, and you also need people to

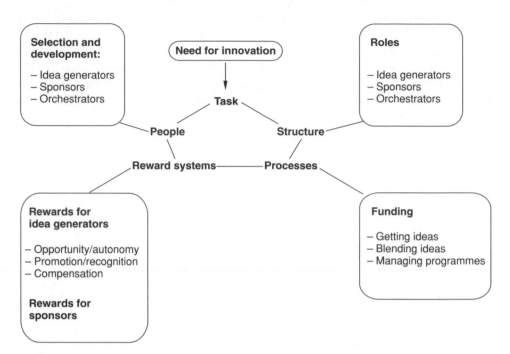

Figure 6.3 Designing innovative organizations. *Source:* adapted from Galbraith and Kazanjian (1986)

champion (sponsor) ideas at a higher level so they get on to the strategic agenda. The generators are not necessarily the best managers of projects. You need orchestrators to make sure the ideas are implemented. You need a management process that will generate ideas, move from the old to the new (transitioning) and put the new idea into practice. You need rewards for people involved in innovation, both the idea generators, the sponsors and also the orchestrators. Rewards include the intrinsic satisfaction of autonomy, the freedom to be creative, recognition, perhaps by promotion, and financial rewards. The organization needs to select and develop the people who are going to occupy these key roles.

The ideal situation for a firm, as has already been mentioned, is to have a range of products, some strong in their markets (the cash cows), others with great potential for the future in fast-growing markets (the 'rising stars', stars of the future). Such a firm has a dual core, one based on its current mainstay businesses, the other geared to innovation. The innovatory unit/division can be structured along the lines just described as conducive to innovation; the business that has reached its potential in a reasonably stable industry can be structured in a different way, more along bureaucratic lines, though with the major excesses of the bureaucracy removed. Top management's role in the latter is to fine-tune the business because the strategy that has gained the unit its success is still viable. There is an accepted industry recipe for success. For example, a company manufacturing various forms of glass products, where it is operating in mature markets, will be structured primarily for efficiency. In other areas, for example, technologically sophisticated products such as electro-optics, where innovation is the key, it needs to be structured in a more flexible way, as a set of small innovatory units with high levels of autonomy to facilitate the maximum levels of new discovery. The long-term aim of such a company, following good portfolio management principles, should be to grow the proportion of their business in the new markets to offset diminishing returns from traditional businesses in the future.

Organizational Development and Strategy

It is wrong to equate change entirely with reorganization, though restructuring can form an important part of strategic change. Often restructuring can hide the lack of new ideas for the future. ('I don't know what to do so let's reorganize to give the illusion of productive new activity!') For real change to occur, structural change must be accompanied by individual attitude changes. Organization development (OD) provides a source of knowledge and techniques to improve an organization's strategic capability through improving its problem-solving and renewal processes, particularly through a more effective and collaborative management of organization culture based on the development of work teams, with the assistance of a change agent, either from inside or outside the organization (a consultant), as catalyst. There are three broad categories of OD approach: laboratory training, diagnostic intervention and process intervention. Laboratory intervention involves human relations training in T-groups focusing upon the examination of 'here and now' interactions, divorced from the organizational context, with a view to improving communication and relating skills and changing attitudes and values. The value of this approach has been questioned because of the difficulty of demonstrating the generalization of the effects of laboratory training (if any) back to the organizational context. Diagnostic intervention involves the change agent working in the organization on live problems. It employs such techniques as observation, interviews and survey questionnaires to collect relevant data concerning the problem, which are fed back to clients. Process interventions involve the examination of relationships and interactions in the organization, via a similar cycle of data gathering, feedback and discussion, and then such techniques as group meetings, team development, inter-group intervention, temporary task forces, counselling and third-party intervention to achieve change.

The development of OD can be seen as a reaction against 'top-down' approaches to change, which are frequently rendered unworkable by resistance and/or lack of interest. The change agent acts as researcher, consultant and/or catalyst in the process of organizational self-examination. OD emphasizes the development of existing work groups through collaboration and participation as methods for achieving ownership of change. This follows the view that the focus of change should be the individual in his or her social group and not the individual in isolation. The key unit of change, therefore, is deemed to be the social group from which the individual derives his or her values. OD's early emphasis on social skills and personal and interpersonal processes as an end in itself has been found wanting. It is not enough merely to get people talking and listening to each other effectively. The purpose of improving communication, a major aim in many OD initiatives, is to improve the efficiency of the organization. This requires an understanding of the technology and tasks of the organization and the role of the groups under development. OD has as its goal the harmonization of people, groups, tasks, technology and structures. Early variants of OD have also been criticized for their failure to confront problems of power and interest as key issues in organization change. The change agent has to be aware of organizational politics.

The sequence of an OD intervention is typically as follows:

1 initial consultation to explore the change issue with the internal 'champions' of the need for change;
2 agreement on the design of the change intervention;
3 collection, feedback and analysis of relevant data;
4 intervention planning;
5 change initiative.

This sequence may be repeated many times during the course of an intervention. The consultant provides process guidance to facilitate the analysis of data and problem solving, helping to define the strategies available to the organization.

An OD initiative aimed at improving the strategy process might proceed as follows:

1 Champions initiate change intervention.
2 Analysis of change issue while learning the skills (vocabulary and action principles) necessary to support change initiative. Typically, small groups of managers from different parts and levels of the company will meet to learn the necessary skills and to analyse what needs to be done. Their own strategic leadership style will generally come under the microscope. An open climate is encouraged at this stage. There is a growing consensus that this process should start with the top management group and then cascade down through the organization with feedback going three ways. vertically up and down, and laterally.
3 A team development phase in which actual work groups focus on how they function. Again this ideally starts with the top group, and openness and trust are encouraged.
4 An inter-group development phase in which groups that have important working relationships come together, e.g. groups from different functions, to explore how to improve relationships.
5 Having radically improved the quality of information and idea sharing, top management is now in a position to develop a strategy for the organization.
6 The strategy is implemented.
7 The strategy is evaluated and refined in the light of unfolding events, both internal, as the OD process evolves, and external, as the environment alters.

Using OD, organizations are designed and redesigned (changed) according to the information needs of tasks and the interdependence of tasks. Related to these core problems are issues of organizational process – communication, control, problem solving and decision making, reward systems and conflict management. Management has to design communication procedures that minimize distortion, provide timely information and see that the organization has sufficient openness to facilitate upward and downward communication. Management has to design structures appropriate to the problems facing the organization. More complex problems require more open structures. Less complex problems can be solved with centralized information networks. Appropriate control mechanisms have to be designed with the participation of those involved and control measurements made explicit and realistic. All OD theorists agree that OD involves a long time scale, usually a minimum of two to three years.

Change in Service Environments

The problem of change is as great in service as in manufacturing industries. Increasingly, differentiation and diversified product ranges in services give rise to new managerial challenges. A recent survey of personal financial service firms highlighted the need for new specialist skills to deal with new specialized products; new training and recruitment to support these products and develop these skills; and the need for a new type of top manager with a more strategic perspective geared to dealing with the increasing complexity of strategic choices in the industry. To find managers with these new skills it may be necessary to search outside the confines of the industry.

One of the most spectacular banking turn-rounds of the 1980s was that of the Bank of Ireland, spearheaded by Mark Hely Hutchinson, whom the bank recruited from Guinness. The new chairman brought to the company important new skills in managing a diversified product range and in becoming marketing-led, providing services responsive to customer need. Marketing has been a low priority until recently in financial services. Bank of Ireland advertised aggressively for new customers, particularly young ones, and its outlets were redesigned as 'selling machines' with bottom-line profitability the key measure of all the bank's activities. More flexible organizational structures were introduced with the introduction of a business unit type of organization and the devolution of decision making to the managers closest to the market. In other service industries major change has necessitated the introduction of new types of managers, i.e. managers with a different industry perspective. In the National Health Service, for example, the Griffiths report highlighted the lessons to be learnt in health care from the successful management of supermarkets. (The author of the report was himself from Sainsbury's.) Recent recruitment of NHS management has attempted to bring in people from non-health-related sectors.

Changing a hospital

1 *External analysis.* Agree on summary of forces placing demands on the hospital.
2 *Internal analysis.* For each external force decide:

(a) How is the hospital responding today?
(b) What will happen if the hospital continues its present response?
(c) What are the alternative responses?
3 *Issue identification and scenario analysis.* Identify compatible and mutually exclusive alternatives; determine ideal responses not currently being demanded.
4 *Generation of alternatives and analysis of mission.* Generate sets of alternative courses of action; determine core mission based on preferred courses of action.
5 *Creation of plan* – implement or move towards goals implied in core mission.
6 *Evaluation* – ongoing! (Based on Fry, 1982.)

Poor quality of service

The following example illustrates the negative effects of poor service on one very influential customer.

When service with a smile is missing by a mile

Why is it that supposedly excellent service organizations seem to slip up when my friends, family or I have dealings with them? If it were just because we are a pernickety lot, then we would presumably harbour the same complaint about the quality of products.

But we don't: in our experience, products with really good reputations generally seem to live up to their promise these days.

The reasons usually given for the patchy quality of most services relate to their supposed intangibility, and to their undoubtedly high reliance on that most fallible of factors, the human being. But there is more to the problem than that – as several supposed paragons need to recognize. Take Federal Express. The air courier company has become the subject of countless business school case studies on service excellence, and in 1990 it was the first leading service company to win America's Malcolm Baldridge National Quality Award.

Yet I have refused to use FedEx ever since the mid-1980s, when I was billed for months in error for a package sent from New York to London. To add insult to injury, the company sent its threatening letters from Paris, and in French! Neither its Paris office nor its UK counterpart ever acknowledged my desperate protestations to them.

Similar stories from a business acquaintance suggest that such problems arise not merely from the human errors of a few operatives, but from system design faults. . . .

Hertz car rental I shall avoid for ever – in America, anyway – because of the chaos of its Boston airport operation one day in 1988, when a thrice-promised shuttle bus failed to show up, and I then had to queue for over an hour to collect a pre-booked car.

[The author then turns his attention to British Airways and three negative moments of truth he has experienced with them: the reduction in the number of ticket desks at Heathrow as an economy measure, thus creating long queues of angry passengers; an unanswered complaint about security lapses; and, worst of all, the meanness of its leg room on long-distance Economy Class flights.] Whereas BA's inadequate response to the security query was, one hopes, a single individual lapse from the normally prescribed level of service, the ticket desks and seating problems are both system faults: dubious economies in the design of products which form part of a service. . . . what are the lessons of these lapses?

First, that product and service quality are intertwined in intimate fashion. Quality service is not merely a question of getting one's front-line staff to behave impeccably in every one of their hundreds of daily customer contacts. . . .

Second, every aspect of the product and service must be designed, produced and delivered correctly – every time, and *ad infinitum*. As BA, and especially SAS, have found, the people-intensity of a service makes its quality far harder to sustain than that of a product. . . . service companies must realise that as the pace of innovation quickens, and as many markets – such as airlines – become liberalised or simply more competitive – like retailing – last year's 'excellent' service may be this year's also-ran.

Underlying everything is the fact that customers who now demand a consistently high level of quality in products – even in low-priced ones – are starting to do the same in services. Such high expectations are fostered still further by the sort of hyperbolic advertising campaigns which service organizations, especially airlines, tend to run. (Chris Lorenz, *Financial Times*, 10 January 1992)

Unfortunately for the firms concerned, the discontented client was an influential *Financial Times* journalist!

QUESTION

1 How might the firms referred to rectify the problems that they are faced with?

'Over-servicing'

One should also be wary of the dangers of 'over-servicing' as illustrated by what happened at KwikFit, the tyre and exhaust service group – slogan 'You can't get better than a KwikFit fitter.' Their 'fast fit' servicing centres were criticized by the Consumers' Association in its magazine *Which?* because more than a quarter of forty-three KwikFit branches recommended unnecessary work on a car brought in for a supposedly free inspection. Other fast-service groups were rated as good or average according to whether or not they too recommended unnecessary work. Interestingly, this problem of moral hazard can arise in other forms of services. In medicine, for example, critics of private medicine, funded by individual insurance schemes, argue that this form of funding provides an incentive for doctors to provide unnecessary services, e.g. operations or drugs, hence the different rates, say, for appendectomies in Great Britain (low) and West Germany (high)!

Strategic Management and Leadership

I didn't enjoy the job. I had to get rid of a lot of mates, and the way in which they left often made things worse – they were like Captain Oates, accepting the group need and sacrificing themselves. (Sir John Harvey-Jones, former chairman, talking about the pains of leadership at ICI)

> Strategic leadership requires . . . a readiness to discuss half-baked ideas, since most fully baked ideas start out in that form; a total honesty, a readiness to admit you got it wrong. (Sir John Hoskyns, former director-general, Institute of Directors, and executive chairman, Burton Group)

Before talking about leadership it is worth making a few points about management. Studies of managers at work have focused on ten major roles in the management process (figure 6.4): interpersonal roles (figurehead, leader, liaison), informational roles (monitor, disseminator, spokesman) and decisional roles (entrepreneur, disturbance handler, resource allocator, negotiator).

The manager's key tasks are to design the work of his organization, to monitor its internal and external environment, to initiate change when necessary and to renew stability when faced with disturbance. How does the manager do this? How

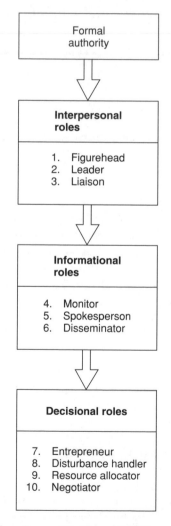

Figure 6.4 The manager's roles. *Source*: Mintzberg (1973)

does he or she spend time? The classical management notion of the manager as a systematic, reflective, proactive planner has come to seem increasingly suspect. Managers are above all reactive, involved in scanning the environment for crucial information concerning their organizations, which they then need disseminate within that organization to manage it properly. The conventional wisdom that senior managers need aggregated information which can best be provided by a formal management information system is also suspect. Managers tend not to use this information even if available. They rely on meetings, often brief, and telephone calls, spending most of their time (more than 75 per cent in some cases) in verbal communication. Successful managers are likely to demonstrate a special ability to operate in peer relationships, to lead others in subordinate relationships, to resolve interpersonal and decisional conflicts, to deal in the verbal media, to make complex, interrelated decisions, to allocate resources (including their own time) and to innovate.

Key features of the managerial decision-making process are the splitting up of decisions (e.g. in the form of improvement projects), the sequencing of the ensuing steps, concern with timing and the juggling of a number of projects. A prime managerial skill is the capacity to keep a number of issues in play over a long period of time until an appropriate moment arrives to activate one of them. Effective managers are those who gain control over their time in the sense that they are able to pick out and concentrate upon key issues in the plethora of demands made upon their time. An important element of time use is to ensure that they regularly communicate with colleagues and subordinates to share information and keep them in the picture. A key demand on the manager's time is the need to influence (rather than give orders). This necessity underlies the 'efficiency of seemingly inefficient behaviour' – in particular the fact that top managers do not plan their days in advance in much detail; they react – and their interactions tend to be short and disjointed. This has to be understood in the context of the generation and maintenance of agendas and networks in the pursuit of influence. Information networks, based on brief but frequent encounters, are of prime importance. They allow managers to disseminate their agendas for action and change.

Let us examine the manager's roles in more detail, starting with the *interpersonal*. As figurehead the manager serves as a symbol for the rest of the organization, a kind of role model demonstrating the corporate culture that he or she is responsible for creating. As leader he/she provides the sense of direction and purpose, exerts power to ensure staff have the necessary skills, and establishes mechanisms and processes so that he/she remains aware of what is happening in the organization. As liaiser the major role is to build a network of contacts between the organization and its external environment.

Next come the *informational* roles. As monitor the key tasks are to acquire information from as wide a variety of sources as possible and to shape this information into 'models' against which the organization can monitor its assessment of its environment, internal and external, and its performance. In the disseminator role the manager is responsible for sharing this information and the models within the organization. As spokesman (or spokeswoman) the manager is also responsible for 'sharing' this information externally in the best strategic way.

Two of the *decisional* roles are particularly important to the change process: those of entrepreneur and disturbance handler. In the entrepreneur role the manager acts as initiator and designer of change, exploiting opportunities and solving non-urgent problems. He or she scans the environment, monitoring internal and external environments for opportunities and potential problems. He or she might, for example, question subordinates at random, hold review meetings, make unannounced tours of the organization. He or she develops, and 'juggles', a portfolio of improvement projects. As disturbance handler the manager spends a great deal of time reacting very quickly to resolve disturbances, making changes because the moment demands them. Managerial processes are enormously complex and mysterious and rely on mental processes that we do not yet understand. These processes are more intuitive than intellectual. As resource allocator the key resource to be managed is the manager's own time, something the good manager seems to know how to do intuitively so that he/she concentrates on the key strategic issues. In this role he or she delegates but retains the power of final authorization before decisions are implemented. In the negotiator role the manager bargains with the various individuals and groups who have an interest or stake in strategic decisions.

Peters and Waterman were crucial in putting the subject of leadership at the centre of debates about strategic management. The quality of leadership was a critical factor in the success of their excellent companies. They sum up their views in the following words:

> Leadership is many things. It is patient, usually boring coalition building. It is purposeful seeding of cabals that one hopes will result in the appropriate ferment in the bowels of the organization. It is meticulously shifting the attention of the institution through the mundane language of management systems. It is altering agendas so that new priorities get enough attention. It is being visible when things are going wrong and invisible when they are working well. It's building a loyal team at the top that speaks more or less with one voice. It's listening carefully much of the time, frequently speaking with encouragement, and reinforcing words with believable action. It's being tough when necessary, and it's the occasional naked use of power or the 'subtle accumulation of nuances, a hundred things done a little better'. (Peters and Waterman: 1982: 82)

Leadership remains a crucial factor at the very highest levels. It has even been argued that some national economies have suffered owing to a lack of leaders. For example, it has been said of British industry that it is overmanaged and 'underled', lacking in a sufficient cadre of managers with leadership ability. But too often our view of leaders harks back to childish fantasies of heroic leadership. When we look at the reality of leadership it is a complicated interaction of skill and willingness on the part of employees to commit themselves to the organization's goals. As we saw in the previous chapter, leadership was a critical factor in companies that were 'built to last' and exhibited qualities of 'good to great' but the image of leadership is not of one visionary leader dragging a company, almost against its will, into a new future. Leadership was distributed throughout the company, a characteristic shared by many at a variety of levels, not just at the top, rooted in a common sense of purpose to build a successful, worthwhile and enduring company.

Leaders do intangible things like define a mission, express a vision, inspire their employees and, perhaps most important, provoke change. There are two essential preconditions for change. Significant people need to feel there is a need for change. They then have to convince others of this need before meaningful, lasting change can occur. The need for it must be felt throughout the organization. A key leadership task is motivating. Peters and Waterman argue that managers in excellent companies are adept at motivating by compelling, simple – even beautiful – values. These managers demonstrate 'transforming leadership' – leadership 'that builds on man's need for meaning [and] creates institutional purpose'. They induce clarity, consensus and commitment regarding the organization's basic purposes. The key role of the chief executive is to manage the *values* of the organization.

Chester Barnard, a seminal figure in management, highlighted what he saw as three main executive functions: (1) to provide the system of communication, (2) to promote essential effort and (3) to formulate and define purpose. The latter function equates with setting the strategic vision/mission of the organization. A fast-changing, complex environment places a premium on leadership which gives greater attention to the role, mission, philosophy and overall culture of the organization. The major faults of leadership are failure to set goals and setting goals that enjoy only superficial acceptance. A strategy needs to be acceptable and to challenge, motivate and excite.

Management has traditionally been concerned with performance, the organization's ability to accomplish its goals. Leadership is concerned with the organization's mission and culture. The main management leadership goal should be the creation of a common culture of shared values geared to the accomplishment of a common goal. Management and leadership come together to the extent that good managers keep themselves well informed with what is happening in their organization, keep what they consider the key interests of the organization alive, ultimately focusing their time and energy on a limited number of key issues. Managers play the power game, effectively knowing where they can mobilize support and how to deflate opposition, and know how to satisfy the organization that it has a sense of direction.

Leaders on Leadership

The enterprise required of innovating managers . . . is not the creative spark of genius that invents a new idea, but rather the skill with which they move outside the formal bonds of their job, manoeuvring through and around the organization in sometimes risky, unique and novel ways. This is what the corporate entrepreneur has in common with the classic definition of an entrepreneur. Organizational genius is 10 per cent inspiration and 90 per cent acquisition – acquisition of power to move beyond a formal job charter and to influence others. (Rosabeth Moss Kanter)

Successful leaders take actions which help achieve tasks, help build *esprit de corps* and help motivate individuals. All the leader's tasks arise from these basic functions; plan schedule; assess team; explain roles; monitor progress; support efforts, evaluate results; and debrief. (Chris Bonington, Britain's most successful leader of mountaineering expeditions)

QUESTIONS

1 Are you happy with the distinction between managers and leaders?
2 Have you worked with or for anybody you consider a good leader?
  If *yes*, what qualities did he or she have?
3 Why is good leadership important?
4 Are leaders born or made?
5 Chris Bonington has also said that the leader and the team must
  find the right balance. What do you think he means by this?

Exhibits 6.1–2 show two European leaders in action, John Harvey-Jones at ICI and Jan Carlzon at SAS, the Swedish airline company. Perhaps the most highly regarded business leader of recent times has been Jack Welch of General Electric (GE) and we analyse his leadership practices in chapter 8. One of the most interesting aspects of Welch's stewardship of GE was that its conglomerate approach went against much conventional business wisdom, which was increasingly focused upon 'sticking to the knitting' and 'back to basics'. Another of the late twentieth century's most notable leaders was Andy Grove of Intel. His account of Intel's 'memory business crisis' in the 1980s illustrates how painful, complex and fundamental the management of strategic change can be. In Intel's case it required a complete rethink of its basic *raison d'être* necessitated exit from the business it was founded on and a refocusing on building an identity in a totally different business.

Intel started in 1968 as a company that developed memory chips for computers. In the process it contributed to the development of the memory chip industry, an industry in which it was such a central player that Intel stood for memory and memory usually meant Intel. The key skills that Intel brought to this task were an ability in solving complex problems and a management style based upon 'ferociously arguing with one another while remaining friends', an approach they call 'constructive confrontation'.

Through the 1970s Intel concentrated its R&D spend on memory chips but also invested in developing another device that it had invented, microprocessors. (Memory chips store information. Microprocessors process information.) At the time, microprocessors represented a slower-growing, smaller-volume market than memory chips. Investment priorities were dictated by Intel's sense of its identity. In Grove's words, 'Our priorities were formed by our identity; after all, memories *were* us.'

Intel's leading product of the early 1980s was designed for the original IBM PC with explosive demand after this was launched. However, from 1984 onwards things changed. Japanese producers of high-quality, low-priced memory chips started to erode both market share and profitability. It slowly became apparent that Intel needed to devise a different memory strategy. A variety of options were discussed, for example outcompete the Japanese either on cost or on product design. Some Intel managers remained convinced that Intel could still develop special-purpose memory, an increasingly unlikely scenario as memory became more and more a commodity product where there were no new niches left.

EXHIBIT 6.1 LEADERS IN ACTION (I) JAN CARLZON AND SAS

Jan Carlzon became president of Scandinavian Airlines Systems at a time when the airline was struggling in the early 1980s. Under his leadership the company went from a loss to a profit of US$71 million on sales of $2 billion in just over a year. His work at SAS provides an exemplar of how to compete in service quality. His focus on strategic change at SAS was more on process and organizational structure than on products. He did develop Euroclass, SAS's version of business class, but more important was his thinking on the nature of service and the type of organization needed to deliver it in a way that satisfied the customer and brought repeat business, thus producing turn-round in his company. His approach is described in his autobiography, *Moments of Truth*. He describes his role not as fount of all knowledge and omniscient decision maker but as facilitator of the best possible decisions by improving the decision-making process and organizational structure: 'The company was not asking me to make all the decisions on my own, only to create the right atmosphere, the right conditions for others to do their jobs better.' He appealed to his employees, involving them in the process of change: 'You are the ones who must help me, not the other way round!' He gave his employees the authority and responsibility to act, making front-line workers, particularly travel agents and stewards and stewardesses, into managers, giving them the authority to 'respond to the needs and problems of individual customers'. Middle managers were no longer to be supervisors but resources to help the frontline workers.

With Carlzon at the helm SAS was voted 'airline of the year' as a result of its efforts to improve its service 'by putting the customer first'. His great achievement was to create awareness of and enthusiasm for the concept of service at every level and in every location in an organization employing 20,000. He did this by a combination of visionary leadership, exceptional powers of communication and intensive training programmes (Sadler, 1988). He convinced his employees that they were responsible for the quality of the '50,000 moments of truth' that the company had to face each and every day. Moments of truth in service are the often fleeting encounters between employees and customers, where the customer senses he or she is truly being served. On their quality depends the customer's impression of the organization. These encounters render the notion of service into a tangible experience that the customers carry away with them. Carlsson's key task was to convince his employees of the strategic importance of embracing this existential approach of service as a competitive edge in the hostile environment of airline competition.

Question
Is Carlzon's approach applicable to other organizations?

EXHIBIT 6.2 LEADERS IN ACTION (II) SIR JOHN HARVEY-JONES: MAKING IT HAPPEN

Sir John's views on the qualities necessary for good management and leadership can be summed up as follows:

1 *Determination to be the best*. In his case to create the best chemical company in the world.
2 *Patience*. The knowledge that such an objective can only be achieved by solidly and carefully building a new company culture.
3 *Breadth of vision*. His idea of 'best' did not just embrace profitability. His vision of the best company included being the best in bringing in new products; in market sensitivity; presence; range; quality; how the company dealt with people; ethical, environmental and safety standards.
4 *Taking the long-term view*. Seeing his success or failure as judged by where the company would be five years later.
5 *A leader, rather than a manager*. Leading by example and persuasion, and hard work, not on the basis of power or authority. Being able to help others release their energies and focus their efforts on corporate objectives; creating conditions in which people want to give of their best.
6 *Humility*. Detesting 'red carpet' treatment, subservience, hierarchy and flattery. Being willing to own up to making mistakes.
7 *Openness*. Trying to make ICI a more open and friendly organization and one in which constructive criticism of top management is accepted.
8 *Compassion*. During his years in office ICI shed 60,000 jobs – something he genuinely feels sad about.

Source: Sadler (1988: 139).

Question
How would you rank-order these eight qualities?

Intel began to think the unthinkable, a fundamentally new strategy that involved exiting form the very business upon which it had been founded and grown so successfully. Intel managers were faced with a profound existential dilemma, one that meant they had to question the very roots of their existence. This was an extremely painful process, especially for top management. In Andy Grove's words:

> to be completely honest, as I started to discuss the possibility of getting out of the memory chip business with some of my associated, I had a hard time getting the words

out of my mouth without equivocation. It was just too difficult a thing to say. Intel equalled memories in all of our minds. How could we give up our identity? How could we exist as a company that was not in the memory business? It was close to being inconceivable.

Meetings to discuss the possibility dissolved into angry, confused and frustrated exchanges with some Intel managers unable to accept the possibility. Open-minded, rational discussion of the topic was impossible for some. Core beliefs – 'as strong as religious dogmas' (Grove, 1997: 90) – were being dissolved. The key belief that needed undoing was that memory was the necessary backbone of Intel's development, manufacturing and sales activities. Even when the rational argument for change was accepted the emotional impact of the decision meant that Intel continued to invest in memory-related R&D when there were no plans for marketing or selling the product. Finally, Intel went public and announced the shift to microprocessors as its main-line business. It was no longer a semiconductor company. (Source: Grove, 1997.)

Leadership means Change

John Kotter, for many years the Konosuke Matsushita Professor of Leadership at the Harvard Business School, has a long history of writing and consulting on the issues of leadership and change – dating back to before 1979, when he wrote an influential *Harvard Business Review* article on choosing strategies for change, through to his work distinguishing managers from leaders and including his eight steps to change described in a series of books and articles (for example, Kotter, 1995).

Echoing the radical/incremental change distinction Kotter describes the situations in which fast or slower change strategies are more appropriate. Change can be fast when the leaders are powerful, knowledgeable and the stakes are high. More consultation and consensus building is needed when others are more likely to resist and when they have the relevant data for designing the solution and the energy needed to implement it. But high stakes and high resistance may also indicate a need for fast top-driven change.

Leaders can bring an array of methods to deal with resistance to change, ranging from education, participation, facilitation and negotiation to co-option and coercion. The skill is to use these wisely and appropriately – not simply to use those methods that have worked well in a previous situation.

Leaders differ from managers to the extent that they set direction and risk disruption (rather than plan to avoid risk); gain alignment by pulling people together (rather than simply organizing) and motivate and inspire (rather than simply solve problems). In essence they produce change rather than create order. Organizations need leaders and managers – but when transformation is called for there is more likely to be a shortage of leaders than of managers.

But leaders still need to follow a systematic approach to change. Based on Kotter's observation that many managers make a predictable set of mistakes, the eight steps are as follows.

Eight steps to transforming your organization

1 Establishing a sense of urgency	Examining market and competitive realities
	Identifying and discussing crises, potential crises or major opportunities
2 Forming a powerful guiding coalition	Assembling a group with enough power to lead the change effort
	Encouraging the group to work together as a team
3 Creating a vision	Creating a vision to help direct the change effort
	Developing strategies for achieving that vision
4 Communicating the vision	Using every vehicle possible to communicate the new vision and strategies
	Teaching new behaviours by the example of the guiding coalition
5 Empowering others to act on the vision	Getting rid of obstacles to change
	Changing systems or structures that seriously undermine the vision
	Encouraging risk taking and non-traditional ideas, activities and actions
6 Planning for and creating short-term wins	Planning for visible performance improvements
	Creating those improvements
	Recognizing and rewarding employees involved in the improvements
7 Consolidate improvements and producing still more change	Using increased credibility to change systems, structures and policies that don't fit the vision
	Hiring, promoting and developing employees who can implement the vision
	Reinvigorating the process with new projects, themes and change agents
8 Institutionalizing new approaches	Articulating the connections between the new behaviours and corporate success
	Developing the means to ensure leadership development and succession.

And of these perhaps the real keys are establishing a sense of urgency through telling/showing people how it really is – building a guiding coalition of key players, who will see the change through – and at some stage ensuring that middle managers are empowered to take over the change themselves.

In his latest book with Dan Cohen (Kotter and Cohen, 2002) Kotter emphasizes the emotional aspects of leadership, arguing that 'the central issue is never strategy, structure, culture or systems . . . the core of the matter is always about changing the behaviour of people, and behaviour change happens in highly successful situations mostly by speaking to people's feelings. . . . The flow of see–feel–change is more powerful than that of analysis–think–change'. So the eight steps stay but get a new feel:

The eight steps for successful large-scale change

1 Increase urgency   People start telling each other, 'Let's go, we need to change things!'

2 Build the guiding team   A group powerful enough to guide big change is formed and they start to work well together

3 Get the vision right   The guiding team develops the right vision and strategy for the change effort

4 Communicate for buy-in   People begin to buy in to the change and this shows in their behaviour

5 Empower action   More people feel able to act, and do act on the vision

6 Create short-term wins   Momentum builds as people try to fulfil the vision, while fewer and fewer resist change

7 Don't let up   People make wave after wave of changes until the vision is fulfilled

8 Make change stick   New and winning behaviour continues despite the pull of tradition, turnover of change leaders, etc.

And the book as a whole emphasizes the importance of stories in tapping into the emotional aspects of change.

CHAPTER 7

THE FUTURE OF STRATEGY: COMPETENCE AND RESPONSIBILITY

This chapter focuses upon what we see as key current issues in the study and practice of strategy, in particular issues of competence and corporate responsibility. Competence has emerged as the most important current concept in strategy and is analysed in terms of discussions of the resource-based view of the firm. The debate about competence pulls together many of the themes we have discussed in previous chapters. It focuses in strongly on how to think about competitive advantage, and raises issues of change through learning, and uniqueness. It also raises questions about how best to organize to capitalize upon competence. We apply the competence perspective to understanding the roots of success of firms that may prove to be the excellent firms of the future.

The concern with responsibility emerges from debates about stakeholders and the goals of business. We live at a time when recent corporate scandals – most notably Enron – have raised profound issues about what motivates management when they pursue strategy. Should it be shareholder value? To the exclusion of everything else? When firms' mission statements emphasize key groups to be taken account of in pursuing a strategy do they mean it? Enron suggests that this is not always the case. Strategic management theory has long emphasized the responsibility of the corporation to society. We examine how a stakeholder perspective provides a way of balancing the complex web of relationships that a firm needs to consider in deciding strategy. We live in a time of great change and of uncertainty. We finish the book on a questioning note. Strategy is the most exciting and challenging of the business disciplines. Debates about its essence will continue.

Competence

It was Prahalad and Hamel (1990) who popularized the concept of competence within the field of strategic management although the term does have a long history. Strategic management is quintessentially concerned with sources of firm competitive advantage. Prahalad and Hamel argue that one of the most powerful sources of competitive advantage is core competence. They define core competences as 'the collective learning in the organization, especially how to co-ordinate diverse production skills and integrate multiple streams and technologies' (Prahalad and Hamel, 1990: 64). The interest in competence in strategy refocused attention on sources of competitive advantage internal to the organization rather than the external focus on product markets and competitive environments. This marked a gradual sea change in thinking about strategy, with the shift away from the emphasis on market selection and positioning to a focus on the internal sources of competitiveness in internal capabilities.

The interest in competence has a long history in strategy which has led to what is now called the resource-based view of the firm. The resource-based view argues that competitive advantage arises from firm-specific resources. This view has its origins in the pioneering work of the economist Edith Penrose (1959), who viewed the firm as 'an administrative organization and a collection of productive resources' and 'a bundle of potential services'. The resource-based view of the firm recognizes resources in their broadest sense to include assets, processes, attributes, knowledge and information. To confer competitive advantage resources must: be rare/scarce, difficult or, better, impossible to imitate, non-substitutable and appropriable by the firm (Barney, 1991). From the resource-based perspective advantage can best be derived from tacit knowledge because such knowledge has rarity value, imperfect mobility, imperfect imitation and imperfect substitutability, making it hard for outsiders to imitate or copy.

The resource-based, competence view is increasingly seen as a knowledge-based view of the firm, with knowledge emerging as the most valuable of resources, and how to access, manage and apply knowledge a major research issue (Grant, 1996). A knowledge-based view conceptualizes the firm as a self-regulating system that optimizes the interactions of individuals and groups to create, circulate and apply knowledge to the strategies of the firm. Much knowledge remains tacit, which means that it is difficult for others to access or replicate. Knowledge works in mysterious ways. For example:

> Toyota's knowledge of how to make cars lies embedded in highly specialized social and organizational relationships that have evolved through decades of common effort. It rests in routines, information flows, ways of making decisions, shared attitudes, and expectations, and specialized knowledge that Toyota managers, workers, suppliers and purchasing agents, and others have about different aspects of their business, about each other, and about how they can all work together. None of these parties knows what Toyota as a whole 'knows' about making car. (Badaracco, 1991: 87)

The overall sum is greater than the sum of the parts.

Knowledge raises important issues of learning as the basis of competence acquisition and development. Prahalad and Hamel (1990: 82) define core competence as 'the collective learning of the organization'. The advantage of a learning organization (Starkey, 1998) built on distinctive core competences is that it generates new knowledge through experience, is adaptive at coping with changing circumstances and generative in creating new solutions and thus combines both refinement and renewal capabilities. A learning organization also enables its members to let go of competences that are no longer relevant and to embrace new skills and techniques offering flexibility to its knowledge base.

Business history contains many rich examples of how knowledge can act as the basis for competence building. Sony learnt to excel in miniaturization, Honda in engines, Federal Express in logistics management. There are also some telling examples of how management failed to develop knowledge and competence into a strategic advantage. One of the most powerful examples of this was Xerox (see chapter 8).

One of the lessons of Xerox is that it is important that firms develop a capacity for change through either developing new or reconfiguring existing competences to match or, better, to create change their business environment. The concept of 'dynamic capability' has been developed to capture this. Indeed, it has been suggested that the ability to change can constitute a core competence 'Dynamic capabilities . . . are the organizational and strategic routines by which firms achieve new resource reconfigurations as markets emerge, collide, split, evolve, and die' (Eisenhardt and Martin, 2000).

Competence, Organization and Human Resources

Thinking in terms of the strategic importance of a limited number of core competences has led firms to question their thinking about the very nature of what they do and what their organizations should comprise. If the strategic imperative is to limit investment to what you do best, then the competence perspective suggests the outsourcing of non-core activities. As firms unbundle, downsize, refocus and reconfigure, one begins to recognize strategy as residing in a network of co-operative relationships. Outsourcing becomes strategic, and firms have to manage those relationships that extend their resource capability.

The focus on competence implies a different way of thinking about both strategy and organization that challenges much previously accepted wisdom – for example, how to think about portfolio management. Prahalad and Hamel (1990: 81) argue that competitive advantage comes from 'management's ability to consolidate corporate-wide technologies and production skills'. Portfolios of competence rather than of separate business units imply a different dominant logic in thinking about strategy. You start with what the firm is good at and use this to unite and focus the organization rather than basing one's corporate decisions on a hands-off financial logic that manages the separate units only according to the numbers and as separate entities. Firms vary in their social architecture of values, cultures and relationships which cannot be readily replicated. It is the nature of the organization that will determine the commitment of individuals and groups to the creation and sharing of knowledge and to the best expression of their competence.

The focus on competence and resources leads naturally to issues of human resource management (HRM). Firms regularly, if somewhat ritualistically, state that 'our people are our most important resource'. A strategic perspective on HRM (Kamoche, 2001: 89) conceptualizes scarcity in terms of human resources, knowledge and skills. Crucial to a competence strategy is the firm's 'capacity to secure, nurture, retain and deploy human resources through HR policies and practices' and HR practices that 'seek to ensure that people are utilizing their skills towards the achievement of the organization's strategies'. Firms can buy in new human resources to acquire new talent, individual or groups of individuals, as, for example, happens in football where star players are key assets. But unlocking the capacity for action is a more difficult challenge: 'even if the resources that constitute the team are transferred, the nature of organizational routines – in particular, the role of tacit knowledge and unconscious co-ordination – makes the recreation of capabilities within a new corporate environment uncertain' (Grant, 1991: 127).

The resource-based view of the firm has informed our understanding of recent developments in corporate refocusing as firms de-diversify to concentrate on areas where they possess a critical competence. New modes of organization – downsizing, restructuring, making our organizations more flexible and more responsive to ever more dynamic markets – challenge our ability to manage. Knowledge builds over time, competence is embedded and embodied in complex routines which are themselves embedded in modes of organising that have a history and a heritage. We dismantle this heritage at our peril.

> resources like knowledge, trust, commitment and so forth are by definition intangible and tacit and have to be built up over time. The tradability of such resources appears rather limited: can one buy trust, or commitment? . . . The stock of skills, talents and competences is tied in with a complex web of other tacit resources in the social context of organizations, including such nebulous constructs as trust and loyalty. (Kamoche, 2001: 48–9)

The new economy and the dictates of responses to short-term (including financial) market needs runs the risk of undermining what takes a long time to develop.

> How can we decide what is of lasting value in ourselves . . . How can long-term goals be pursued in an economy devoted to the short-term? How can mutual loyalties and commitments be sustained in institutions which are constantly breaking apart or continually being redesigned? These are the questions . . . posed by the new flexible capitalism. (Sennett, 1998: 10)

But certain key questions about competence remain unanswered. For example, do firms know what they are good at? One major telecommunications firm was very surprised, when it performed a competence audit, to find that what it considered its core competences were different from what those external to the firm judged as core. The firm was not sure what it was best at! The focus on competence can go too far and even make us myopic. An organization that focuses purely on refining existing competences may become strategically vulnerable as these become too specific to a particular context. If change occurs an organization can find it hard to respond. This is captured by Leonard-Barton's (1992) notion of 'core rigidities' whereby over time core competences can become dysfunctional to performance. There need to be shifts in competence and knowledge during periods of discontinuous change. The dynamic capability necessary to chart this kind of change is linked to the concept of 'absorptive capacity' (Cohen and Levinthal, 1990), the capacity of the firm to absorb new knowledge, competences and to develop out of these new routines and actions.

The notion of competence now extends beyond the limits of the firm. We need to think of competence as a firm-specific attribute and also as an attribute of a network of relationships. Here, the need is to think of competence as a clustering phenomenon in which the firm is only one player. Porter (1990) links firm competitive advantage to developments at the regional and national level whereby firms cluster in specific regions and jointly develop robust new business models for particular industries. Examples here include information technologies in Silicon Valley, film and media around Hollywood, fashion clusters around Milan and motor racing clusters around the Thames Valley in the United Kingdom. In these clusters, firm competence is developed in intense competition with competitors, in collaboration with key suppliers with their own unique competences and in response to demanding customers.

Future Excellence

The competence perspective raises issues of what competences make the excellent companies of today and of the future. This is a hard question to answer, particularly for the future. (See exhibit 7.1 for a slightly tongue-in-cheek example of the migration of competence from one business, sport, to another, clothes retailing!)

EXHIBIT 7.1 WHAT IS DAVID BECKHAM BEST AT?

Sport provides many lessons for strategy. It provides stark and precise lessons about the importance of competence. Football stars command salaries that compete with business's most valued superstars. When it was rumoured that Real Madrid were interested in signing the England player Michael Owen, having just signed the Brazilian Ronaldo for a record-breaking fee, Owen's club manager, Gerard Houllier of Liverpool, dismissed the rumour unceremoniously. 'Real Madrid might be able to afford Ronaldo, but they can't afford Michel Owen. Thirty million pounds might buy his left foot, but what about the rest of him?'

Football also illustrates the importance and the difficulties of combining competences. The football manager faces the unenviable challenge of developing and moulding talented individuals into a winning team. France, with the football academy it developed to bring together its up-and-coming younger players, did this remarkably well, winning its first World Cup in 1998 and following that with winning the European Nations' Championship, Euro 2000. There was a clear consensus that, by the year 2000, France were the world's best team and that, still young, they would go from strength to strength. In the words of Bobby Robson, a former England manager, reflecting upon the lessons of Euro 2000, 'They have the best players, the best squad, the best options.' Yet France was eliminated in the first round of the 2002 World Cup, a dismal failure on the world's most visible and important footballing stage.

David Beckham is captain of England and a stalwart of one of the world's best club teams, Manchester United. His footballing competence is undisputed. However, the latest addition to his portfolio of activities may come as a surprise. Not content with his mastery of the long-range free kick, Beckham was appointed by a leading UK retailer, Marks & Spencer, as clothes designer. The retailer identified Beckham as the personality whom most young boys wanted to emulate. He was also considered an excellent family role model because of his happy home life with one of what was once one of the world's most successful female singing groups, the Spice Girls.

In 2002 M&S launched his first collection, a new range of boys' clothes. Beckham rejected the idea of adding his considerable brand name to an already partly designed collection and was heavily involved in the design and manufacture of a brand-new collection of casual boys' clothes. Beckham brought his own particular ideas and fashion flair to the design. In the words of Pauline Ainslie, design manager for M&S boys' wear, 'The one thing David was adamant about was that he wanted everything to be really baggy. That meant completely rethinking the usual pattern shapes we use to make the garments, adding loads on to the trouser waist front and back seams.'

Beckham was actively involved in the design specification, insisting on broadening the colour range beyond the original combination of slate grey and navy, which he considered too dull for the age range. He contributed other ideas as well, such as the garments' eye-catching details and insistence on top-quality finish – for example, Beckham tags on the zips and belt loops and the Beckham name embossed on the trouser buttons. He also demonstrated an eye for functionality, identifying the need of young children for pyjamas with short sleeves and short legs, 'because kids often get really hot in bed, so I thought they'd like to wear shorts, as they're cooler'.

Both the company and the superstar seem happy with their collaboration. Beckham signed up to work on another five collections for Marks & Spencer over three years. It will be interesting to ask future readers of this book, in five or ten years' time, how many know or remember who Beckham is/was and to see then what he is famous for, or remembered for, if at all – footballer or design icon?

Source: *Marks & Spencer Magazine*, autumn 2002.

As we saw when we talked about Peters and Waterman's research on 'excellence', only a minority of companies seemed able to sustain excellence even over the relatively short term. Tom Peters has reputedly said that you can only guarantee excellence will last for six months!

Perhaps this should come as no surprise. It is almost a management truism that we live in a time of great unpredictability and fast change. If we had been writing this book in the year 2000 rather than 2003 we would have spent more time addressing the view, held by many at the time, that the old models were becoming redundant and that we should be looking at the new ways of doing strategy and even the 'new economy' being formed in places like Silicon Valley. Here the emphasis was upon the flexible alignment of ideas, talent and capital. Key drivers of success were seen as the ability to change and 'reinvent' the firm; innovation was everybody's responsibility. Graduates of top MBA programmes queued up to join new technology start-up companies . . .

Then came the dot-com collapse and so much of the rhetoric of the time was revealed as hype. And behind the hype there lay issues more sinister than hype. The most admired firm of the late 1990s, lionized for its innovative management practices, its aggressive growth strategy and its stellar performance was Enron! What can we conclude from the sorry stories of 'dot-connery' and 'Enronitis'? That we don't know what the new business models of the future will look like! Strategy consulting firms are struggling as corporate clients dispense with their services, feeling betrayed by consultants' advice to invest in dot-com projects (*Economist*, 2 November 2002). In other industries, leaders struggle. In fast foods, for example, McDonald's reported its first set of losses. Sales of burgers and chips declined as customers moved to more 'wholesome' products. The company's expansion plans were cut back. The company now says it wants to be more 'relevant' to its customers. In the words of its new chief executive, 'The world has changed. Our customers have changed. We have to change too. . . . Are we trying to attract a twenty-first-century customer with a twentieth-century menu?' (*Financial Times*, 8 April 2003).

Some Old Economy firms have proved surprisingly resilient. New technology can present major challenges. For example, the music industry is still engaged in a desperate rearguard action to control the impact of online access to its products. Whether the music companies can limit 'piracy' remains open to question. Some of the biggest names in the business think it impossible and are looking at innovative ways of tapping the potential of the technology. But in another industry undergoing major technological change – telecoms – the old incumbents, the former telecommunications monopolies, criticized as dinosaurs, are managing to survive as new entrants fade away. In Europe the vast majority of consumers still use the older firms rather than the new nimble and agile entrants (*Financial Times*, 28 February 2003). Even in the new markets – for example, for high-speed internet access – the old telecoms dinosaurs survive and even prosper.

Firms still find themselves faced with the core strategy dilemmas, in particular whether and how to compete on cost and/or on innovation. In our opinion, too many firms have overemphasized the reduction of costs at the expense of innovation.

In pharmaceuticals, for example, we have seen much merger and acquisition activity, which, with subsequent restructuring, can help drive down costs, but firms such as GlaxoSmithKline (GSK) find it hard to renew their drug pipelines with innovative new products. Pharmaceutical firms struggle with their bureaucratic heritage to create environments that will foster better collaboration between groups of scientists. Investors are sceptical of drug company strategies for creating new business when they see large increases in spending on lawyers to defend and prolong existing patents. But there does seem to be a failure of corporate imagination, with companies queueing up to compete in the same market – for example, for erectile dysfunction drugs – rather than creating new market space.

In other industries, we do see the emergence of innovative new industry leaders. In the auto industry it is innovative firms like Renault that are creating a new future by transforming their capacity for design innovation. Even in an Old Economy industry like this, innovation can be a key driver of success. In other industries it is the innovators who are the industry leaders. The French company L'Oréal is a global leader in many segments of the cosmetic industry. As of 2002 it had sustained seventeen years of double-digit sales and earnings growth, a unique achievement in a fast-moving consumer goods environment. It is a company characterized by a passion for developing innovative products. L'Oréal's success is driven by its investment in research, developing literally hundreds of new products each year. And, unlike other innovative companies, such as Nike, it also manufactures its own products, mostly in France, to guarantee the quality standards it desires.

A Swedish company, H&M, the largest clothing retailer in Europe, has also developed a reputation as a design leader in its fashion-conscious industry. Its strategy combines 'fashion and quality at best price', or 'cheap *chic*' (*Business Week*, 11 November 2002). The company is strong on design. Its design team spends a large amount of its time travelling the world or working in company stores to remain close to the customer. H&M updates its clothing range with great speed and frequency, compressing lead times – how long it takes for a garment to move from design table to shop window – to a matter of weeks. The idea is to treat fashion like perishable produce: keep it fresh and keep it moving! To control costs it keeps inventory to an absolute minimum, despite the turnover of fashion ideas and the fickleness of the fashion-conscious public. It outsources manufacture on a global basis to minimize costs and also controls costs by having employees travel economy class and without mobile phones, which is bad news for the Finnish company, Nokia, the leading manufacturer of the mobile phone!

Nokia has developed an enviable reputation in the mobile telephony market and is clear innovation leader. With a mission statement that emphasizes openness, integrity, teamwork, humility, communication and openness, Nokia is now leader in the global mobile-phone market, accounting for three times the sales of its nearest competitor, Motorola. But it has got to that position by accepting the challenge of change. It was during the late 1980s that the company refocused its strategy on to the telecommunications area. It was one of the first companies to develop a truly portable mobile phone handset and to foresee the possibilities of major changes in the market, to which it could respond quickly and flexibly, owing to its R&D capabilities. Nokia's strategic intent is to create personal communication technology that enables people to shape their own mobile world and to strengthen its leadership position in converging digital solutions. It pursues this intent through capitalizing upon its understanding of user needs and through its ability to meet and exceed user expectations by building upon core competences in key areas such as design and product innovation, brand development and effective demand/supply network management. Organizationally, competences are focused vertically in independent business units responsible for product and business development within a defined market segment, with cross-cutting horizontal functions to promote economies of scale in application software development and demand–supply network management (see chapter 8).

The Future of Strategy

Strategy theorists continue to try to define new ways of thinking about competitive advantage. One concept that has emerged to define a new key competence is what Gawer and Cusumano (2002) describe as 'platform leadership'. The term describes how industry leaders, such as Intel, Microsoft, Cisco and Oracle, develop products which provide the basic technological architecture on which other products and systems depend, for example the microprocessor or the Windows operating system. Firms which have attained platform leadership thus create standards for entire industries and occupy pivotal positions at the centre of those industries, around which other firms develop complementary innovations dependent upon their platforms. Platform leadership is particularly important in high-tech industries and it may be in the battle for platform leadership that we shall see new models of strategy emerging. Here it has been suggested that the growing 'battle' between Microsoft and Linux indicates one of the ways strategy might go in the future.

Software Wars: Davids *v.* Goliath

Until recently it looked as if Microsoft had a stranglehold on the software market and, thus, on the computer industry overall. Microsoft is now under siege on two fronts. It is challenged in the US courts over apparent abuse of its quasi-monopoly power. And it is under attack from a new type of organization with a new strategy for software development.

Microsoft's dominance of the market has been predicated on its omnipresence as personal computer operating system of choice. Every few years Microsoft launches a new variant of its Windows software and, in between times, it provides updates. In essence, it has been difficult for the non-sophisticated user to contemplate an alternative.

Now there is a developing alternative to the private, closed space, in-house software development approach that characterizes Microsoft, and its products are making significant inroads into the business software market. The alternative model arises out of open-source software development, itself the offspring of the free software movement that began in the 1980s. Its most famous example is Linux, invented in 1991 by a young Finnish student, Linus Torwalds. When Torwalds started work on what was to become Linux he decided, in the spirit of the free software movement, to give his software away for free, and he included the source code – in essence, its powerhouse – for free too.

Torwalds was a student at the time and he was making a virtue of necessity. He could not have sold what he was developing and he was not interested in raising venture capital to grow a business. He wanted to involve other like-minded programmers (hackers) in a collective effort to improve what was on offer. To do so he made his work available on the Internet and what became the Linux community started to grow. Today about 1,000 people devote their spare time to developing the Linux kernel, with contributions from thousands of others on an *ad hoc* basis

Today open-source servers power more than 50 per cent of the Web servers on the Internet. The open-source movement has created software that many, including a growing number of corporates, think is as good as or better than anything Microsoft has developed. Linux has been embraced as a significant business opportunity by firms such as Red Hat and Oracle. Indeed, Oracle, the world's leading enterprise software company, and Red Hat collaborate on the implementation of office systems powered by Linux, in Oracle's words, because Linux is the best means of helping customers to implement the lowest-cost hardware and operating system infrastructure – in other words, as the most cost-effective solution. Oracle and Red Hat have been collaborating to enhance the Linux kernel to support enterprise-class functionality and Oracle pronounces itself committed to working with the 'Linux community' to develop the kernel further. Oracle does not have its own distribution of Linux. This is why it collaborates with partners such as Red Hat. According to Oracle's advertising, 'Everyone knows that Linux costs less.' Oracle's aim is to make it increasingly fast and even more reliable.

The spectacular development of Linux raises profound questions, not just about the strategies for and business opportunities in software development but about the evolution and ownership of knowledge in our society. In the words of the *New York Times* journalist Peter Wayner:

> Is society better off with a computer infrastructure controlled by a big corporate machine driven by cash? Or does sharing the source code create better software? Are we at a point where money is not the best vehicle for lubricating the engines of societal advancement? Many in the free software world are pondering these questions.

Why did Linux develop in the way it has and what are the lessons we can draw from its development? Bob Young, Chairman and CEO of Red Hat, argues that the Linux approach will open the door to unprecedented innovation in the software industry. In contrast to the computer hardware industry, where no one firm exercises the degree of control of a Microsoft, competition reigns and customers benefit from a profusion of choice and unparalleled innovation in product and customer value. Change in the software industry takes far longer, up to decades. For example, the 1980s killer app(lication), the office suite, remained unchallenged until the 1990s and the introduction of the Web browser and server. In Young's words, the benefits of the open-source revolution are as follows:

It gives customers control over the technologies they use, instead of enabling vendors to control their customers through restricting access to the code behind the technologies. Supplying open-source tools to the market will require new business models. But by delivering unique benefits to the market, those companies that develop the business models will be very successful competing with companies that attempt to retain control over their customers.

In his landmark study of the development of open source and of Linux, Eric Raymond, himself a leading open-source activist, characterizes the process of systematically harnessing open development and decentralized peer review and contribution to software advancement as akin to the activity of a bazaar.

> Linux is subversive. Who would have thought . . . that a world-class operating system could coalesce as if by magic out of part-time hacking by several thousand developers scattered all over the planet, connected only by the tenuous strands of the Internet? . . . Linus Torwald's style of development – release early and often, delegate everything you can, be open to the point of promiscuity – came as a surprise . . . the Linux community seemed to resemble a great babbling bazaar of differing agendas and approaches (aptly symbolized by the Linux archive sites, which would take submissions from *anyone*) out of which a coherent and stable system could seemingly emerge only by a succession of miracles. ˙

When he looked closer, Raymond identified a number of core processes that make the Linux community work. There was, first of all, a leadership style and a set of co-operative customs that allowed a developer (Torwalds), and then the other core developers who joined him, to attract co-developers and get maximum leverage out of their interactions, in the process producing 'a self-correcting spontaneous order more elaborate and efficient than any amount of central planning could have achieved'. Individuals, in the jargon of economics, were maximizing their own utility, but the utility function they were maximizing was not the one usually emphasized by economic explanation. They were massaging their own ego satisfaction and seeking to build their reputation for elegant and path-breaking work among the community of hackers. Torwalds, along with a small self-selecting central group, exercised the function of gatekeeper and network broker. Also motivating involvement and the contribution of time and brainpower was intellectual interest. The Linux community is promordially a community of interest whose members deeply enjoy what they do. Finally, the other way of characterizing the Linux community is as a *gift culture* in which your standing is determined by what you freely give away! (Sources: Raymond, 1999; O'Reilly, 2000.)

QUESTIONS

1 Which kind of organization is likely to survive longer, one modelled on Microsoft or on Linux?
2 Which kind of firm benefits society most?

Strategy and Responsibility

Finally we address the issue of responsibility in strategy, a subject that is increasingly demanding the attention of top management. This is not surprising, given the demise of the dot-coms, the distaste felt by many at the apparently exorbitant salaries awarded to 'fat cat', and sometimes not very successful, top managers, and the scandals associated with firms like Enron. Many wonder what really drives strategic decision making.

One of the earliest and most influential models of the strategic management decision process, the Harvard 'Design School' model, suggested that the basic building blocks of strategy encompass four factors: (1) an organization's strengths and weaknesses, (2) opportunities and threats in its environment, (3) the values of its managers and (4) its broader social responsibility. Most attention in strategic management has been paid to the analysis of internal and external factors. We have suggested that the values of top managers are also a crucial determinant of strategy. We also suggest in our model of strategic management that one has to balance the interests of various stakeholders in taking strategic decisions. Firms need to address their responsibilities to these stakeholders.

The first issue in corporate responsibility is that of 'private solutions to public problems'. The arguments concern corporate responsibility for aspects of social welfare that the State cannot or will not provide. In this context business is increasingly expected to be responsive to the needs of the community and society. It is not enough for companies to be concerned only with the needs of shareholders and employees. This view is most developed and accepted in the United States but one of the themes of Thatcherism in the United Kingdom in the 1980s was that the State expected business leaders to help in the revitalization of the economy of inner cities. Businesses were urged to look on this as an investment, providing returns in terms of good public relations and in providing an edge in recruiting the best local labour. Out of this approach came initiatives such as 'Business in the Community'. Even under a Labour government the United Kingdom has seen further blurring of the line between private and public sectors.

The second dominant theme in corporate responsibility is that of business ethics and the claim that ethical decision making is a business as well as a moral imperative. Equal opportunities is a case in point. Also, investment decisions are increasingly examined in an ethical light. Ethical investment trusts appear to have performed above the average in the latter part of the 1980s. Green issues and industrial disasters have heightened moral concern. Only ethical management, the strong proponents of this argument suggest, will survive and prosper in an increasingly ethical world.

In her autobiography *Body and Soul* Anita Roddick, founder of Body Shop, tells of her search for 'the modern-day equivalent of those Quakers who ran successful businesses, made money because they offered honest products and treated their people decently, worked hard, spent honestly, gave honest value for money, put back more than they took out and told no lies', only to conclude that 'This business creed, sadly, seems long forgotten.' Ms Roddick set out to 'remoralize' an industry that, she claimed, had absolutely no sense of moral responsibility and went as far as to claim that by the turn of the millennium any company that does not operate in the same ethical way as the Body Shop will risk failure. Sir Adrian Cadbury makes a similar point about the effect of insider trading scandals on the junk bond market in the United States. The financial services industry in the United Kingdom is held in very low esteem as pension misselling and other examples of consumer mismanagement appear as leading news items. It is not just the companies associated with such scandals that have been damaged, but the entire industry.

The importance of corporate responsibility, broadly defined, to strategy can be illustrated in three hypotheses:

- *The stakeholder hypothesis.* Organizations are stronger to the extent that they demonstrate a broad sense of responsibility to a variety of stakeholders, both external and internal. The Japanese *kaisha* provides a potent illustration of the importance of management accepting responsibility for internal stakeholders.
- *The vision hypothesis.* 'Visionary' organizations whose missions capitalize on emerging social trends have been among the success stories of the 1970s and 1980s, e.g. Body Shop with its new vision of the cosmetic industry as socially responsible.
- *The value hypothesis.* The values of top managers have a crucial role to play in the strategic management process. The extent to which these values are 'responsible' will increasingly impact upon the fate of the organization. The study of corporate responsibility and business ethics has important role to play in the surfacing of core values and their clarification. One should also be aware, however, of the ambiguity of supposedly responsible and irresponsible behaviours.

Stakeholders

The term 'stakeholder' refers to any group or individual who has a legitimate expectation of a firm. Stakeholders include stockholders, employees, customers, suppliers, creditors, managers, local community, special interest groups such as environmentalists, the general public, government and any other groups who have entered into relations with the firm. A stakeholder map of a large organization is set out in figure 7.1.

Such a map provides an image of stakeholder groups. It thus illustrates graphically the range of stakeholders the corporation is responsible to and needs to seek to satisfy. The emphasis on stakeholders also suggests that Porter's 'five forces' model of industrial structure needs to be extended to embrace the relative power of those stakeholders that Porter's five forces do not accommodate.

The implication of the stakeholder approach is that organizations must ask themselves searching questions about the range of their stakeholders and their relative power. In firms such as Ford one can construe major changes in management style and corporate ethic as, in part, a redefinition of the corporation's responsibility to its employees and other stakeholders. Japanese management practices have played an important role in changing accepted managerial wisdom in the West. Japanese

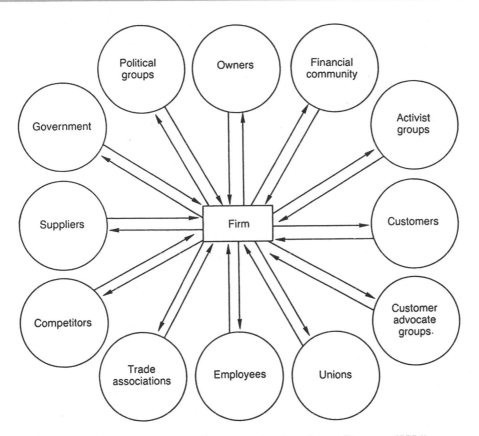

Figure 7.1 Stakeholder map of a very large organization. *Source*: Freeman (1984)

strategic management seems more oriented to the maximization of the interests of employees than of shareholders and it has been suggested that this has helped Japanese firms develop a long-term approach to strategy, free of the short-term market-led corporate control constraints that operate in the West.

In the West the demand for more responsible behaviour from employees in the form of increased efficiency and quality is often perceived by the employees as a threat to their own welfare. This presents a major problem in developing a sense of mutual responsibility between management and work force. In the words of one Western manager from Xerox, a leading company in responding to the lessons of the Japanese style of management, 'We need to get over the hurdle that means that efficiency, quality and competence result in loss of jobs. You need to have a sense of security to take risks with new jobs and new skills.'

There is, then, an important issue of the relative merits of internal and external stakeholders. Japan, a leader in recognizing and responding to the notion of responsibility for internal stakeholders, is now, in its global expansion strategies, targeting broader social responsibility as an important element of what Sony calls 'glocalization' – adapting global strategies to local conditions. The global strategies of Japanese firms have led to investment friction in the countries they have targeted. One way in which the Japanese have responded to this friction is through attempting to become good corporate citizens in foreign countries. The Keidanren, the Japan Federation of Economic Organizations, estimates that US corporate donations amount to about 2 per cent of gross national product. In Japan the figure is a mere 0.1 per cent. However, in Japan the concept of corporate responsibility includes such things as job security (for core workers), import promotion and price stability.

Visionary organizations

The strategy literature has paid increasing attention to 'organizational vision'. 'Visionary' organizations whose missions capitalize on emerging social trends were among the success stories of the 1970s and 1980s. Body Shop, with its new vision of the cosmetic industry as socially responsible, has been mentioned. Apple, with its vision of democratizing the computer industry by bringing computer power to the people, springs to mind. At the turn of the century Henry Ford's vision of democratizing the automobile industry led to mass production. Other visions focus on internal transformation. The 'Aspirations Statement' of Levi Strauss begins: 'We all want a company that our people are proud of and committed to, where all employees have an opportunity to contribute, learn, grow and advance based on merit, not politics or background.'

Mission statements increasingly refer to a broad range of stakeholders. Ford's statement of 'Mission, Values and Guiding Principles' includes a clear commitment to stockholders, the owners of the business, employees, dealers and suppliers, as well as to a broader social responsibility. This represents a broadening of the responsibility agenda, particularly in the area of internal stakeholders, driven by a reanalysis and redefinition of core values. It is the combination of mission, vision and values that can create the common identity necessary to unite the large number of people that constitute a large organization. Peter Senge emphasizes the importance of shared vision as a key aspect of the learning organization. The impetus to learning is to foster an environment in which people share their visions of the organization, and through this process of sharing create a common future. Through the creation of a common vision organizations can overcome the sectionalism that is inimical to the sense of shared responsibility for the organization's fate.

Getting started is as simple as sitting people in small circles and asking them to talk about 'what's really important to them'. . . . When people begin to state and hear each other's visions, the foundation of the political environment begins to crumble – the belief that all we care about is self-interest. Organizations that fail to foster genuinely shared visions, or that foist unilateral visions on their members and pretend that they are shared, fail to tap this broader commitment. Though they decry internal politics, they do nothing to nurture a non-political environment.

It is only in a non-political environment that responsibility for the common good can be generated. 'One of the deepest desires underlying shared vision is the desire to be connected, to a larger purpose *and* one another. The spirit of connection is fragile' (Senge, 1990: 275).

Values

Chester Barnard taught us that a primary role of senior management is the fostering of shared values in the organization. The Ford example illustrates how major strategic change necessitates a fundamental re-examination of the organization's value system. At Ford the re-examination of values came before the framing of the mission and the guiding principles and, indeed, was a necessary precursor of the later initiatives. Strategic change focused on the need for better-quality products to compete with Japanese automobile firms. The key to unlocking the potential to manufacture to this quality was the redefinition of the value of people to the organization. Strategic management, Ford was accepting, needs to be responsible management.

But even a visionary company like Body Shop is not without its critics, who, for example, contest the claims about animal testing, criticize franchising as favouring the company at the expense of the franchisee, argue that it is unethical to use ethics as a promotional device and claim that the company may not spend money on advertising but is very adept at promoting media attention, a form of covert advertising, usually focused on Anita Roddick herself. And Body Shop's decision to close its main UK manufacturing operation raises significant questions about its commitment to the local community

---

QUESTIONS

1 Anita Roddick is a woman with a burning social purpose. She is championing a new philosophy of retailing, illustrated by the following quotations: 'I think loneliness is a time bomb ticking away in our society, especially in the shopping malls. Anyone who can figure a way of reducing loneliness, either through their stores or their marketing, will have a business that will thrive for ever. Never treat customers as enemies, approach them as potential friends. Think of customers as guests, make them laugh. Is any retailer thinking about how to make a shopping mall function socially as an arena of human contact or centre for useful, social information, like a village well in traditional societies? I doubt it.' Anita Roddick claims that her ethical approach to business will become the norm for the twenty-first century. Do you agree with her views and the Body Shop approach or do you count yourself as one of its critics?
2 What kinds of organizations and strategies will win in the competition for the future?

Epilogue

Strategic management should be synonymous with responsible management. In the final analysis, 'the buck stops' with those managers who are empowered to sanction the critical strategic decisions that will, in the long term, make or break a company. This is a heavy weight for managers to bear. One of the most significant trends of recent years has been the embracing of shareholder value as the key measure of firm performance and, therefore, as the main goal of effective strategy. Many firms have gone down this route and there have been few dissenting voices.

The notion that a firm exists primarily to maximize the returns of its shareholders (stockholders in the United States) is seductive. It simplifies and focuses top management attention, especially if the rewards are linked with performance according to this measure. But many organizations do not have shareholders. See, for example, the UK National Health Service in chapter 8, one of the world's largest and most complex organizations, which has provided a management headache for successive governments. And what of the 'carpetbaggers', speculators with no long-term allegiance to companies themselves, who move their share portfolios according to the vagaries of the market? What kind of consideration does this group deserve?

Strategy is frequently presented as an analytical exercise, the outcome of rational decisions. This ignores fundamentals of human behaviour, which is as often motivated by emotion as by reason. In the final analysis, firms reflect and shape their social context. There is a concern among critics of big business that top managers have become too conditioned by the notion that 'greed is good', a phrase coined by a leading US financier (Ivan Boesky) before he fell from grace, and immortalized in the film *Wall Street*.

In *Wall Street* the lead character, Gordon Gekko, makes a speech to a group of stockholders of a company he has targeted in which he extols the virtues of greed. He associates these virtues with survival in a corporate jungle as red in tooth and claw as the view of nature propounded by Charles Darwin. There are dangers in this view, as the sad lesson of the dodo reminds us. (See chapter 8, which illustrates how unrestrained competition can kill the very thing it feeds on.) It sets very few limits on managerial excess, with negative effects on the environment and on the reputation and even the legitimacy of business.

Strategy theory, supported by finance theory, must itself accept some responsibility for the problems facing business. Business schools have been charged with complicity in the Enron disaster, most notably in being an active party in promoting the feeding frenzy of fast-track corporate growth without educating the executives involved in any broader perspective on the social implications of their financial and economic practices. The business school is charged with teaching in a moral and cultural vacuum.

> So many people – most notably investors and employees, but also society at large – have been badly hurt by the Enron debacle. How could it happen? Business schools must accept some of the responsibility. Recent survey data suggest that MBA students graduate with less concern about social and ethical issues than when they entered business school. . . . Like it or not, business school faculty – myself included – must accept some responsibility for the managers we train. Too often we turn out ambitious, intelligent, driven, skilled over-achievers with one underdeveloped aptitude. Too many of the business leaders we graduate are hitting the ground running, but we have forgotten to help them to build their moral muscles. (Salbu, 2002: xiv)

There is certainly some truth in the view that Enron is a symptom of broader business and education. In his much discussed critique of the contemporary conditions of work in advanced economies, Sennett (1998) eloquently portrays the consequences of a new management culture and management practices that promote permanent restructuring, acute downsizing and new flexible ways of working as the holy grails of effective organization. Of course, not all businesses are guilty of the same excesses but enough are to leave us with a sense of anxiety about the future of strategy. In the final analysis, is strategic management only about maximizing financial capital or should we also be concerned with the generation of social capital? We leave the reader to ponder this question.

Final Thought

The major issue we should be considering, as managers and as citizens, is how to build sustainable enterprises and an economic reality that connects industry, society and the environment (Senge and Carstedt, 2001). Strategy, in the final analysis, is about deciding what kinds of organization and business we want for the society of the future.

CHAPTER 8

CASE STUDIES

In this final part of the book we have included a selection of short case studies. These are current business stories that are interesting in their own right and give insights into strategic issues facing business (and in one case the public sector) in the twenty-first century. In fact you may want to read them first so that you have a larger fact base for considering the different models and theories contained in the text.

The case studies are deliberately short so that they can be used to promote discussion within a typical teaching session. They can then be supplemented by the longer Harvard and Insead cases, which demand more detailed analysis and judgement.

As the cases were written in 2003 the stories were still unfolding. We would encourage you to read some of the articles on which the cases are based, to look at the company Web sites and to update your understanding of how the stories develop by looking at press and magazine Web sites. Most of the material for the cases is drawn from company Web sites and magazine articles, especially in *Fortune*, the *Economist*, *The Times*, the *Financial Times* and *Business Week*.

The cases are also intended to encourage you to prepare your own cases on companies in which you are interested and, where appropriate, on your own organisation. We have used this approach as a teaching method both for undergraduate and MBA examinations and assignments.

Each case has questions for consideration at the end. You may also like to identify themes across the cases, especially about industry structure, competitive advantage and strategic leadership.

What Business are we in? Boots: the Journey to Well-being

Historically, a leading UK retailer, the Boots Company, had a clear sense of its business mission. This was framed very much in terms of being 'chemists to the nation', providing, through its extensive range of retail outlets, medicines and attractive health and beauty products. Approximately 12.5 million customers visit a Boots The Chemists store every week and its offering includes over 25,000 health and beauty items. Boots possesses unique strength among retailers in being able to create a succession of brands – such as No. 7, the UK leader in cosmetics, over-the-counter medicines such as Strepsils, the painkiller Nurofen, the UK's leading painkiller, and, more recently, its Natural Collection – and supporting its retail operations with a strong manufacturing capability.

Boots' approach to strategy has been driven by the search for shareholder value as its prime goal. This focuses upon pursuing new opportunities with strong margin potential. It also means pulling out of areas where margins become unattractive and has led to withdrawal from leisure areas such as music, videos and cookware. This liberates retail space for new activities that increase focus and create more value. However, Boots has struggled with just what its focus is and what it stands for as a company. In essence, the last few years have seen it wrestling with the question 'What business are we in?' The company's own answer was 'Look good, feel good,' and the company is now focused upon a new strategic intent, 'well-being'.

It is the attempt/intent to own the term 'well-being' in the mind of the consumer that defines where Boots aspires to give its customers and it is where the Boots story currently stands. In the company's own words:

> Pharmacy remains the cornerstone of our business in the UK but now, as well as being 'chemists to the nation', we are laying the foundations of a future where we grow our range of health and beauty products and develop into related service markets. We are also Opticians, Dentists, Chiropodists and we offer an expanding range of specialist services, to cater for all the diverse wellbeing needs of our customers. Because 'looking good' is an important part of 'feeling good', Health and Beauty are natural companions and together they constitute Boots' established market territory. Interest in personal health and wellbeing continues to increase around the world and, at the dawn of a new century, we are taking Boots to the world in many different ways.

To support its well-being aspirations the company is developing its stores to provide an increasing range of health-related services such as chiropody, dentistry and osteopathy. It is Boots' perception that its entry into these markets is itself capable of stimulating market growth. For example, 50 per cent of its chiropody customers had never sought chiropody treatment previously. Half its dental customers had not visited a dentist in the previous five years.

Its chief executive talks about the change process Boots has embraced in recent years as 'more than skin-deep'. The 2001 annual report talked about 'reinventing the business' as part of a response to fundamental social and economic changes which include: increases in disposable income, particularly among women, key Boots customers; growing awareness of personal responsibility for individual health and fitness; demographic change towards an ageing population allied to increasing government reluctance to foot the whole bill for health care. In the words of Steve Russell:

Distinctions between health, beauty and general fitness are blurring in a broader pursuit of 'well-being'. People are becoming more aware of alternative treatments and therapies. They're more ready to experiment. But this is taking them into uncharted territory; they want to be reassured that they are in good hands. As one of the most trusted brands in Britain Boots is ideally placed to help them. . . . There is compelling evidence of the Boots brand's power to add authority and reassurance – even in such a well established and highly professional field as dentistry.

However, if the company now feels better able to answer the 'What business are we in?' question, investors also need to be convinced that it is capable of achieving its ambitions. Key investors see Boots as possessing traditional virtues such as knowing how to manage costs and margins. But investors also know that to achieve strong long-term growth the company will have to refocus on more than being more efficient. The future is finely balanced between unanswered and, for the present, unanswerable questions and a new strategic intent that will determine the company's future. The company is bullish. 'Can we find new ways to stimulate and inspire consumers? We can and we will – by becoming more relevant to the way people's health and beauty needs are evolving, with fresh ideas that command decent margins.' Investors wait to see if Boots can recreate itself in the new image to which it aspires.

End note

Boots CEO gets axe, chairman to quit

British health and beauty products retailer Boots said on Sunday it is to replace Steve Russell as chief executive as it strives to 'drive strategic change faster'.

Boots Chairman John McGrath will also step down when his term expires at the end of July 2003.

The management overhaul comes amid criticism that Boots has failed to meet rising competition from the major supermarkets such as Tesco.

The issue raised questions about strategy and pace of growth at the 150-year-old Nottingham-based retailer.

Boots' shares closed on Friday at 550p, down 6 per cent since the start of the year, to value the company at about £4.5 billion (US$7.15 billion). The shares are worth just over half of their peak of £10.80 seen in June 1998.

(Reuter's, 17:18:32 GMT, 15 December 2002)

Source: Boots' annual reports, 1998–2002.

QUESTIONS

1 How would you characterize the well-being mission?
2 What went wrong?
3 What is the future for Boots?

The Sad Fate of the Dodo

> What creature has ever been subjected to more ridicule and derision? (Stephen Jay Gould)

Some see the dodo as the ultimate lesson in extinction. It rivals the dinosaur as a symbol of how not to survive. The phrase 'dead as a dodo' has entered the language as a damning way to describe any project that has no hope of realization – totally dead, and for ever. First sighted by Portuguese or Dutch sailors in the forests of the island of Mauritius in the late 1500s, the dodo was totally extinct by 1681.

There are now no complete specimens of the dodo, so what we know about it is based on travellers' tales, drawings and painstaking scientific research. Scientists believe that the dodo evolved from a bird capable of flight into a flightless one. When the ancestors of the dodo landed on Mauritius they found a habitat plentiful in food and no predators. There was no need to expend the energy necessary for flight, so the bird stayed on the ground and, eventually, the flightless dodo evolved. However, when sailors landed on its island, the flightless bird had no means of escape. Indeed, escape was an alien concept to the bird, because it had never experienced predators.

So innocent and lacking in fear was it in the presence of the new arrivals that the sailors took its equanimity as evidence of stupidity. The dodo eventually became synonymous with slow, stupid and fat. Indeed, its name has been linked with this perception. Three origins have been suggested. The one most favoured is that the word 'dodo' comes from the Dutch word *dodoor*, meaning 'sluggard'. The second is that it may derive from the Portuguese *doudo*, meaning foolish or simple. Finally, there is the possibility the word is a variant of the Dutch *dodaer*, a seventeenth-century term used by sailors, meaning 'fat arse'.

The dodo was hunted as easy prey, though it was not considered particularly palatable. In the words of the eminent historian of evolution, Stephen Jay Gould, 'What could be easier to catch than a lumbering, giant, flightless pigeon?' It was hunted relentlessly, with sailors killing up to fifty birds at a time. Destruction of its forest habitat cut off its food supply. The animal's habitat was further ravaged by the animals the sailors brought with them – cats, pigs, monkeys and rats – which pillaged the dodo's ground nests of eggs.

A non-flying bird, a deterministic theory of evolution suggests, cannot hope to survive in such an environment. The extinction of the dodo is frequently cited as a prime example of natural selection. Recently, however, there have been new interpretations of the dodo's story. New evidence suggests that the dodo was not fat and slow-moving, that it was actually lithe and active. Rather than demonstrating the weakness of the dodo, its defenders suggest that the bird's fate illustrates the irresponsibility of those who disrupted its habitat. According to Stephen Jay Gould, the dodo was the first animal driven to death in modern times by human agency, a harbinger of far worse to come. The dodo's fate has even been read as a fable about the negative impact of human beings on the earth's eco-systems.

To add insult to injury, many commentators denigrate the dodo as doomed to extinction by its own inadequacies and by the species deterioration brought about by the easy life on Mauritius, a life free of predators and competition. Gould's commentary on this interpretation is dismissive: 'I suggest we need new concepts and metaphors to replace the false and constraining notions, however comforting, of predictable progress in the history of life (with sad but inevitable loss of inferior creatures) and sensible causality for all major events.' One wonders what new concepts and metaphors will deepen our understanding of business and what might replace the Darwinian notions endemic in the free-market ethos of contemporary capitalism?

How should we interpret the dodo's story? Now all that remains of what was once a perfectly adapted creature is a few bones and the Alice-in-Wonderland Dodo in Oxford University's Museum of Natural History. The latter consists of just a head, a leg and a foot! The rest is lost in time, an object of curiosity, self-fulfilling prophecies, some regret and increasing controversy.

Sources: 'The Mauritius Web Directory' (www.mauritiusdelight.com/dodohist.htm, 24 October 2002); S. J. Gould, 'The dodo and the caucus race', *Natural History*, 105, 11 (1996), 22–33.

QUESTIONS

1 Did the dodo deserve to survive?
2 What firms resemble the dodo?
3 How useful is the Darwinian idea of the 'survival of the fittest' for thinking about strategy?
4 Are there other metaphors that we might use to think about business?

Home Depot in the midst of Transformation

Home Depot is one of the world's leading and most admired retailers, and sixth in *Fortune*'s list of America's most admired companies. During its growth in the 1990s its earnings per share rose at a compound rate of 29 per cent (Pelepu, 2001). Based in Atlanta GA, it is the world's largest home improvement retailer, with a turnover of $15 billion in fiscal 2002. Home Depot employs 30,000 people ('associates') in its 1,500 warehouse-style stores located in the United States, Canada, Mexico and Puerto Rico. Yet, according to *Fortune*, 'The country's second largest retailer is in the midst of its own transformation – namely, from that of a hypergrowth upstart to a mature industry leader – and in the process the stock is getting hammered' (*Fortune*, 9 January 2002).

Bernie Marcus and Arthur Blank founded Home Depot in 1978. They conceived of it as a builders' supply store that was open to the public. 'Marcus was the CEO, a charismatic visionary that everyone seemed to like, and Blank was an accountant and a good second-in-command.' They made a good team, and during the first twenty years Home Depot grew faster than any retail chain, including Wal-mart. The concept is based on large stores in out-of-town locations, low competitive prices, large inventory, all on display, and an aggressive advertising programme to attract customers. This is normal warehouse retailing. But Home Depot went beyond that. W. C. Kim and R. Maubourgne (1999) describe how:

> Home Depot has created a new market of do-it-yourselfers out of ordinary home owners. So executives in Home Depot have made it their mission to bolster the competence and confidence of customers whose expertise in home repair is limited. They recruit sales assistants with significant trade experience. These assistants are trained to walk customers through any project – installing kitchen cabinets, for example, or building a deck. In addition Home Depot sponsors in-store clinics that teach customers such skills as electrical wiring, carpentry and plumbing . . . Essentially Home Depot offers the expertise of the professional home contractor at markedly lower prices than hardware stores'.

There was a lot of autonomy. The company was divided into nine regions that each did their own buying. Store managers were encouraged to run stores like independent businesses.

In 1997 Marcus became chairman and the board (reluctantly, it later transpired) appointed Blank to the CEO position. By this time they had led Home Depot to forty quarters of consecutive record financial results, the business had over 500 stores and was doing $431 million in sales. In 2000, now with 1,000 stores, Home Depot had been named Most Admired Speciality Retailer for nine years running. Yet the board was worried. Lowe's, Home Depot's main competitor, now competed with about 70 per cent of its stores in 70 per cent of its markets. In Robert Tillman it had an experienced retailer in charge who was listening to his customers and targeting the female market. The stores had wider aisles, neat displays and bright lighting.

Same-store sales growth (also called like-for-like sales) – which excludes sales from stores open less than a year – is the most closely watched measure of a retailer's performance. After years of superior performance, Home Depot's same-store sales had slowed and were now below Lowe's. Increasingly new stores were cannibalizing existing store sales. There was a danger of the market becoming saturated: on one analysis this would happen at 2,600 stores. (Home Depot and Lowe's now have 2,200 outlets between them.)

There was speculation that the problem might be that Home Depot's basic business model – 'a builders' warehouse that's open to the public' – might be less viable in a mature market place. It worked originally simply because it was unique. The market had become more sophisticated and had to meet the needs of at least three types of customer: the traditional DIY customers, buy-it-yourself customers', people who wanted to select the materials that went into their homes but who wanted someone else to install them, and professional customers (e.g. contractors, electricians, plumbers, landscapers, property maintenance managers). The market for professional customers was huge and it also involved a greater propensity for repeat business. Yet in 2000, according to Krishna Pelopu, in a Harvard Business School case study, 'It wasn't clear whether the decline in the company's stock price was primarily a function of the slowing economy, a reaction to an overvaluation of the stock, or a reflection of possible problems with the company's strategy for the future.' Nevertheless Blank as CEO was seen as arrogant and dismissive. He responded slowly to directors' calls and denied many of the problems they raised after their contracted visits to evaluate five stores a quarter. The board agreed to approach Bob Nardelli of General Electric.

Bob Nardelli had been vice-president, manufacturing, at GE in the 1980s, left for a general management role at Case equipment, returned to GE to become CEO of Transportation in 1992 and became CEO of Power Systems in 1995. He fully expected to move up to the top job and was devastated when Jack Welch passed him over in favour of Jeff Immelt. Ken Langone, a GE director, one of the original financial backers of Home Depot, and now their senior non-executive director, offered him the CEO's position. He took over in December 2000 and bcame chairman in January 2002. Nardelli's creed is 'There is an infinite capacity to improve upon everything you do' and he quickly set the goal to double sales and more than double profits by 2005. And, according to *Fortune*, 'he's also driven by a burning personal need: to prove that Jack Welch picked the wrong guy'. Nardelli's diagnosis was that:

> Home Depot had not put in place the systems, processes and disciplines that a $50 billion company needed. It had been in start-up mode for twenty years. Previous management seriously under-invested – no distribution centres, no appropriate IT. Computer systems were 'woeful'. Stores were getting shabby. And there was no general counsel, no chief marketing or chief financial officer function. 'It wasn't like you had 1,500 stores; you had 1,500 businesses,' says Mr Nardelli. 'It was clearly bugled that if you get a fax from Atlanta, tear it up; if you get a voice-mail, dump it. Home Depot was failing to harness its full buying clout and struggled even to do nationwide promotions on products. Not every store would stock a particular product, let alone sell it at the same price. (*Financial Times*, 8 July 2003)

His style is aggressive:

> He leads by example. Up at 5.00 a.m., he is in the office by 6:15 and usually works until at least 9.00 p.m. Saturday and Sunday are workdays –.and, unlike Blank, Nardelli has his executives in for weekend meetings. 'It's not a job,' he says. 'It's a life.' He is intensely hands-on: While Blank had ten people reporting to him and gathered them quarterly for business reviews, Nardelli meets with his twenty-one direct reports every Monday at noon, zeroing in on KPIs (key performance indicators, such as customer counts and average tickets) and action plans. 'I love data,' he effuses. 'I love to know what's going on in the company totally.' Former executives say that the new environment is 'command and control' and 'all business all the time'. (*Fortune*, June 2002)

So Nardelli started taking massive action. He:

- Centralized purchasing and merchandising.
- Eliminated the company's famous cash return policy, changing it to one of 'No receipt, then credit only,' saving an estimated $10 million annually.
- Launched a big initiative to receive products and stock shelves at night, freeing staff to spend more time with customers during the day.
- Invested $360 million in systems in the first year alone, including new data warehousing capability in partnership with IBM.

- Brought in a group of non-retail people, including marketing and finance officer roles and Dennis Donovan from GE (at a salary of $2.4 million), to head up a revamped HR function.

In terms of people Nardelli and Donovan have initiated:

- A revamped performance management and reward process. (Home Depot used to have 157 appraisal forms; now there are two for 295,000 employees.)
- 360 appraisal, using common grades such as 'gets results', 'develops people', 'drives change' and 'displays character'.
- Succession planning, where the CEO participates in performance reviews of each of Home Depot's 130 senior managers.
- A leadership institute at Atlanta headquarters that's modelled on GE's Crotonville. ('They're building the most systematic teaching organization that I've seen in a retailer,' says Noel Tichy, a management professor at the University of Michigan Business School, who once ran the Crotonville facility. 'Wal-mart does a great job training people in the stores, but at Home Depot there's more of a mind set to build leadership throughout the organization'.)

As for growth, Nardelli is continuing with the 200 stores a year opening programme, piloting Home Depot Pro stores for the $200 billion professional market, building a corporate business selling timber, lighting and other products to any company that builds or operates facilities. He has done deals with Disney on branded merchandise, and with Dunkin' Donuts to provide in-store restaurants. He also sees a major ($180 billion) market in home services (e.g. appliance repair, home security, pest control and home improvement finance). There has been some overseas expansion in South America and there are rumours that he is looking at acquiring B&Q in the United Kingdom.

So much change resulted in huge disruption. Products were out of stock. Customer complaints rocketed. Same-store sales went negative. The share price more than halved during 2002 (having risen from $39 when Nardelli took over in 2000 to $53 in 2001, then slipped to $40 in 2002 and $21 in 2003). Nardelli was accused by analysts of 'tinkering with one of the world's most successful retail formulas . . . with near disastrous results' and of doing too much too fast. 'But it wasn't a matter of too fast,' he insists. 'Quite honestly, we should have done more, better. My error was, we didn't execute well enough' (*Financial Times*, 8 July 2003). And by centralizing the chain's purchasing function and cutting down the number of suppliers Nardelli has increased gross margins by one percentage point. He inherited and has maintained a strong balance sheet (*Fortune*, 21 January 2003). The company message now is that the biggest changes are complete:

> 'The Home Depot is beginning to gain traction from the transformational initiatives launched last year,' said Bob Nardelli, chairman, president and CEO. 'We introduced new products, increased the overall inventory levels in our stores, and introduced a cohesive, nationwide marketing program. Collectively, these initiatives helped us perform through a tough environment. Our store reinvestment strategy is delivering a cleaner, brighter shopping environment as we continued with our store resets and

remodels. Our 315,000 associates focused on sales, service and execution during the quarter and delivered the highest average ticket in company history' (Home Depot press release, 20 May 2003).

Home Depot is doing things it could not have done before. It has launched its first national marketing campaign, under the slogan 'You can do it. We can help.' Same-store sales are still negative but improving ahead of forecast. The share price was back up to $31 in 2003. Sales of higher-value items are increasing. A specially designed $2,000 tractor mower from John Deere – a brand that would once have turned up its nose at working with Home Depot – has been a smash hit. Home Depot has also 'dramatically increased its appliances sales in the past two years, rising from being a minor player to the third largest seller (6.4 per cent of a $21 billion market, behind Sears and Lowe's). Really the jury is still out: Nardelli is highly motivated to succeed but he negotiated his contract at the height of the dot-com era, so even if dismissed is likely to walk away a multi-millionaire.

Sources: Home Depot news release, 20 May 2003; 'Home Depot now third in appliances', *Atlanta Journal*, 5 August 2003; K. W. Chan and R. Maubourgne, 'Creating new market space', *Harvard Business Review*, January–February 1999; K. Pelepu, 'Home Depot Inc in the new millenium', Harvard Business School case 2001; 'Home Depot: something to prove', *Fortune*, 9 June 2002; 'Home Depot: a do-it-yourself disaster?' *Economist*, 9 January 2003; 'Can Home Depot get its groove back?' *Fortune*, 21 January 2003; Neil Buckley and Betty Liu, 'Fixer puts the final touches to a DIY refit', *Financial Times*, 8 July 2003.

QUESTIONS

1 How would you describe the development of Home Depot prior to Nardelli's appointment?
2 How would you characterize Nardelli's approach to managing strategic change?
3 What are the key business drivers in this industry?

The National Health Service: a case of too many trusts?

The National Health Service is not short of strategies or structures. It has a national ten-year plan drawn up in 2000 by the Secretary of State at the Department of Health (DoH) and the Wanlass report commissioned by the Treasury. The purpose and vision of the NHS plan are 'to give the people of Britain a health service fit for the twenty-first century: a health service designed around the patient'. The Wanless report extends the vision of the NHS to 2020, conducts a gap analysis, and produces three scenarios with costings for bridging the gap.

The plan led to a major restructuring of the NHS in an initiative called 'Shifting the Balance of Power'. There are now over 600 NHS trusts. These comprise: twenty-eight Strategic Health Authorities, Hospital Trusts, 303 Primary Care

Trusts (covering GPs, community nursing, opticians, pharmacies, etc.), Mental Health Trusts, Ambulance Trusts, Workforce Confederations (workforce planning) and Special Trusts (e.g. the Blood Service). Each has its own organizational charter with local strategies and plans. All have their own executive and non-executive committees and consultative committees involving patients, carers and professional groups.

There is now a Modernisation Board charged with delivering best practice, including National Service Frameworks that lay down best practice for key treatments like coronary heart disease. The Commission for Health Improvement (CHI) with the support of the Audit Commission inspects every NHS organization every four years. The National Institute of Clinical Excellence (NICE) is there to give clear guidance on the best treatments and interventions, vetting the medicines the NHS should pay for. Human Resources has its own policy document (*Human Resources in the National Plan*) and there is a Human Resources performance framework with targets for improving working lives, working together and developing the work force. While the NHS plan espouses the principle of subsidiarity there are over 400 centrally driven targets.

There is one chief executive, Nigel Crisp, but, to quote a perceptive article in *The Times* by Patience Wheatcroft (5 November 2002):

> The outwardly affable Crisp clearly has a steely core and might stand a chance of pushing through the reforms on which he has started if he had a board prepared to support him from the sidelines. But Crisp has to rely on politicians to stay solidly behind him and that is not their way, particularly with something so sensitive to the voters as the NHS. . . . The NHS is in danger of having two chief executives rather than one, and however hard Crisp is striving to achieve change internally, public perception is generally that it is the minister who is in charge. And so, in the end, he is.

And there are of course a number of professional and managerial cultures. The hospital consultants who turned down a new contract which would have reduced their professional autonomy, the GPs who run their own practices, the nurses who feel undervalued, the allied health professionals who feel unrecognized and the ancillary staff who feel (like the rest) underpaid. And, of course, the managers, who are often a cross between civil servants and business managers.

The national plan contains a 'snapshot' which gives a clear picture of the scope of the NHS. On a typical day there are:

- 90,000 doctors
- 300,000 nurses
- 150,000 healthcare assistants
- 22,000 midwives
- 13,500 radiographers
- 15,000 occupational therapists
- 7,500 opticians
- 10,000 health visitors
- 6,500 paramedics

- 90,000 porters, cleaners and other support staff
- 11,000 pharmacists
- 19,000 physiotherapists
- 24,000 managers
- 105,000 practice staff in GP surgeries

And on a typical day in the NHS:

- Almost a million people visit their family doctor.
- 130,000 go to the dentist for a check-up.
- 33,000 people get the care they need in Accident and Emergency.
- 8,000 people are carried by NHS ambulances.
- 1.5 million prescriptions are dispensed.
- 2,000 babies are delivered.
- 25,000 operations are carried out, including 320 heart operations and 125 kidney operations.
- 30,000 people receive a free eye test.
- District nurses make 100,000 visits.

And we know there is a shortage of professional staff, especially consultants, GPs and nurses, and it takes three years to train a nurse, five to train a GP and fifteen to become a consultant. Yet by and large the NHS does a good job:

> Despite all its problems, satisfaction with today's health service is often high. A survey found that 83 per cent of people were satisfied with their GP, and recent users are more satisfied than the general public. While satisfaction with GPs is generally higher than satisfaction with hospitals, patients are satisfied with the friendliness of hospital staff and the quality of care provided. (Wanlass report)

As Wanlass continues:

> The ethos of the NHS – comprehensive care available to all – commands universal support. Over 90 per cent of people believe that he NHS should be available free of charge when they need it. The Review has assumed that, even though people will expect ever more from the health service over he next twenty years, public support for the values of the NHS will remain firm. Whether this is right will depend on the achievement of both the improvements promised and a general belief that money is being well spent.

So the government has ruled out alternative forms of funding such as insurance or privatization, arguing:

> The public service ethic [is something that] most private companies envy. The NHS is an organisation glued together by a bond of trust between staff and patient or, what some have called, 'principled motivation'. Our aim is to renew that for today's world, not throwing away those values to market mechanisms, but harnessing them to drive up performance.

The public are clear about what they want: The NHS plan contains the top ten things the public want to see:

- more and better-paid staff – more doctors, more nurses, more therapists and scientists;
- reduced waiting times – reductions in waiting overall, for appointments and on trolleys and in casualty;
- new ways of working – including 'bringing back Matron';
- care centred on patients – action on cancelled operations, more convenient services;
- higher quality of care – especially for cancer and heart disease;
- better facilities – more cleanliness, better food, getting the basics right;
- better conditions for NHS staff – reward and recognition for the work they do;
- better local services – improvements in local hospitals and surgeries;
- ending the postcode lottery – high-quality treatment assured wherever people live;
- more prevention – better help and information on healthy living.

And there is a vision – 'a health service designed around the patient' – which Wanless expands in a section on 'the health service in 2022':

Patients are at the heart of the health service of the future. With access to better information, they are involved fully in decisions – not just about treatment, but also about the prevention and management of illness. The principle of patient and user involvement has become ever more important and the health service has moved beyond an 'informed consent 'to an 'informed choice 'approach. The health service is able to recruit and retain the staff that it requires with the right levels of skills. No longer do chronic shortages among key staff groups act as a constraint on the timely delivery of care. Health care workers are highly valued and well motivated as a result of better working conditions and the opportunity to develop their skills to take on new and more challenging roles for which they are appropriately rewarded.

Modern and integrated information and communication technology (ICT) is being used to full effect, joining up all levels of health and social care and in doing so delivering significant gains in efficiency . . .

With support from the NHS, people increasingly take responsibility for their own health and well-being . . .

When patients need to see their GP, or seek other forms of primary care, they get appointments quickly with staff who are pro-active in identifying what care is required and who is best placed to deal with it.

Both major reports agree on the underlying problem:

In essence the problem is that despite the best efforts of doctors, nurses and other staff the NHS is not sufficiently centred around the needs of individual patients. There are two major reasons why this is the case. First, decades of under-investment and second, because the NHS is a 1940s system operating in a twenty-first-century world.

Today, successful services thrive on their ability to respond to the individual needs of their customers. We live in a consumer age. Services have to be tailor-made not mass-produced, geared to the needs of users not the convenience of producers. The NHS has been too slow to change its ways of working to meet modern patient expectations for fast, convenient, twenty-four-hour, personalised care.

In addition to the new structures described above the NHS plan offers more money to fund extra investment in facilities:

- 7,000 extra beds in hospitals and intermediate care;
- over 100 new hospitals by 2010 and 500 new one-stop primary care centres;
- over 3,000 GP premises modernized and 250 new scanners;
- clean wards – overseen by 'modern Matrons' – and better hospital food;
- modern IT systems in every hospital and GP surgery;

and investment in staff:

- 7,500 more consultants and 2,000 more GPs;
- 20,000 extra nurses and 6,500 extra therapists
- 1,000 more medical school places childcare support for NHS staff with 100 on-site nurseries.

Granted the changes in structures and extra investment, the key argument is that change is now a matter of culture and behaviour: embracing modernization or, as the Director of Primary Care terms it, 'collaborative contestability'.

Sources: NHS plan, available on the NHS Web site; Wanlass report, available on the Treasury Web site.

QUESTIONS

1 In what ways is strategy in the public sector different from in the private sector?
2 How would you wish to deal with the complexity of the NHS?
3 Is the NHS 'business model' still 'the envy of the world' or is it 'broken'?

Nokia: a Great Company in a Turbulent Market

In its November 2002 special report on Nokia versus Microsoft, the *Economist* reported that in 2002: 400 million phones were sold (10 per cent with built-in mobile cameras), there were now more than 1 billion mobile phone users, more mobile phones than fixed-line phones, and the number of internet-connected phones is overtaking the number of internet-connected PCs. The latest phones, with colour screens, cameras, music players and downloadable games, have as much computer power as the desktop computer did ten years ago. Yet 'the troubled switch to 3G technology means the mobile telecom industry is in turmoil':

- The market for handsets is saturated after nearly a decade of double-digit growth. Seventy per cent of Europeans and 50 per cent of the US population now own a mobile phone.
- Revenues from voice calls are flat – so companies are looking to new services such as photo messaging, gaming and location-based information for revenue growth.
- Wireless Application Protocol (WAP), a cut-down, simple application of the Web, has failed to excite users or generate revenue streams.
- 3G services have been delayed everywhere and are only just appearing in Europe.

So who are the key players in this complex and turbulent industry?

Nokia, Motorola, Siemens, Sony, Ericsson and Samsung make about 80 per cent of the phones. They also have a joint venture in Symbian software, an open and flexible standard that permits compatibility and constant innovation. There are other alliances such as the Mobile Processor Interface Alliance and the Digital Home Working Group which are also promoting compatibility and ease of use. The mobile phone operators (Vodaphone, Orange, T-mobile and O2 in the United Kingdom) act as the hub between customers, handset makers and content providers. Many of them are saddled with huge debts after paying billions for 3G licences.

Success in 3G will depend on finding ways of selling content and services: both the media companies and the banks could enter the market as 'mobile virtual network operators' (MVNOs). Currently BskyB, Vodaphone and 3 are bidding for the rights to show ninety-second clips of premier football matches (*Times*, 6 August 2003).

But 3G is also an opportunity for the Japanese and Korean manufacturers to enter Europe and for the Europeans to enter Japan. Ericsson is teaming up with Sony and Toshiba with Siemens. Samsung, already dominant in Korea and America, has a track record of producing reliable, easy-to-use phones. And on the UK high street Phones 4U is launching a high-street price war aimed at rivals Carphone Warehouse and the Link in a drive to become market leader (*Times*, 4 August 2003).

Nokia is the major player in the mobile phone market. Its share of the global market increased from 36 per cent in 2002 to 39 per cent in 2003 (50 per cent in Europe) – it outsells its three closest rivals combined. It now has annual sales of US$30 billion across 130 countries, selling five phones every second. It has core competences in radio technology, digital signal processing, electronics manufacturing, software platforms and architecture. According to the *Economist*, Nokia's Series 60 software could yet emerge as the mobile equivalent of Microsoft's Windows. The company has a track record of design innovations, including user-changeable handset covers, scroll-down text bars and predictive text messaging. It introduced thirty-four new phones in 2002 and is heading for a similar number in 2003. Forty per cent of its employees are involved in R&D, which accounts for a steady 10 per cent of sales and an annual spend of US$3 billion in 2002.

Since 1999 Nokia has presented itself as the world's leading design house for mobile communication, launching its model 8210 during the 1999 Paris fashion week and portraying its phones in the media as cultural artefacts and icons. Surveys show that consumers rate Nokia above all other mobile phone brands, its customers are more loyal to Nokia than to their mobile phone operator, and in 2002 Nokia was the world's sixth most valuable brand valued at some US$30 million (Interbrand). Club Nokia enables it to keep close to its customers and sell units and accessories that would normally go via the telephone operator or retailer.

The company has a flat, non-hierarchical structure based around Nokia Mobile Phones, Nokia Networks, Nokia Ventures Organization (including an Insight and Foresight team which seeks out disruptive technologies, new business models and promising entrepreneurs) and Nokia Research Centre. Its mobile phone business has been further divided around nine business segments, including one focused on CDMA networks, an entry product group aimed at emerging markets, an imaging group producing camera phones, a gaming and entertainment group (responsible for the N-gage games machine) and a business devices group (responsible for a new phone, mobile e-mail and messaging machines).

Jorma Olla has been with the company since 1985 and since 1990 has led the turn-round and growth strategy with four close colleagues. 'Almost every assignment is given to a team, and managing the company is no exception.' Collaborative working is encouraged, and Nokia is involved in a wide range of joint and collaborative ventures aimed at growing the market and making life easier for the consumer. Now half the employees are outside Finland, leading *Fortune* to quote one of Nokia's American directors: 'Nokia is in the unique position that it has got a group of managers that have been working together for years – and now they've got a lot of senior people from outside who can shake things up' (*Fortune*, May 2000).

Nokia is in the European *Fortune* 'top ten' companies to work for, and the Nokia way comprises a set of values and a strategic planning process that encourages participative contribution, a clear sense of direction and disciplined execution. A new HR director has introduced upgraded performance management and reward processes. However, its mobile telecom equipment business (where Nokia competes against Ericsson, Lucent, Nortel and Motorola) is loss-making because of capital spending cuts by the telecoms operators. Nokia is also playing catch-up in the CDMA market (the digital standard championed by Qualcomm of San Diego and adopted by most US cellular operators), the fastest-growing sector in the United States and Asia, of which its share is less than 10 per cent.

Nevertheless the *Economist* predicts an interesting battle, concluding that 'Nokia has achieved its dominance not through ownership of proprietary technology but from its ability to innovate around open standards, from its strong brand and from its impressive logistics' (23 November 2002).

Sources: 'The Internet untethered', *Economist*, 11 October 2001; 'Nokia *v.* Microsoft: the fight for digital dominance', *Economist*, 23 November 2002; 'Computing's new shape', *Economist*, 23 November 2002; 'Calling for a renewable future', *Fastcompany* 70, May 2003; 'Ten great companies to work for', *Fortune*, March 2002; 'What makes Nokia so good?' *Fortune*, May 2000.

QUESTIONS

1 To what extent is this an attractive market to be in?
2 What are Nokia's main strengths, weaknesses, threats and opportunities?
3 From Nokia's perspective, produce a best and worst case scenario for 2007.

Rexam: a Classic Transformation

Rexam's 'transformation from cluttered conglomerate to pure consumer packaging maker' is a classic case of combining market positioning, portfolio management and internal resource building. It also then leaves the classic growth question: what next? Rexam gained entry into the FTSE 100 index in 2002. The company name is not well known, partly because of its history and partly because the company is in the support services – 'the polite name for a raft of largely dissimilar companies that do not have a sector of their own' (*Times*, 2003).

Rexam was originally part of Bowater, thirty years ago a major UK paper and pulp business. After a period of unfocused and unsuccessful diversification Bowater Inc demerged into a US-listed paper business while the remainder was later renamed Rexam. Rolf Borjesson, who joined as chief executive in 1996, described the business: 'We were in everything. Just name it. We were in it. We were printing stamps in New Zealand, phone cards in Sao Paulo, corrugated boxes in the Midlands, diesel engines in Australia, a windows business, there was even a nursery' (*Sunday Times*, 2000). Of the diversified group, about 50 per cent was in packaging, and only about half of that in consumer packaging. Borjesson decided to make the 25 per cent in consumer packaging the core. This meant selling off the remaining 75 per cent, and replacing it with acquisitions (*Financial Times*, 2001).

Consumer packaging, defined as 'the packaging that carries the brand message to the customer', is a large global market worth around £300 billion. It has proved to be an essentially predictable and non-cyclical business, as people tend to consume as much in good times as in bad. It is a relatively mature business with annual long-term growth of around 4 per cent (annual report, 2002). To quote Borjesson, 'Why consumer packaging? Because it's a very stable business. It's difficult to imagine a world without consumer packaging – at least, I can't think how you would sell margarine, ice cream, wine or water without it . . . if you can grow with GDP plus a few percentage points you are doing better than average in the economy' (*Sunday Times*, 2002). An article in the *Rexam World* analyses the packaging business:

It is a £250+ billion global business whose top ten players account for just over12 per cent of the market. Brand owners are constantly striving for ways to differentiate their products, and packaging is one of the key tools at their disposal. Consolidation and customers shrinking their supplier rosters have meant that size is become increasingly crucial. Large customers are more likely to forge long-term alliances with large and reliable suppliers who can provide packaging to certain specifications on a global basis. Populations around the globe continue to grow, and as emerging countries pass certain GDP thresholds packaging consumption is set to accelerate. Lifestyles also affect packaging. The rise in urban population and urban life is set to further accelerate the rate of growth of packaging. Smaller households also encourage packaging growth. With the world population growing older, there is an increase in the demand for health care, personal care and beauty products. Packaging will come under greater pressure from an environmental point of view, which will challenge packaging companies to come up with new solutions. But it will not disappear. It has become an indispensable part of everyday life, even though we may seldom reflect on the fact.

Rexam is now one of the world's top five global consumer packaging groups, serving global and regional customers in the beverages, beauty, health care and food segments. Customers include Anheuser-Busch, Avon, Cadbury-Schweppes, Cardinal Health, Carlsberg, Coca-cola, Coor's, Heineken, Holsten, Interbrew, L'Oréal, LVMH, Pepsi-cola, Procter & Gamble, Red Bull, SAB Miller, Scottish & Newcastle and Unilever.

Rexam's two major acquisitions were PLM (where Borjesson had been chief executive before joining Rexam) and American National Can (ANC). PLM, acquired for £380 million, was one of Europe's largest packaging groups. ANC, bought for £1.5 billion, was the world's second largest beverage can producer. 'The acquisition of . . . PLM, in February 1999, gave us critical mass in our packaging operations. The purchase of American National Can in mid-2000 consolidated our position and made us a global leader in beverage cans' (annual report, 2002). At the same time, in the three years up to 2002, Rexam sold over thirty of its non-core businesses, bringing in nearly £800 million to pay down debt. For the year to 31 December 2002 the company had turnover of approximately £3 billion, with pre-tax profits around £274 million.

Beverage packaging accounted for nearly 75 per cent of sales, making Rexam Europe's largest drinks can maker, and the third largest in the United States. To make the US business profitable:

> Rexam took out about 10 to 12 per cent of its capacity in the US, which prompted others in the highly concentrated US can market to cut capacity, hence ending the price war. The result was that Rexam was able to push through a price rise of 5 per cent in the US, starting from the beginning of 2001, which triggered a rapid and sustained rise in the company's shares. It was this price rise that earned Borjesson the loyalty of his shareholders and which was largely responsible for Rexam's entry into the FTSE 100. (*Times*, 2003)

Its growth is also being driven by the company's decision to consolidate the European glass bottle industry. Rexam made several further acquisitions, including Nienburger Glass, in 2001, for £65 million, and Luner Glas in 2002, for £33 million. Rexam now has twelve glassworks, seven of them in Germany, the largest glass market in Europe. The industry in Germany is now relatively well consolidated, with the top three having some 75 per cent of the market. Borjesson says: 'The glass market in Europe is fragmented. We can build a situation that is very similar to the beverage can structure. We can take out cost. We can get a better pricing environment and we can get better margins.' He dismisses any glass acquisitions in the United States because the industry there has already been consolidated and is making very reasonable returns.

Plastics is now the fastest-growing sector of the packaging market, and Rexam is one of only two global manufacturers in beauty packaging, supplying miniature spray samples and cosmetics pumps, lipstick cases and compacts. In foods it produces containers for yellow fats and dairy products. Rexam's Medical Packaging division offers a complete line of pharma blister films, barrier films for tubes, and sterilization and waste management supplies.

Rexam's vision incorporates shareholders, customers, staff and the environment (although it is suffering from the German decision to levy a deposit on disposable drink cans).

> Our vision is to become the leading consumer packaging Group in each of our chosen market segments. . . . Quality will always take precedence over quantity. However, we have to be both sufficiently large and have the global presence to meet our customers' requirements wherever they may be or want to be.
>
> Leading equally refers to our manufacturing capabilities, the quality of our products, the level of service we offer, our ability to innovate and the efficient management of the supply chain.
>
> Enlightened, motivated and satisfied employees will ensure that customer needs are readily met, and the business will then prosper to the benefit of shareholders. To maintain this cycle of success we will be No. 1 with our employees in terms of providing the kind of working environment in which people can grow, feel respected and fulfilled.
>
> We also want to be seen as a leader in the eyes of society at large in terms of the way in which we act in the community and the responsibilities we assume as an employer and citizen.

The vision is backed up by a centrally co-ordinated customer satisfaction survey: a lean enterprise initiative (which incorporates Six Sigma, supply chain innovation and new products such as refillable plastic bottles), a thorough GE-type management review process, an intensive leadership assessment programme, a training programme that addresses the fundamentals of motivation, and a common team meeting process to structure internal communications in all businesses. The 'Rexam Way', a group-wide cultural programme:

> covers the way we work and behave towards each other, and the way we develop, implement and manage various projects and programmes. It also determines the way we act towards customers, shareholders and other stakeholders. It is based on a set of four core values – Continuous Improvement, Teamwork, Trust and Recognition – that form the foundation of all that we do, and which we consider key to driving our company forward.

As for the future, Borjesson argues that Rexam has completed its transformation to a consumer packaging group and does not need to do any more company-changing deals. 'There will not be another big spectacular step. The strategy is in place and we are going to grow our business. We are well positioned in our chosen segments. I am confident that we have the management team and that we are sufficiently well acquainted with the various materials, end uses and the global dimensions of packaging to be able to exploit the opportunities that are there' (chief executive's report in the annual report, 2002).

Sources: *Rexam World*, autumn 2001; Rexam annual review, 2002; interview with Rolf Borjesson, *Sunday Times*, 2002; company profile, *Times*, 7 July 2003; 'Rexam travels long road on journey to recapture focus', *Financial Times*, 28 August 2001.

QUESTIONS

1 How attractive is the industry?
2 How would you analyse Rexam's business and management strategies?
3 Is this classic Porter strategy?

Sainsbury: Stuck in the Middle Again

> Nothing in business beats the thrill of a good old-fashioned take-over battle. And the fight to win Safeway, Britain's fourth-largest supermarket chain, seems destined to become a classic. After Safeway's management agreed to a friendly merger for £2.6 billion (US$4.2 billion) with a rival, Wm Morrison, on 9 January, no fewer than five other potential bidders have emerged. (*Economist*, 23 January 2003)

These naturally included Safeway's other main rivals: J. Sainsbury, Wal-mart (which owns Asda) and Tesco. The others, Kohlberg Kravis Roberts (KKR), a private equity firm, and Philip Green, owner of the retail chains BhS and Arcadia, intend to take the firm private.

Sir Peter Davis, Sainsbury's group chief executive, called the bid 'a defining moment in British retailing'. And for weeks the *Times* reported the odds on each bidder on the front page of its business section. In March the bid was referred to the Competition Commission. In August the commission delivered its report to the Trade and Industry Secretary, who was expected to give a final verdict by the end of September 2003. What is the background? According to the *Economist*:

> Sir Peter is right to argue that retailing is at a watershed. After enjoying boom conditions in Britain and America for far longer than other industries, retailers are finally facing recession. So far the industry has found no real solutions to the problems of slowing demand and price deflation, apart from aggressive discounting, which further damages margins.
>
> Richard Hyman, head of Verdict, a British retail consultancy, believes it is no coincidence that there is a fight over Safeway at a time when margins are under pressure. 'The retail industry is maturing. Operating-cost inflation is outpacing retail-price inflation. The only response is to raise volumes, either by pinching market share or buying it'. The Safeway deal fits the pattern. Morrison and Sainsbury's expect synergies of between £250 million and £400 million a year from merging stores and greater buying clout'. (*Economist*, 16 January 2003)

And as the *Sunday Times* comments, 'When Davis took the helm at Sainsbury in March 2000, sales growth of 6 per cent was not uncommon among food retailers. But that was during a boom when consumers were not so penny-conscious. In today's economic environment, people have become much more cautious' (*Sunday Times* 20 July 2003). So who are the key players?

Safeway UK, originally but no longer owned by the US Safeway chain, has 480 stores. Under the leadership of Carlos Criado-Perez it had been winning at least a public relations battle through a strategy of store refurbishment, selective price reductions and giving store managers more autonomy to fight local competition. But, says Criado-Perez, 'It is the relatively small size of Safeway that prevents it lowering prices to the same level as its rivals,' and he admits his strategy would never enable Safeway to catch up with its rivals. 'Each year Tesco grows by 10–15 per cent of Safeway, so we will never catch up' (*Times*, 15 August 2003). So the board decided to look for a 'white knight' when it feared that Wal-mart might put in a bid. Hence the agreement with Morrison's (which retracted when the other bids were announced).

Morrison's has 119 stores, mainly in the north of England, and is planning to open another fifteen over the next two years, including expansion into Scotland. Buying Safeway would give Wm Morrison a foothold in the south and a national presence, taking its market share as high as 15 per cent. In 2003 Morrison's announced thirty-six years of unbroken profit growth, a 14 per cent year-on-year profit increase and like-for-like sales up 5.3 per cent (*Guardian*, 18 March 2003). Alan Leighton, former Asda chief executive, describes Sir Ken Morrison, whose family owns 30 per cent of the company, as 'streets ahead of everybody in terms of retailing'. Sir Ken favours no-nonsense low-price offerings in stores which are laid out like a classic high-street operation. 'As for home shopping on the Internet, he comments that he last delivered groceries on a bike and does not intend to start again now' (*Guardian*, 10 January 2003).

Morrison's bid is favoured by suppliers (NOP research) because it would preserve a broad base of retailers and prevent Tesco, Asda and Sainsbury from further increasing their buying power. Similarly the Competition Commission is thought to favour Morrison's, as there would be at least three major players promoting 'everyday low prices'.

Led by Terry Leahy, Tesco, with nearly 2,000 UK stores and a number of retail formats (Superstore, Extra, Metro and Express) is the United Kingdom's largest and most successful retailer. Safeway would lift Tesco's share to an uncompetitive 36 per cent and many see its bid as a ploy to ensure that all the bids were referred to the Competition Commission. Its strategy is clearly stated in its annual report. Firstly to develop and maintain the core business; secondly to expand its non-food range (televisions, computers, clothes; cosmetics and toiletries – in 2001 its sales in this category overtook those of Boots The Chemists). Thirdly to expand services: on-line shopping, credit cards, utility payments, etc. (in association with the Royal Bank of Scotland). And finally, international expansion through a steady series of joint ventures and acquisitions in Central Europe and Asia, where it now has over 40 per cent of its retail space. All this puts Tesco in a strong position. According to the *Economist*:

Though it is possible that Tesco could stumble in its turn, it is currently extending its lead, using size as a weapon. While British rivals such as Sainsbury's and Safeway try to improve profitability, Tesco is deliberately keeping its margins flat, ploughing back into lower prices the gains it reaps from economies of scale. That brings more sales, and so more scale economies. This virtuous circle is similar to the one followed with such deadly efficiency by Wal-mart in America. (*Economist*, 9 August 2001)

Meanwhile, in July 2003 Asda overtook Sainsbury for the first time to become the country's second largest supermarket group, after Tesco. Even more than Tesco it has the buying power to offer a wide range of goods at low prices. Yet its UK growth potential is limited by its store portfolio (259 stores and nineteen depots), granted the tight planning restrictions on further out-of-town shopping (although there is a hint that a deal was done with politicians when Wal-mart entered the United Kingdom). Wal-mart is also under pressure because of doubts over the execution of its international strategy, especially in Germany. It put in a last-minute proposal to the commission based on an offer to sell 100 stores to Morrison's (otherwise the bid would take Asda's market share to 26 per cent, just behind Tesco) (*Financial Times*, 15 August 2003).

And so to Sainsbury. Its recent history is described by Seth and Randall (1999). The founding family owned it wholly until 1973. By the 1970s and 1980s Sainsbury's had developed into a highly integrated enterprise with a uniquely powerful food brand thanks to early visionary thinking, persistence with established values and consistent leadership. Sainsbury's possessed leading scale efficiencies, the lowest costs, best systems and a unique and highly valuable brand reputation. Sainsbury's was led by six family chairmen over four generations. Its commitment to long-term objectives in addition to the dominant presence of family directors led to powerful autocratic leadership, risk-averse decision making, management by results and a dependence culture. Within the prevailing environment this generated exceptional growth and profits and led to a dominant position in the retail market.

However, the decade of the 1990s was characterised by a period of intense strategic challenge for the retail company as Sainsbury's experienced problems in its core business. Sainsbury's suffered a decline in performance and lost its premier position with UK customers when Tesco's market share overtook that of Sainsbury's in 1995. Between 1995 and 1999 Sainsbury's suffered an overall decrease in profits before tax of 6.4 per cent whilst Tesco, its main rival during that period, expanded profits by 52.8 per cent. Sainsbury's had 16 per cent of the market, but Tesco was No. 1, with 21 per cent, and the gap between them was widening. In 1999 Sainsbury's confronted its performance when the firm's financial crisis finally forced action.

Sir Peter Davis, who had left because he believed the top job would be reserved to the family, was bought back to reverse the company's falling share price, profitability and market share. He took immediate action under the banner of a 'total business transformation programme' in which the company:

- focused on its core competence in food retailing: 'Our objective is to be the first for food, we are aiming at people who are interested in food as opposed to people who eat to live';

- signed up Jamie Oliver, the celebrity chef, to publicize the company and appeal to younger customers;
- invested £2 billion on refurbishing its stores and opening modern distribution centres while upgrading and outsourcing its IT function to Accenture;
- was one of the launch partners in the Nectar loyalty card scheme;
- announced plans to open up to 100 convenience stores on the forecourts of Shell petrol stations;
- slashed costs – savings are on course to reach £960 million by 2005, above the original £700 million target.

Other initiatives have been less successful. Sainsbury:

- sold its DIY chain, Homebase, to Permira, the private equity group, for £750 million (Permira sold Homebase just two years later for £900 million);
- set up a pilot venture with Boots to sell health and beauty products in the supermarket (the arrangement was ended early in 2003);
- devised Savacentre, a new brand to try to appeal to customers in lower-income areas. Sainsbury expected that Savacentre stores could ultimately generate £500 million of sales. But only about fourteen stores have been tested;
- relaunched its non-food items, but to date has struggled to match its rivals' success in this area;
- held talks but then abandoned a joint venture to build homes on surplus land around its supermarkets, by building on top of car parks;
- proposed the purchase of 171 Somerfield stores, but this has been referred to the Competition Commission.

Although profits have grown, from £549 million to £695 million, like-for-like sales growth was only 1.3 per cent at year-end in 2003 – far lower than the figures at Tesco (4.6 per cent) and Wm Morrison (5.3 per cent). The share price has fallen 2.1 per cent, while over the same period Tesco has climbed 17.4 per cent. And the company has failed to build up non-food sales, which account for 13 per cent of Sainsbury's turnover, compared with 18 per cent at Tesco and a fifth at Asda (*Times*, 20 July 2003).

So what's the verdict? 'What Davis has got right is to get some urgency into the business and accelerate the systems development, but the concern is whether he is leaving some of his customers behind by going into premium products,' says Paul Smiddy, a food analyst at Baird, the investment bank (*Times*, 15 August 2003).

> Sir Peter may have stabilised the business in profit terms in the three years that he has been in charge. But he appears incapable of stopping the onward march of Tesco and Asda, which drive their top line with a ferocious focus on everyday low prices. Arguably, there has been too much investment in stores in the south of England, and too little investment in genuine innovation to update areas such as the bakery and delicatessen counters that shoppers see. (*Financial Times*, 21 July 2003)

But the issue on which Sir Peter is most vulnerable is his decision to ignore the widespread criticism that the store is expensive. As a consequence Sainsbury is losing ground to Tesco and Asda, both of which have everyday low pricing. The quality-food end of the market is dominated by Waitrose and Marks & Spencer, niche retailers able to charge premium prices for their quality products. Sainsbury will be left stranded in the middle.

And the criticism of Sir Peter Davis is getting personal: investors grumble about his award of extra shares worth £3.9 million, and about the board's decision to make him chairman in 2004.

> Outsiders wonder if Sir Peter has the feel for the customer that a great retailer needs John Sainsbury, the family scion who ran the firm in the 1970s, did: he could pass a shelf of goods and see at a glance if their price was wrong. So does Sir Terry Leahy, the boss of Tesco, the store that has gained most as Sainsbury has fallen. Sir Terry, like Sir Peter, comes from modest origins in Merseyside, but whereas the quiet, lean Sir Terry still collects visitors personally from the lobby of Tesco's shabby headquarters in Cheshunt, the charismatic, rotund Sir Peter directs Sainsbury's fortunes from a glass-and-steel office block in central London and seems most at home at the Royal Opera House, where he is a director. (*Economist*, 28 June 2003)

'It is like they are in complete denial,' said one analyst, who says most clients buying the shares do so on the basis that a deal is the most likely outcome. 'I do not know what it will take to make the management realise that this is not just about investing in the infrastructure. The market is changing around them and the group is in real trouble' (*Financial Times*, 21 July 2003). 'This is a perfect bid situation. The group is strategically challenged but it has a strong brand' (*Financial Times*, 21 July 2003). In the end it will depend on the Sainsbury family, who own about 35 per cent of the shares.

But who would buy Sainsbury's? The *Times* argues that its unlikely that an international retailer would want to buy the third (or eventually fourth) player in the most competitive retail market place in Europe. 'Sainsbury could be attractive to venture capital buyers – although it would be a huge deal for any of them without an obvious exit strategy: it is difficult to see much appetite for a float. Perhaps the answer lies with somebody who wants to take it private and keep it that way – a retail entrepreneur of the likes of Philip Green, who seems quite happy with the money he is earning from the BHS and Arcadia groups and does not currently plan to float them' (*Sunday Times*, 20 July 2003). And, more broadly, the *Economist* speculates that:

> In the longer term, the Safeway deal could spark other retail mergers. If Wal-mart loses, it may accelerate its moves elsewhere in Europe. Moreover, if Tesco has a more formidable rival in Britain, it too might be tempted to switch from an international strategy based on organic growth to something more aggressively based on acquisition.
> But experience shows that retail mergers are tough to pull off and frequently end up destroying value. Ahold of the Netherlands, for example, has come spectacularly unstuck after a three-year buying spree, and Carrefour is still licking its wounds after difficulties in integrating Promodes, which it bought in 1999. A troubled British pharmacy group, Boots, recently pulled out of Japan, and Marks & Spencer has retrenched to nurse its British stores back to health. (*Economist*, 16 January 2003)

Sources: 'Tesco: Leahy's lead', *Economist*, 9 August 2001; 'When you can't sell the goods sell the shop', *Economist*, 16 January 2003; 'The case for going private', *Economist*, 23 January 2003; 'The mediocre middle', *Economist*, 26 June 2003; 'Wm Morrison turns in thirty-sixth year of profit growth', *Guardian*, 18 March 2003; 'Competitors put the squeeze on Sainsbury', *Financial Times*, 21 July 2003; 'Focus: the heat is on', *Sunday Times*, 20 July 2003; 'Mr Safeway waits to be taken off the shelf', *Times*, 15 August 2003; 'Profile: Sir Ken Morrison', *Guardian*, 10 January 2003; *Guardian*, 18 March 2003; 'Pack of five still circle supermarket', *Financial Times*, 15 August 2003; Andrew Seth and Geoffrey Randall, *The Grocers: the Rise and Rise of the Supermarket Chains*, London: Kogan Page (1999).

QUESTIONS

1 In the early 1990s Sainsbury could put up a good case for its combination of price and value ('Good food costs less at Sainsbury'). What, if anything, has changed?
2 How has Sainsbury allowed itself to be moved from the No. 1 spot to the No. 3 or even No. 4 position?
3 Who are the key stakeholders in the supermarket wars and what are their interests?

Sony: Idei's Vision

In Nobuyuki Idei Sony is blessed with a visionary leader. He was *Fortune*'s 'Asia's businessman of the year' in 2001:

All great businessmen need a vision for the future. In Idei's case, he's leading Sony into the digital world. He dreams of a day when consumer electronics and computer technology will converge with the entertainment businesses of film and music to form a whole new industry. This restless polymath, who is just as at home with egghead computer scientists as with entertainment czars like Disney's Eisner, believes that Sony must become a master of the digital universe. 'The most important priority for Sony is to jump fast into this stream and find a way to swim at the same speed as or faster than others.' (*Fortune*, 7 February 2002)

His challenge is to keep Sony's large and independently-minded businesses profitable, growing and heading in the same direction so that:

Sony can be the No. 1 company in the broadband network society. That will be a much bigger role than Sony has ever had. But we can't just wait until broadband arrives. And we can't merely follow the dot-com companies or Microsoft or anybody else. We have to take advantage of everything the technology and the new economy provide. We have to prepare while we still have time.' (Idei, quoted in *Fortune*, 1 May 2000)

The following extract from a press release about the new Clié handheld device gives a flavour of how the vision is being realized. It:

> integrates both Wi-fi® and Bluetooth® wireless technologies. The device represents the first in Sony's anticipated line of many that will enable users to access Web-based content and to communicate via the Internet. It also incorporates hallmark features that helped to set Clié handhelds apart in the market, including an integrated digital camera, voice recorder, digital audio player and high-resolution color screen.
>
> When people think of data, they typically think of office documents or, in the handheld world, things like address books or calendars. But, at Sony, we see beyond the 'tool' aspect of the handheld market, we have the capability of injecting wonder, joy and levels of customization into a portable device so it becomes like a companion or a friend to a lifestyle that uses digital technology. (Sony, San Francisco, July 2003)

Current best sellers include the Viao computer (especially the laptop) and, of course, PlayStation 2, which accounted for more than half of Sony's 2001 profits. Other advanced products include a wristwatch video, the Sony Airboard (a wireless portable video and internet display) and Cocoon (a gateway to the Internet which the company describes as 'the future of television'). Then, not to mention Aibo, the robot dog that can fetch its master's e-mail, there are two-legged singing and seeing robots on the horizon.

Idei is structuring the company in line with the vision. A March 2003 press release describes the new structures based on the 'integrated and decentralized' model and the 'company with committees' principle. The top three company roles overseeing total group management are Group CEO (Nobuyuki Idei), Group COO (Kunitake Ando) and Group CSO (Chief Strategy Officer) (Teruhisa Tokunaka). Then 'to strengthen the team responsible for total group management, Howard Stringer will be appointed as Vice-chairman and Ken Kutaragi as Executive Deputy President of Sony Corporation in addition to their current positions'.

Next the appointment of Regional Representatives for Europe, the Americas and East Asia, 'who will work to optimize operations in each of Sony's main business regions in line with the overall group vision. The regional representatives will oversee the appropriate implementation of group strategy according to local circumstances.' This is supported by a reorganization of Sony group business structure into seven entities (four Network Companies and three Business Groups). Further authority will be delegated to these entities to formulate strategy in their respective fields on a mid to long-term basis. They are

- *Home Network Company.* Create a new home environment with networked electronic devices centred on next-generation television.
- *Broadband Network Company.* Development of next-generation electronics devices and linkages to game devices.
- *IT and Mobile Solutions Network Company.* Realize a connected world with PC and mobile devices and strengthen the B2B solutions business.
- *Micro-systems Network Company.* Enhance key devices and modules as core components of attractive set products.

- *Game Business Group.* Promote game businesses for the broadband era.
- *Entertainment Business Group.* Develop entertainment content businesses based on pictures and music and develop a new content business model for the network era.
- *Personal Solutions Business Group.* Integrate various business units providing services based on direct contact with customers (finance, retail, etc.). Strengthen synergies and develop attractive new business models for customers through the application of IT.

And finally there is a Service/Platform Function to support Network Companies and Business Groups on a horizontal basis.

But according to *Fortune*:

> The biggest cultural change Idei has fostered is how Sony deals with other companies. Under Morita and Ohga, Sony was arrogant and standoffish, seldom deigning to take on partners to develop and popularize new technologies. . . . Sony now crows about partnership with a Who's Who of high-tech companies. (*Fortune*, 1 May 2000)

So, for example, the Digital Home Working Group (DHWG) – an alliance covering the computer, consumer electronics and telecommunications industries – is aiming to make home networking simple. The group of over 100 companies, including Sony, Microsoft, Intel and Nokia, are developing guidelines for a new generation of interoperable products. 'Consumers will be able to share digital content (such as music, pictures, video) across a vast range of devices, quickly, easily and seamlessly' (*Financial Times*, 4 August 2004).

But there are significant challenges:

> 'Idei's job is much harder than that of, say, GE's Jack Welch, simply because Sony is Japanese,' says Howard Stringer, CEO of Sony America and a close confidant of Idei's. 'Back home in Japan, the political system and economy are under enormous stress. Meanwhile, he's coping with revolutionary forces inside Sony – the PlayStation group, for example, doesn't even use the Sony brand name or logo. And Sony's young people aren't so patient and want to make a contribution sooner.' Stringer shakes his head and continues, 'Then there's the Internet and broadband and wireless. I could go on. It's an astonishingly complicated task. This is all moving so fast that not even Idei is really in charge. But he's the only one with it all in his head. (*Fortune*, 1 May 2000)

Business Week characterizes the company:

> Under a magnifying glass, Sony starts to look a lot like one of Japan's giant integrated electronics makers – a Toshiba, Hitachi, or NEC – which are jacks of all trades and 'Microsofts' of none. These sprawling manufacturers churn out thousands of products, from chips and computers to robots and power plants, many of them unprofitable. Sony doesn't make nuclear power stations. But it does crank out more than 100 million devices a year – and loses money on TVs and cathode-ray tube displays, hard-disk drives, and cell phones. 'Sony has succumbed to the big-company disease.' (*Business Week*, 11 March 2002)

And the *Economist*: 'Dismal results at Japan's top electronics firm have stunned investors. . . . Japan's high cost base, plus growing competition, are chomping away at the unit's profit margins, which have now fallen below 1 per cent' (1 May 2003).

Competition in Sony's core consumer electronics business is fierce:

> The Sonys, Sanyos, and Samsungs of the world – not to mention Chinese upstarts – all have access to the same huge pool of chips, liquid-crystal displays, audio pickups, power supplies, and packaging. To see what impact that has on prices, look no further than the DVD market, where Sony once ruled the roost. Recently, some of the hottest models are Chinese DVD players selling for less than $100. (*Business Week*, 11 March 2002)

Meanwhile the network vision puts Sony into a new and powerful set of competitors:

> Nokia and Samsung in telecommunications, Hewlett-Packard and Dell in computers, and Microsoft in the fast-growing game-console business. Add to those the rivals Sony faces in its mainstream businesses. In entertainment, it is up against AOL Time Warner and other giant providers of content, services, and online distribution. In consumer electronics, which still accounts for nearly two-thirds of Sony's revenue, the competition with Matsushita, Philips, and others remains fierce; last year the sector lost money as profit margins vanished. And did we mention that Microsoft, Intel, Apple, and Samsung are all pushing broadband visions of their own?' (*Fortune*, 10 November 2002)

And as for the vision itself, maybe the products are too complicated for the consumer audience – many of whom still struggle to programme the video recorder and who have learned over time that combination products are never as robust as ones designed to do a single job. (Are we all rushing out to buy the Sony Ericsson combined pda and mobile phone?)

It also means 'selling the broadband vision to consumers who have been slow to embrace high-speed networks and to dealers, who may actually have to reconceive and reconfigure their stores to accommodate the new Sony products' (*Fortune*, 10 November 2002).

> What's missing in the broadband network strategy is the network, at least in the United States. There's a reason Cocoon and other broadband products are released first in Japan: More than half of all households there are expected to have broadband Internet access by the end of 2005, compared with only about 30 per cent in the US. This is the first time in Sony's history that they are producing products that are ahead of the infrastructure's ability to use them, indeed, the rollout of broadband service in the US has been stymied by ineptitude on the parts of cable and telephone companies, high infrastructure costs, lack of availability in some areas, and perhaps most of all by the high cost of monthly service to consumers. Prices for broadband access in the US average around $50 a month, vs as little as $20 per month in Japan. Especially in this economy, price matters. (*Fortune*, 10 November 2002)

'Trouble is, Sony managers have been preaching about this glorious networked future for half a decade with little to show for it. The company, in short, is caught between a past that no longer works and a future that hasn't arrived' (*Business Week* online cover story, 11 March 2002).

Sources: Sony plays to win, *Fortune*, 1 May 2000; 'Asia's Businessman of the Year', *Fortune*, 7 February 2002; 'Sony re-dreams its future', *Fortune*, 10 November 2002; 'The problem with convergence', *Fortune*, 10 March 2003; 'Sony announces executive appointments and organizational reforms effective as of April 1, 2003', Sony Corporation of America press release, 31 March 2003; 'New Clié handheld features more power, mobility and intelligence', Sony Corporation of America press release, 18 July 2003; 'Sony, surprise: dismal results at Japan's top electronics firm have stunned investors', *Economist*, 1 May 2003; 'Sony: the complete home entertainer?' *Economist*, 27 February 2003; 'People want simple home networking', *Financial Times*, 4 August 2003; 'Can Sony regain the magic?' *Business Week* online, 11 March 2002.

QUESTIONS

1 How attractive is the Sony vision?
2 How would you characterize the Sony organization?
3 Will you bet on the vision or the reality?

GE: the Leadership Practices of Jack Welch

What can we learn about strategic leadership from the practices of Jack Welch, who was chairman of US General Electric for twenty years from 1981 to2001? According to Noel Tichy and Stratford Sherman, 'The twentieth century has produced two business leaders who will be remembered for their ideas: Alfred Sloan of General Motors and Jack Welch of GE. As CEO, he pushed for radical change long before most people recognized it as necessary' (Tichy and Sherman, 1993). Succeeding in a gruelling contest for the leadership, Welch knew from the start that radical change was necessary if GE was to remain America's No. 1 company. He set the direction in his first year as chairman. Quoting Clausewitz on strategy, he argued that 'Men could not reduce strategy to a formula . . . strategy was not a lengthy action plan. It was the evolution of a central idea through continually changing circumstances.'

Welch identified businesses as either core (e.g. lighting), service (e.g. financial) or high-technology (e.g. medical) and then set the challenge: to be No. 1 or No. 2 in the chosen market. If not, then 'fix, close or sell' the business:

> The winners in this environment will be those who search out and participate in the real growth industries and insist upon being No. 1 or No. 2 in every business that they are in – the No. 1 or No. 2 leanest low-cost, worldwide producers of quality goods and services or those who have a clear technological edge, a clear advantage in a market niche. (Welch 2001)

While known at this stage as 'Neutron Jack' for the number of businesses sold and employees made redundant, his first major speech on the direction he wanted GE to pursue also focused on the 'soft values':

Around this tangible central idea we will wrap these intangible central values . . . Reality (see the world the way it is, not the way we wish or hope it will be), Quality/excellence (creating an atmosphere where every individual is striving to be proud of every product and service we provide) and the human resource element (where people feel assured in knowing that only the limits of their creativity and drive, their own standards of personal excellence, will be the ceiling on how far and how fast they move. (Welch 2001)

Having set the direction, over a twenty-year period Welch managed four major initiatives, left three 'cultural legacies' and instituted an operational system that embeds learning and leadership into the organization, turning GE into what Tichy (1997) calls 'a leadership engine' where leaders with a proven track record take direct responsibility for the development of other leaders, have 'teachable points of view' and invest considerable time developing other leaders. The four company-wide initiatives were:

- 1987. *Globalization*, based on a deal which swapped the US consumer electronics business for the French medical imaging unit Thompson GCR. No. 1 or No. 2 now meant: in the global market place. By 2001 GE had doubled the percentage of revenue from non-US markets, from 20 per cent to 40 per cent.
- 1995. *Growing services* based on Welch's vision of GE as 'a global service company that also sells high-quality products'. In 2000 services delivered 70 per cent of revenue from a 1980 base of 15 per cent (Krames, 2002).
- 1995. *Six Sigma*. Six Sigma is a statistically based programme that attempts to achieve near perfect quality (less than four mistakes per million) in GE's products and processes. The challenge was to introduce Six Sigma working over a five-year period (learning from Motorola, which took seven years). In the first year GE trained 30,000 employees at a cost of about US$200 million, obtaining savings in the region of US$150 million. Three thousand Six Sigma projects in 1996 rose to 6,000 in 1998 with an estimated US$320 million in productivity gains and profits. No one was considered for a management position without at least green belt training and a successful project. Compensation schemes were altered so that 40 per cent of bonus was based on Six Sigma (Welch, 2001).
- 2000. *Digitization*. 'Digitization is transforming nearly everything we do, energizing every corner of the company, and making it faster.' GE did US$8 billion of business over the Internet in 2000 (Krames, 2002).

Welch defines an initiative as 'something that grabs everyone – large enough, broad enough, and generic enough to have a major impact on the company. An initiative is long-lasting, and it changes the fundamental nature of the organization.' He led each initiative with passion and rigour: 'not only did we put the best people on each initiative, we trained them, measured them, and reported their results. In the end each initiative had to develop people and improve the bottom line.'

One feature of Welch's leadership is the time and effort put into putting his best people on to the most valuable initiatives. He developed GE's own model of leadership, comprising:

- *energy*: possesses an enormous amount of energy;
- *edge*: competitive spirit, understanding the value of speed;
- *energizer*: able to motivate others through their own enthusiasm;
- *execution*: delivers on commitments and targets.

Welch believes passionately in discriminating between high and low performance, using what he calls the 'vitality curve' (where the top 20 per cent are highly rewarded, the next 70 per cent are encouraged and developed, and the bottom 10 per cent are dismissed). And at the Session C meetings (see below) he makes sure that he has data on all the senior managers, covering track record, current performance (including 360 appraisal) and potential rating. He is known for distinguishing between four types of manager:

- Delivers on commitments and shares the values of the company: onward and upward.
- Does not meet commitments and does not share values: out.
- Misses commitments but shares values: second chance, preferably in a different environment.
- Delivers on commitments but does not share values (autocrat): convince to change or part company.

He estimates that he spends 40 per cent of his time on people issues.

Welch's three 'cultural' legacies comprise: his support of Crotonville; the concept of the boundaryless organization; and the 'Work out' programme.

Crotonville. 'The Harvard of corporate America' was GE's model corporate university, which Welch spent US$45 million upgrading at the same time as he was cutting back on people and selling businesses in other areas. He hired in key management gurus (Noel Tichy, David Ulrich) to redesign the curriculum on action learning lines, ensured that nominations for the key programmes were based solely on merit and visited Crotonville twice a month during his twenty-year tenure to spend time with every GE manager programme debating current strategy and issues. It is one of the ways, as well as frequent visits (managing by walking around), by which he kept closely in touch with what was really happening.

Bourndaryless organization:

'Boundaryless' is an uncommon word – perhaps even an awkward one – but it has become a word we use constantly, one that describes a whole set of behaviours we believe are necessary . . . In a boundaryless company, suppliers aren't 'outsiders' . . . Customers are seen for what they are – the lifeblood of the company . . . In a boundaryless company, internal functions begin to blur . . . Even the barriers between GE work life and community life have come down.

Eccles and Nohria (1992) cite Jack Welch's description of the boundaryless organization as a key example of effective management rhetoric, commenting, 'despite its awkward label, the vision is imaginative and coherent . . . discloses several layers of emotional appeal . . . invites a new set of possibilities and encourages them to take actions that they believe would be in keeping with the vision'.

Work out programme. The vision of the boundaryless organization is in keeping with Welch's consistent attack on 'bureaucracy', which we also see in the 'Work out' programme. Work out was designed after a meeting at Crotonville, where Welch had become exasperated that his views and initiatives were being blocked by senior middle managers arguing: 'and yet they still lingered, these unimaginative, frightened, bureaucratic bosses-from-hell, the ones who demand that fewer people do everything that once had been done by many more. We've got to force leaders who aren't walking the talk to face up to their people' (Tichy and Sherman, 1993). Work out began in 1988. The programme comprised a series of three-day off-site workshops patterned after New England town meetings designed to 'work out' of the organization unnecessary work and other problems. In groups of 30–100 employees identified and discussed common problems. Bosses were locked out during discussion times and returned to hear their subordinates' proposed solutions. Then they had to make on-the-spot decisions about each proposal, right in front of everyone. Eighty per cent of proposals got instant yes/no decisions.

None of the business initiatives or cultural legacies would have succeeded without the strong operating system Welch inherited and developed to suit his challenging yet informal style. This system comprises an annual series of meetings to develop operating plans, drive initiatives and especially to share learning and best practice. The annual cycle begins with a two-day meeting in January for the top 500 operating leaders. Much of the meeting is taken up with short ten-minute presentations outlining progress and sharing learning on specific company-wide initiatives. There is a deliberate intention to encourage learning across GE's many diverse businesses. Jack Welch was able to reinforce existing and introduce new initiatives. Videos of the meeting are quickly available for top managers to use to disseminate the key points of the meeting throughout their business units.

March sees the first of the quarterly Corporate Executive Council meetings (comprising GE's top thirty) where business leaders update their operations and describe their newest thinking around the initiatives. 'Session Cs' take place in each business during April and May. Welch describes these intense one-day meetings as the most important meeting of the year: a demanding annual management appraisal and succession planning review which determines who gets promoted and who receives stock options. The focus is on how the human resource strategy is being applied to all major initiatives by talking about the organization and the people in it. During the morning there are in-depth discussions on careers, promotions, vitality curves and each key player's strengths, weaknesses and development needs The afternoon is spent scrutinizing each initiative and the person leading it. Decisions are then made on moving people to new positions. These meetings are followed up in July by a video-conference to see if the personnel changes agreed have been implemented.

During June and July business leaders come to Fairfield (HQ) for strategy reviews of each business (session I). In October the top 170 executives meet at Crotonville to share the best ideas found in the strategy sessions. Finally in November business leaders present their operating plans for the up-coming year (session II). Again the point is that these processes are institutionalized. As Collins and Porras note in their classic book *Built to Last*:

> We respect Jack Welch for his remarkable track record. But we respect GE even more for its remarkable track record of continuity in top management excellence over the course of a hundred years. More GE alumni have become chief executives at American corporations than alumni of any other company.

Sources: Jack Welch with John A. Byrne, *Jack: What I've Learned leading a Great Company and Great People*, London: Headline Press (2001); Jeffrey A. Krames, *The Jack Welch Lexicon of Leadership*, New York: McGraw-Hill (2002); R. G. Eccles and N. Nohria, *Beyond the Hype*, Boston MA: Harvard Business School Press (1992); Noel Tichy and Stratford Sherman, *Control your Destiny: How General Electric is revolutionizing the Art of Management*, New York: Harper Collins (1993); Noel M. Tichy, *The Leadership Engine: How Winning Companies build Leaders at every Level*, New York: Harper (1997); J. C. Collins and J. I. Porras, *Built to Last: Successful Habits of Visionary Companies* (1994).

QUESTIONS

1 How would you characterize Jack Welch's leadership style?
2 What made him so effective?
3 Would you like to have worked for him?

Xerox: Capabilities Discovered but not Developed

In 1970 Peter McColough, Chief Executive Officer (CEO) of Xerox Corporation, announced a new vision of the company. Xerox would become a world leader in developing the architecture of information appropriate for a new information technology era. During the 1970s Xerox Corporation made a major investment in its Palo Alto Research Center (PARC). PARC recruited the world's leading computer scientists and earned a reputation as one of, if not the world's leading, computer research centres. PARC pioneered major breakthroughs in copier and computer technology, both hardware and software, yet few of these discoveries, such as the first personal computer, the now ubiquitous 'mouse' and the first word-processing program for non-experts, became commercial Xerox products. Xerox's mission of developing the archetype for the office of the future had not been realized. PARC scientists left Xerox to join other companies, such as Apple, which capitalized upon their scientific leadership. Three PARC scientists left Xerox to join Digital Equipment Corporation and were awarded the 1984 Software System

Award from the Association for Computing Machinery for the invention of personal distributed computing. In September 1983 *Fortune* published a lead article entitled 'The lab that ran away from Xerox'!

Its CEO's 1970 vision set the company two major tasks. The first, to invent new breakthrough technologies, had been achieved. The other, to transform Xerox from a copier company into an office systems company, proved far more problematic. Xerox proved incapable of learning how to develop, manufacture and market office systems that customers actually needed or wanted. It bought a computer company without the necessary competences in this area. It funded long-term research at PARC but failed to develop it into marketable products. In short, it failed to make the company anything other than a copier company. One of the scientists who left PARC to join Digital summed up the failure when he told colleagues who followed the same path, 'It's great . . . to finally work for a computer company' (Smith and Alexander, 1988: 201, 254). PARC helped Xerox develop innovative products for its traditional imaging business, such as the laser printer. But the company failed to capitalize on the greater prize PARC led the way towards. PARC offered Xerox the opportunity to define and dominate the emergent personal computing business. Pursuing the opportunity required Xerox to change its identity. In the end it failed to do so, at a time when it was losing its dominant position in its core copier markets to new competition. In the end the company that invented the first version of a personal computing future was reduced in its aspirations to 'struggling to recapture the glory of its copier past' (Smith and Alexander, 1988: 19).

Xerox's attempts to change direction and identity began, like IBM's, in a time of plenty. Xerox seemed invincible in the copier industry that it had invented. But top management began to worry about possible technological threats that might impact upon their core business, particularly from computer firms. To become a world-class communications company, it was felt, Xerox needed to build a competence in the ability to handle information in digital as well as graphical form (Smith and Alexander, 1988: 24). The computer industry clearly represented greater growth opportunities than copiers. Success in computing depended upon the success of R&D. In the words of CEO McColough, 'R&D *has been*, *is*, and *will be* a way of life. Our company already owes much to the prompt exploitation of new technology' (Smith and Alexander, 1988: 49). Investment in PARC was meant to give Xerox a lead in digital technology applications in computer and information processing.

The management philosophy adopted at PARC was a bottom-up one – the recruitment of leading scientists who would then, within very broadly defined limits, be free to generate their own research agendas. In the words of PARC's first director, '[l]ittle success . . . is likely to come from showing researchers to a laboratory, describing in detail a desired technology or process not now existent, and commanding, "Invent!"' (Smith and Alexander, 1988: 55). The research process initiated at PARC involved the explicit surfacing of difference in an atmosphere where people felt understood, even if they disagreed, the fear of failure was diminished by emphasis on learning through mistakes and egos were not threatened. If disagreement became inevitable, members worked on generating 'Class 2' disagreements. Class 1 disagreements are when neither party can describe to the other's satisfaction the other's point of view. Class 2 disagreements are when each party can describe to the other's satisfaction the other's point of view. Experimentation and discovery flourished. Interactive computing was extended to an 'entirely new frontier'. In the words of one of the participants, 'It was certainly from my own experience the largest continuous piece of creative output that I have seen anywhere. And it was like being right there at the Creation. A lot of people worked harder than I had ever seen, or have seen since, doing a thing they all thought was worthwhile, and really thought would change the world.' By 1972 PARC was in a position to provide Xerox with 'an unprecedented variety of new technologies' (Smith and Alexander, 1988: 78–9, 103, 113, 154). The vision of an entirely new form of 'architecture of information' became a reality. Unfortunately, the capability discovered by PARC was not developed into a commercial proposition by Xerox.

Xerox top management's intuitive vision at the beginning of the 1970s of what needed to be done in the light of changes in the copier industry and the computer industry and the future technological convergence of those industries was timely and appropriate. It was a vision endorsed by the most stringent strategic analysis. A major strategic review of 1974 recommended a two-pronged approach for the company. Cost reduction and quality improvement in copier development and manufacture were necessary to survive the new competition. The second recommendation was that Xerox could seize a unique opportunity for change and growth by capitalizing on PARC's innovations and developing the office of the future 'as a business instead of a technology alone' (Smith and Alexander, 1988: 141).

The latter involved the integration of digital capabilities into the mainstream of the organization. There were a number of factors militating against successful integration. Two were location and politics. The location of PARC on the west coast created major problems of integration of researchers' and Xerox senior management's needs and a lack of mutual responsiveness. Location gave PARC access to some of the best brains in the computer industry but left it decoupled from the changing corporate agenda. Integration problems were exacerbated by the politicality of the Xerox organization, described in the following manner by a Xerox manager who had served in the Nixon administration: 'I was used to the politics of Washington, but at Xerox it was worse. In Washington, you knew your adversaries and accepted that they would work against you. At Xerox, you only found out who was not on your side after you noticed the knife in your back' (Smith and Alexander, 1988: 156).

PARC met with severe resistance from a broad base of managers steeped in the old Xerox ways who thought diversification into the non-copier business made no sense, an attitude exacerbated by equally strong 'not invented here' views that further marginalized PARC's endeavours. Feuds developed between PARC management who wanted to take risks and a development function that became increasingly risk-averse. There were also new managers, recruited from companies such as IBM, oriented primarily to marketing and sales, and Ford, brought into the company for their expertise in cost containment and control, who were constitutionally unsympathetic to the long lead times and uncertain outcomes associated with leading-edge research, for whom short-term performance would always outweigh long-term opportunity. These managers favoured a more top-down approach to development, with the agenda set centrally by senior management.

The PARC research effort suffered from its decoupling from Xerox's sales, manufacturing and finance organizations. There was little commitment to PARC among Xerox's business managers. There was no organization structure or process to link PARC with a development function able to turn PARC's inventions into products. In some ways PARC itself did not help its better integration into Xerox's central community. PARC's young and arrogant computer scientists were intolerant of those without their specialist knowledge. They seemed blissfully unaware of the fact that they were the exceptions to the traditional Xerox culture – indeed, that they were seen as representatives of a counter-culture by Xerox's more conventional managers. The appearance of an article in *Rolling Stone* in December 1992 entitled 'Space war: fanatic life and symbolic death among the computer bums' which featured several PARC alumni did little to give the group extra credibility in the rest of the company (Smith and Alexander, 1988: 148). The situation was graphically and starkly summed up by one Xerox manager as follows: 'PARC was floating around in free space . . . PARC was a head [with a brain fertile in groundbreaking ideas]. But a head to which body? Who was going to pick up from whatever was done at PARC to do all of the rest of the hard work to make a business out of it?' (Smith and Alexander, 1988: 143–4).

The overarching theme here is that the shift in Xerox's identity required to support its transformation from a single-product (copier) company to a diversified communications company was just too fundamental a change for Xerox management to accept and one that its top management lacked the skills and perhaps the courage or the real desire to convince the company to accept. Top management, responsible for the creation of PARC, remained strangely aloof from the political in-fighting and the inertia that stifled the opportunities pioneered at PARC, 'uninvolved while the management machinery of Xerox – the decision systems, the prevailing prejudices, the reigning executives – conspired to keep the company's great accomplishment[s] a secret from the world' (Smith and Alexander, 1988: 177).

Source: D. K. Smith and R. C. Alexander, *Fumbling the Future: How Xerox invented then ignored the first Personal Computer*, New York: Morrow (1988).

QUESTIONS

1 What went wrong?
2 What are the lessons for companies which need to innovate?
3 What is the future for Xerox?

REFERENCES

Abernathy, W. J., Clark, K., and Kantrow, A. (1981) 'The new industrial competition', *Harvard Business Review*, September–October, pp. 68–81.

Alexander, N. (1997) *International Retailing*. Oxford: Blackwell.

Ansoff, I. (1965) *Corporate Strategy*. New York: McGraw-Hill.

Badaracco, J. L. (1991) *The Knowledge Link*. Boston MA: Harvard Business School Press.

Barnard, C. I. (1938) *The Functions of the Executive*. Boston MA: Harvard University Press.

Barnatt, C., and Starkey, K. (1991) 'The case for flexibility: a study of the UK television industry', working paper, Nottingham: School of Management and Finance, University of Nottingham.

Barney, J. B. (1991) 'Firm resources and sustained competitive advantage', *Journal of Management*, 17 (1): 99–120.

Bartlett, C. A., and Ghoshal, S. (1989) *Managing across Borders*. London: Hutchinson.

Best, M. H. (1990) *The New Competition*. Oxford: Polity Press.

✓ Brandenburger, A. M., and Nalebuff, B. J. (1995) 'The right game: use game theory to shape strategy', *Harvard Business Review*, July–August, pp. 57–71.

Cadbury, A. (1991) 'Business strategy', Esmee Fairbairn Distinguished Lecture Series, inaugural lecture, University of Lancaster, 7 November.

Carlsson, J. (1989) *Moments of Truth*. New York: Harper & Row.

✓ Chan, K. W., and Maubourgne, R. (1999) 'Creating new market space', *Harvard Business Review*, January–February.

Cohen, W. M., and Levinthal, D. A. (1990) 'Absorptive capacity: a new perspective on learning and innovation', *Administrative Science Quarterly* 35: 128–52.

✓ Collins, J. C., and Porras, J. I. (1991) 'Organizational vision and visionary organizations', *California Management Review*, fall, pp. 30–52.

Collins, Jim C., and Porras, Jerry I. (1994) *Built to Last*. New York: Harper.

Collins, Jim C. (2001) *Good to Great*. New York: Random House.

✓ Collis, D. J., and Montgomery, C. A. (1995) 'Competing on resources: strategy in the 1990s', *Harvard Business Review*, July–August, pp. 118–28.

Cronshaw, M., Davis, E., and Kay, J. (1990) 'On being stuck in the middle, or, Good food costs less at Sainsbury's', Working Paper 83, London: Centre for Business Strategy, London Business School.

✓Cronshaw, M., Davis, E., and Kay, J. (1994) 'On being stuck in the middle', *British Journal of Management*, 5: 19–32.

D'Aveni, R. J. (1994) *Hypercompetition: Managing the Dynamics of Strategic Maneuvering*. New York: Free Press.

✓D'Aveni, R. J. (1999) 'Strategic supremacy through disruption and dominance', *Sloan Management Review*, 40: 127–35.

David, F. R. (1989) 'How companies define their mission', *Long Range Planning*, 22: 90–7.

Davidson, I., and Mallin, C. (1993) *The Business Accounting and Finance Blueprint*. Oxford: Blackwell.

Dixit, A. K., and Nalebuff, B. J. (1991) *Thinking Strategically*. New York: Norton.

Drucker, P. F. (1974) *Management: Tasks, Responsibilities, Practices*. London: Heinemann.

✓Drucker, P. F. (1994) 'The Theory of the Business', *Harvard Business Review*, September–October, 95–104.

Eccles, R. G., and Nohria, N. (1992) *Beyond the Hype*. Boston MA: Harvard Business School Press.

✓Eisenhardt, K. M., and Martin, J. A. (2000) 'Dynamic capabilities: what are they?' *Strategic Management Journal*, 21: 1105–21.

Ennew, C. (1993) *The Marketing Blueprint*. Oxford: Blackwell.

Ennew, C., Watkins, T., and Wright, M. (1990) *Marketing Financial Services*. London: Heinemann.

Freeman, R. H. (1984) *Strategic Management: a Stakeholder Approach*. London: Pitman.

Fry, R. E. (1982) 'Improving trustee, administrator and physician collaboration through open systems planning' in N. Margulies and J. D. Adams (eds) *Organizational Development in Health Care Organizations*. Reading MA: Addison Wesley.

Galbraith, J. R., and Kazanjian, R. K. (1986) *Strategy Implementation*. St Paul MN: West Publishing.

✓Gawer, A., and Cusumano, M. A. (2002) *Platform Leadership*. Boston MA: Harvard Business School Press.

Ghemawat, P. (1997) *Games Businesses Play: Cases and Models*, Cambridge MA: MIT Press.

Goold, M., and Campbell, A. (1987) *Strategy and Style: The Role of the Centre in Managing Diversified Corporations*. Oxford: Blackwell.

Goold, M., Campbell, A., and Alexander, M. (1994) *Corporate-level Strategy: Creating Value in the Multibusiness Company*. New York: Wiley.

Gould, S. J. (1996) 'The dodo and the caucus race', *Natural History*, 105 (11): 22–33.

✓Grant, R. M. (1991) 'The resource-based theory of competitive advantage: implications for strategy formulation', *California Management Review*, 33: 114–35.

✓Grant, R. M. (1996) 'Toward a knowledge-based theory of the firm', *Strategic Management Journal*, 17 (winter special issue): 108–22.

Grove, A. (1997) *Only the Paranoid Survive: How to exploit the Crisis Points that challenge every Company and Career*. London: Harper Collins.

✓Hambrick, D., and Fredrickson, J. W. (1996) 'Are you sure you have a strategy?' *Academy of Management Executive*, 15: 48–59.

✓Hamel, G. (1996) 'Strategy as revolution', *Harvard Business Review*, 74, July–August, pp. 69–82.

Hamel, G. (2000) *Leading the Revolution*. Boston MA: Harvard Business School Press.

✓Hamel, G., and Prahalad, C. K. (1989) 'Strategic intent', *Harvard Business Review*, May–June, pp. 63–76.

Hamel, G., and Prahalad, C. K. (1994) *Competing for the Future*. Boston MA: Harvard Business School Press.

Harvey-Jones, J. (1988) *Making it Happen*. London: Collins.

Hedley, B. (1977) 'Strategy and the "business portfolio"', *Long Range Planning*, 10 (February): 9–15.

Hickman, C. R., and Silva, M. (1984) *Creating Excellence: Merging Corporate Cultures, Strategy and Change in the New Age*. London: Allen & Unwin.

Johnson, G., and Scholes, K. (1988) *Exploring Corporate Strategy*, 2nd edn. New York: Prentice Hall.

Johnson, G., and Scholes, K. (2002) *Exploring Corporate Strategy*, 6th edn. New York: FT Prentice✓ Hall.

Kamoche, K. (2001) *Understanding Human Resource Management*. Buckingham: Open University Press.

Kaplan, R., and Norton, D. (1992) 'The balanced scorecard: measures that drive performance',✓ *Harvard Business Review*, 70 (1): 71–9.

Kaplan, R., and Norton, D. (1993) 'Putting the balanced scorecard to work', *Harvard Business* ✓ *Review*, 71 (5): 134–47.

Kaplan, R., and Norton, D. (1996) 'Using the balanced scorecard as a strategic manage-✓ ment system', *Harvard Business Review*, 74 (1): 75–85.

Kay, J. (1993) *Foundations of Corporate Success*. Oxford: Oxford University Press.

Kay, J. (1996) 'Adding value', in *The Business of Economics*. Oxford: Oxford University Press.

Kay, J. (2000) 'Strategy and the delusion of grand designs', in *Financial Times Mastering Strategy*. London: Financial Times/McGraw-Hill.

Kay, J. (2003) *The Truth about Markets*. London: Penguin/Allen Lane.

Knee, D., and Walters, D. (1985) *Strategy in Retailing*. Oxford: Philip Allen.

Kotter, J. (1995) 'Why transformation efforts fail', *Harvard Business Review*, March–April, pp. 59–68.

Kotter, J., and Cohen, W. (2002) *The Heart of Change*. Boston MA: Harvard Business School Press.

Krames, Jeffrey A. (2002) *The Jack Welch Lexicon of Leadership*. New York: McGraw-Hill.

Lanzilloti, R. F. (1961) 'The automobile industry' in W. Adams (ed.) *Structure of American Industry*, 3rd edn. London: Macmillan.

Leavy, B. (1998) 'Learning in the strategy field', *Management Learning*, 29: 447–66. ✓

Leonard-Barton, D. (1992) 'Core capabilities and core rigidities: a paradox in managing new product development', *Strategic Management Journal*, 13: 111–25.

Milburn, Todd T. (2001) 'EVA's charms as a performance measure' in *Financial Times Handbook of Management*, 2nd edn. New York: FT Prentice Hall.

Miles, R. E., and Snow, C. (1986) 'Organizations: new concepts for new forms', *California Management Review*, 28 (3): 62–73.

Mintzberg, H. (1973) *The Nature of Managerial Work*. New York: Harper & Row.

Morgan, G. (1986) *Images of Organization*. Beverly Hills CA: Sage.

Morgan, G. (1989) *Creative Organization Theory*. Beverly Hills CA: Sage.

Morita, A. (1987) *Made in Japan*. London: Fontana.

Naylor, T., Vernon, J., and Wertz, K. (1983) *Managerial Economics: Corporate Economics and Strategy*. New York: McGraw-Hill.

Ouchi, W. G. (1981) *Theory Z: how American Business can meet the Japanese Challenge*. Reading MA: Addison Wesley.

Pascale, R. T. (1990) *Managing on the Edge*. New York: Viking.

Penrose, E. (1959) *The Theory of the Growth of the Firm*. New York: Wiley.

Peters, T., and Waterman, R. H. (1982) *In Search of Excellence*. New York: Harper & Row.

Pettigrew, A. M. (1985) *The Awakening Giant: Continuity and Change in ICI*. Oxford: Blackwell.

Pilkington, J. R. A. (1991) 'A study of strategy formulation in an automotive manufacturer', unpublished Ph.D. thesis, Birmingham: University of Aston.

Porter, M. (1996) 'What is strategy?' *Harvard Business Review*, November–December, pp. 61–78.

Porter, M. E. (1979) 'How competitive forces shape strategy', *Harvard Business Review*, March–April, pp. 137–45.

Porter, M. E. (1980) *Competitive Strategy: Techniques for analyzing Industries and Competitors*. New York: Free Press.

Porter, M. E. (1985) *Competitive Advantage: Creating and Sustaining Superior Performance*. New York: Free Press.

Porter, M. E. (1990) *The Competitive Advantage of Nations*. New York: Free Press.

✓Prahalad, C. K., and Hamel, G. (1990) 'The core competence of the corporation', *Harvard Business Review*, May–June, pp. 79–91.

Pucik, V., and Hatvany, N. (1983) 'Management practices in Japan and their impact on business strategy' in *Advances in Strategic Management* I. Greenwich CT: JAI Press.

Quinn, J. B. (1980) *Strategy for Change: Logical Incrementalism*. Homewood IL: Irwin.

Quinn, J. B., Mintzberg, H., and James, R. (1988) *The Strategy Process*. Englewood Cliffs NJ: Prentice Hall.

Raymond, Eric S. (1999) *The Cathedral and the Bazaar: Musings on Linux and Open Source by an Accidental Revolutionary*. Sebastopol CA: O'Reilly.

Roddick, A. (1991) *Body and Soul*. London: Ebury Press.

Rumelt, R. (1988) 'The evaluation of business strategy', in J. B. Quinn, H. Mintzberg and R. B. James (eds) *The Strategy Process*. Englewood Cliffs NJ: Prentice Hall.

Sadler, P. (1988) *Managerial Leadership in the Post-industrial Society*. Aldershot: Gower.

Salbu, S. (2002) 'Foreword' to B. Cruwer, *Anatomy of Greed*. London: Hutchinson.

Scherer, F. M., and Ross, D. (1989) *Industrial Market Structure and Economic Performance*, 3rd edn. Boston MA: Houghton Mifflin.

Schumpeter, J. (1943) *Capitalism, Socialism and Democracy*. London: Allen & Unwin.

Seeger, J. A. (1984) 'Reversing the images of BCG's growth share matrix', *Strategic Management Journal*, 5: 93–7.

Senge, P. (1990) *The Fifth Discipline*. New York: Doubleday.

✓Senge, P., and Carstedt, G. (2001) 'Innovating our way to the next industrial revolution', *MIT Sloan Management Review*, 42: 24–38.

Sennett, R. (1998) *The Corrosion of Character*. New York: Norton.

Seth, Andrew, and Randall, Geoffrey (1999) *The Grocers: the Rise and Rise of the Supermarket Chains*. London: Kogan Page.

Singh, S., Utton, M., and Waterson, M. (1991a) 'An introduction and a pen portrait of the whole sample by industry', Discussion Papers in Industrial Economics 27, Reading: Department of Economics, University of Reading.

Singh, S., Utton, M., and Waterson, M. (1991b) 'Entry-deterring strategies by established firms', Discussion Papers in Industrial Economics 28, Reading: Department of Economics, University of Reading.

Singh, S., Utton, M., and Waterson, M. (1998) 'Strategic behaviour of incumbent firms in the UK', *International Journal of Industrial Organization*, 16: 229–51.

Smiley, R. (1988) 'Empirical evidence on strategic entry deterrence', *International Journal of Industrial Organization*, 6: 167–80.

Smith, D. K., and Alexander, R. C. (1988) *Fumbling the Future: How Xerox invented then ignored the first Personal Computer*. New York: Morrow.

Starkey, K., ed. (1998) *How Organizations Learn*. London: Thomson.

Thompson, A. A. (1989) *The Economics of the Firm*, 5th edn. New York: Prentice Hall.

Tichy, N. M. (1997) *The Leadership Engine: How Winning Companies build Leaders at every Level*. New York: Harper.

Tichy, N. M. and Sherman, Stratford (1993) *Control your Destiny: How General Electric is revolutionizing the Art of Management*. New York: Harper Collins.

Tse, K. K. (1985) *Marks & Spencer*. Oxford: Pergamon Press.

Van der Heijden, K. (1996) *Scenarios: The Art of Strategic Conversation*. New York: Wiley.

Wayner, Peter (2000) *Free for All: How Linux and the Free Software Movement undercut the High-tech Titans*. New York: Harper.

Welch, J., with Byrne, J. A. (2001) *Jack: What I've learned leading a Great Company and Great People*. London: Headline.

Whittington, R. (2000) 'In praise of the evergreen conglomerate', in *Mastering Strategy*. New York: FT Prentice Hall.

Wileman, A., and Jary, M. (1997) *Retail Power Plays*. London: Macmillan.

Yoshimori, M. (1995) 'Whose company is it? The concept of the corporation in Japan and the West', *Long Range Planning*, 28 (4): 33–44.

INDEX

3: 207
3M 139, 148

absorptive capacity 180
Accenture 215
acceptability issues, corporate-level strategy 87, 112
acquisition/diversification subsystem 156
acquisitions 97, 98
 internationalization through 89–90
Adidas 12
advertising
 carbonated soft drinks industry 29, 30, 31
 Gillette 77
 importance 82, 83
 newspaper industry 36
 Slater Menswear 60–1
A. G. Barr 29–30
agents 99
aggressive strategies 81, 84–5
A. G. Stanley 109
Ahold 89, 216
Ainslie, Pauline 181
Airbus consortium 99
Aldi 54, 69
alien territory businesses 105, 106
Allen, Woody 131
Amazon 75, 76
American National Can (ANC) 210
Ando, Kunitake 218

AOL Time Warner 220
Apple 11, 12, 79, 190, 220, 225
appropriability test for resources and capabilities 71
Arcadia Group 47, 109, 212, 216
architecture, organizational 71–2
Argos 109
Asda
 competitive position 33
 growth 214, 215, 216
 internationalization 90
 non-food sales 215
 parenting strategies 108
 and Sainsbury's, competition between 65, 66
 takeover bid for Safeway 47, 212, 213
Associated Newspapers 37
AT&T 114
attractiveness–strengths matrix 100, 102–3, 104
Audit Commission 203
automobile industry 9, 127, 157
autonomy 129–30

B&Q 68, 108, 201
BA 85, 94, 164, 165
Badaracco, J. L. 177
Baird 215
balanced scorecard approach, corporate-level strategy 87, 119–20
ballast businesses 105, 106

Bank of Ireland   163
Barclay brothers   109
Barnard, Chester   169, 191
barriers to trade   30
Bartlett, C. A.   144–5
Bass   148
BCG growth–share matrix   100–2, 103, 104
Beckham, David   181
Benetton   89, 142
Berkshire Hathaway   93
Berlin, Isaiah   140
BhS   47, 109, 212, 216
Bic   54, 76–7, 78
Blank, Arthur   198, 199–200
BOC   147
Body Shop
   corporate responsibility   187–8, 190, 191
   focus strategy   59
   franchises   99
   internationalization   89
   mission statement   11
Boeing   139
Boesky, Ivan   192
Bonington, Chris   169
Boo.com   75
Boots Company
   case study   194–6
   hybrid strategies   66, 67, 68
   identity   14–15
   internationalization   90, 109, 216
   parenting strategies   109, 110
   and Sainsbury, co-operation between   215
   and Tesco, competition between   213
   Unipart   107
   Value Based Management   114, 117
Borjesson, Rolf   209, 210–12
Boston Consulting Group (BCG)
   growth–share matrix   100–2, 103, 104
Boston Market   118
bottom-up approach to strategy   2
Bowater   209
BP   147
Brandenburger, A. M.   150
Branson, Sir Richard   93, 95
Briggs & Stratton   114
British Airways (BA)   85, 94, 164, 165
British Gas Communications   21

British Leyland   64, 107
British Petroleum (BP)   147
British Telecom (BT)   21–2, 73–4
Britvic Soft Drinks   29
Brooks Brothers   90
BskyB   207
BT   21–2, 73–4
BTR   147, 148
Buffett, Warren   93
Burberry   109
bureaucratic organizations   140–1, 142
business, theory of the   15–16
business-level strategy   83–5
   competitive advantage through resources and capabilities   70–4
   competitive strategies   52–62
   gaining competitive advantage   62–70
   market turbulence and hypercompetition   74–80
   opposition, dealing with the   80–3
   strategic choice   51–2
business schools   192
business services   44–5
BUT   108
buyers, power of
   competitive environment, structural analysis of   28, 30–1
   cost leadership strategies   56
   differentiation strategies   58
   focus strategies   59

C&A   89
Cable & Wireless   21, 73
cable television companies   22
Cadbury, Sir Adrian   188
Cadbury's   66
Cadbury Schweppes   114, 144, 147
Campbell, Andrew   15, 147, 148
Canon   11, 130, 148, 149
Cantalupo, Jim   117
capabilities *see* resources and capabilities, organizational
capacity creation   82, 83
capital requirements   27
carbonated soft drinks industry   29–31
Carlzon, Jan   170, 171
Carphone Warehouse   21, 207
Carrefour   89, 90, 216
carrier pre-selection (CPS) services   21–2, 73

cash cows   101, 102, 160
Castorama   108
category killers   68–9, 75
Caterpillar   11, 130
Centrica   21, 73
change   151
  incremental   152, 153–5, 156, 159
  innovating organizations   159–61
  leadership   165–75
  managing   157–9
  organizational development and strategy
    161–3
  radical   152–3, 154–5
  service environments   163–5
  strategy subsystems   155–7
  triggers   151–2
  see also innovation
chemicals sector   82
Children's World   109
China   99
Chipotle   118
chosen strategy   7
Chrysler   152
cigarette industry   88–9
Cisco   184
clustering phenomenon, competence as
    180
Coca-Cola   29, 85, 114
Cohen, Dan   174–5
Collins, Jim   138–40, 149, 225
Collis, D. J.   71
Comet   108
Commission for Health Improvement
    (CHI)   203
commitment, strategic   81
communication issues   129, 161–2, 163
Compaq   79, 80
competence   176–8
  core   110–11, 177
  future excellence   180–4
  organization and human resources
    178–80
competition and co-operation   149–50
Competition Commission   212, 213, 215
competitive advantage   83–5
  competence   177
  competitive strategies   52–3, 58, 59
  corporate-level strategy   86
  demand-led strategy   69
  gaining   62–70

growth vector   9
  IKEA   136–7
  market turbulence and
    hypercompetition   74–5
  Marks & Spencer   136
  of nations   49
  through resources and capabilities
    70–4
  strategic choice   52
  strategy, definition   1
  Value Based Management   116
competitive environment, analysis of   19,
    26–32
  business-level strategy   80–3
  carbonated soft drinks industry   29–31
competitive position, analysis of   19, 32
  life-cycle model   32–8
  market share analysis   40–1
  strategic group analysis   38–40
competitive positioning   6
competitive strategies   52–4
  cost leadership   54–7, 61
  demand-led   68–70
  differentiation   57–9, 61
  economic logic behind   62–3
  focus   59–62
  hybrid   64–8
  key features   61–2
  strategic choice   51–2, 63–4
competitive superiority test for resources
    and capabilities   71
complexity
  of environmental conditions   23, 24
  structuring for   144–6
Computer World   68
consolidation   88
consortia   99
contingency planning   23–5
continuous improvement   139
contracting markets, competition in   36–7
Co-op   34
co-operation and competition   149–50
co-operative strategies   81
co-opetition   150
core competences   110–11, 177
core rigidities   179
corporate-level strategy
  corporate objectives   112–20
  development, methods of   97–100
  directional strategies   87–97

parenting strategies   104–11
portfolio strategies   100–4
selecting appropriate strategies   111–12
strategic considerations   86–7
corporate relatedness   93–4
corporate responsibility *see* responsibility,
   corporate
Costco   90
cost leadership strategies   53, 54–7
choice, influencing factors   63, 64
competitive advantage   70, 71–2
demand-led strategy   68
economic logic behind   62–3
hybrid strategies   64–6
key features   61
Cott Beverages   30, 96
Courtauld's   147
credence goods   64
Criado-Perez, Carlos   213
Crisp, Nigel   203
culture, national   125
environmental analysis   21
internationalization   90
Japan   128–9
objectives, corporate   112–13
culture, organizational   6, 125–7
current strategy   5
customer perspective, balanced scorecard
   approach   119–20
Cusumano, M. A.   184

Daily Mail   37
Daily Star   37
Daily Telegraph   36, 37
Darty   108
D'Aveni, Richard   74, 75
Davis, Sir Peter   212, 213, 214–16
De Beers   75
DEC   225, 226
Decathlon   68
decentralization   156
decisional roles of managers   166, 168
decision making   130
decline stage of life cycle   35
Dell   75, 78–80, 85, 220
demand-led strategy   52, 68–70
Desmond, Richard   37
development, methods of   97–100
diagnostic intervention, organizational
   development   161

differentiation strategies   53, 57–9
choice, influencing factors   63, 64
competitive advantage   70–2
competitive environment, structural
   analysis of   27, 29
demand-led strategy   68
economic logic behind   62
hybrid strategies   64–6
key features   61
Digital Equipment Corporation   225, 226
Digital Home Working Group (DHWG)
   207, 219
directional strategies   86, 87–9
internationalization of retailing   89–90
related diversification   91–2
unrelated diversification   93–7
directions for development   6
Direct Line   75
direct selling   75
discounting   69
disequilibrium situation, market turbulence
   76
Disney   134–6, 139, 201
dissemination role of managers   167
distribution issues   27
disturbance handler role of managers   168
diversification
directional strategies   88, 89, 91–7
growth vector   8
related   89, 91–2, 107–8
subsystem   156
unrelated   89, 93–7
Dixon's   90
dodo   197–8
dogs   101, 102, 104
Do-it-all   109
Donovan, Dennis   201
dot-com collapse   182
Drucker, Peter   10–11, 15, 141
Dunkin' Donuts   201
Du Pont   30
durability test for resources and capabilities
   71
dynamic capabilities   178, 179–80
dynamic corporations   87
dynamic environments   23–4, 72
dynamic networks   142

easyGroup, diversification   93, 94–7, 107
easyJet   54, 85, 94, 95

eBay   75
e-business   75
Eccles, R. G.   224
economic factors, environmental analysis
      20
economic profit (economic rent/economic
      value added)   115, 116
economies of scale *see* scale economies
edge of heartland businesses   105, 106
efficiency issues   91–2
Egg   54
Eisenhardt, K. M.   178
electricals sector   82, 83
electronic commerce   75
emergent strategy   5
employee involvement   133
enemy, focus on a common   12
Energis   73
Enron   176, 182, 192–3
entrepreneurial companies, characteristics
      158
entrepreneurial pillar of excellence   122
entrepreneurial skills   93
entrepreneur role of managers   168
entry barriers
   competitive environment, structural
      analysis of   27, 29, 30, 32
   cost leadership strategies   56
   differentiation strategies   58
   first-mover advantage   80–1
   focus strategies   59
   strategic group analysis   40
   strategic tools   82–3
environmental (external) analysis   18,
      49–50
   environment defined   18–19
   identifying the firm's competitive
      environment   32–41
   model of strategy   6
   nature of environment   22–6
   procedure   19–20
   scanning the general environment
      20–2
   structural analysis of competitive
      environment   26–32
   SWOT analysis   46–8
equilibrium situation, market turbulence
      75, 76
Ericsson   75, 146, 207, 208
   Sony Ericsson   99, 220

ethical issues   187–8
Euro-Disney   134, 135–6
European   37
European Union, harmonization   30
Evening Standard   37
excellence, organizational
   future   180–4
   IKEA   136–7
   Japanese companies   125–8, 138
   Marks & Spencer   134, 136, 138
   new perspectives   138–40, 149
   Peters and Waterman's perspective   121,
      122–5, 134, 135, 137–8
   Walt Disney   134–6
exclusivity, competitive advantage through
      72–3
exit barriers   27–8
Experian   109
experience factors   100
experience products   64
Express   37
Express Newspapers   37
external analysis *see* environmental
      (external) analysis

Fads   109
Fannie Mae   140
fashion industry   142
feasibility issues, corporate-level strategy
      87, 111–12
Federal Express   164, 178
Ferranti   147
Ferrari   59
figurehead role of managers   167
film production organizations   142, 143
financial control   147
financial perspective, balanced scorecard
      approach   119
financial resources   43
financial services sector   82, 188
Financial Times   36
Fiorina, Carly   79
first-mover advantages   72–3, 80–1
fixed costs   27
flexibility issues   56
fluctuating equilibrium situation, market
      turbulence   75, 76
focus strategies   53, 59–61
   choice, influencing factors   63
   key features   61–2

food and drink sector   82
football   180–1
Ford, Henry   57, 159, 190
Ford Motor Company
    change, lack of   159
    cost leadership strategy   56–7
    excellence   139
    hybrid strategies   66
    mission statement   12, 13
    stakeholders   188
    strategic human resource management
        132–3
    values   191
France   114, 180–1
franchising   89, 99
future of strategy   176, 184, 193
    competence   176–8
    competence, organization and human
        resources   178–80
    excellence   180–4
    responsibility   187–93
    software wars   184–6

game theory   81
Gap   89
Gawer, A.   184
GE *see* General Electric
GEC   147
General Electric (GE)   146
    case study   221–5
    diversification   93
    excellence   139
    leadership   170, 201
    Nardelli, Bob   200
General Electric/McKinsey
    attractiveness–strengths matrix   100,
        102–3, 104
general environment   6, 19, 20–2
General Motors (GM)   15, 56, 57, 221
Germany   114
Ghoshal, S.   144–5
Gillette   76–8, 84, 140
glass industry   152
GlaxoSmithKline (GSK)   183
global companies   144, 145, 146
    see also multinational corporations
globalization   89–90, 189–90
glocalization   189
GM   15, 56, 57, 221
Go   94

Gould, Michael   15, 104, 105, 146–8
Gould, Stephen Jay   197, 198
Grant, R. M.   179
Great Universal Stores   109
Green, Philip   47, 109, 212, 216
Griffiths report   163
grocery retail industry   33–4, 38–9
Grove, Andy   170–3
growth, industry   27
growth–share matrix   100–2, 103, 104
growth stage of life cycle   35
growth vector   7–9
GSK   183
Guinness   163
Gulf War   25
GUS   109

H&M   183
H&P   139
habit-breaking pillar of excellence   122
Haji-Ioannou, Stelios   93, 94
Halford's   109
Hall & Woodhouse   30
Hamel, Gary
    competence   110, 111, 176–7
    competitive advantage   178
    innovation   84
    strategic success   85
    strategy   1
Hanson, Lord   148
Hanson Trust   93, 147, 148
Harvard Design School model of strategic
    management   187
Harvey-Jones, Sir John   126, 151, 152, 165,
    170, 172
heartland businesses   105, 106, 108
hedgehog concept   140
Hertz   164
Hewlett-Packard (HP)   78–80, 220
Hewlett-Packard/Compaq   79, 80
Hickman, C. R.   122
history, strategic   5
Hitachi   219
Hobby Craft   68
Homebase   109, 215
Home Depot   198–202
Honda   12, 110–11, 127, 178
Hoover   74
horizontal integration   91–2
Hoskyns, Sir John   166

hospitals   163–4
Houllier, Gerard   180
human resources (HR)
   competence and organization   178–80
   situation analysis   43
   strategic management   128–34
Hutchison, Mark Hely   163
Hyman, Richard   212
hypercompetition   74–80

Iacocca, Lee   152
IBM
   business, theory of the   15
   change   226
   Home Depot   200, 201
   industrial orthodoxy   85
   and Intel   170
   and Linux, partnership between   150
   managers recruited by Xerox   227
   market turbulence and
      hypercompetition   74
   model   12
   strategic intent   132
   strategy subsystems   157
   subcontracting   142
ICI
   cultural change   126, 152, 165
   leadership   170, 172
   parenting   147
Idei, Nobuyuki   217, 218, 219
identity   14–15
IKEA
   demand-led strategy   68
   excellence   136–7
   industrial order, overturning the   85
   internationalization   89, 90
   network organizations   142
   strategy   1
Immelt, Jeff   200
Imperial   147
incremental change   152, 153–5, 156, 159
Independent   36
induction programmes   129
inflexibility issues   56
informational roles of managers   166, 167
information networks   167
information technology   44–5
inimitability test for resources and
      capabilities   71
innovation   84

competitive advantage through   72
competitive environment, structural
      analysis of   28, 31
corporate-level strategy   87
differentiation strategies   59
first-mover advantage   80
future excellence   182–3
Japanese firms   130
and learning perspective, balanced
      scorecard approach   119, 120
market turbulence and
      hypercompetition   76–8, 79, 80
technological resources   43
see also change; research and
      development
intangible resources   43
Intel   74, 79, 170–3, 184, 220
intended strategy   5
internal analysis *see* organizational
      (internal) analysis
internal business perspective, balanced
      scorecard approach   119, 120
internal development   97, 98
internal transformation   12
internationalization   89–90, 189–90
internationalization organizations   144–5,
      146
   see also multinational corporations
Internet   75
interpersonal roles of managers   166, 167
InterSpar   90
intrapreneurs   158
introduction stage of life cycle   35
investing in resources and capabilities   71
investment skills   93
Irn-bru   29–30
ITT   93, 146

Jaguar   107
Japan
   automobile manufacturers   9
   challenge for Intel   170
   consumer durables sector   49
   corporate objectives   113–14
   criticism of companies   138
   investment in the UK   132, 145
   products as triggers for change   152
   stakeholders   188–90
   strategic human resource management
      128–31, 132

success of firms   121, 125–8
VCR producers   75
Walt Disney   136
job rotation   129
John Deere   202
joint development   97–9
joint ventures   89, 96, 99, 150
J. Sainsbury *see* Sainsbury
just-in-time production   42

Kahane, Adam   25
Kamoche, K.   179
Kanter, Rosabeth   169
Kao   146
Kaplan, Robert   119
Kay, John   1, 71, 72
Keidanren (Japan Federation of Economic
    Organizations)   190
Kellogg's   82
Kennedy, John F.   11
Kentucky Fried Chicken (KFC)   99
KESA Electricals   108
Kim, W. C.   199
Kingfisher   108–9, 110, 148
knowledge-based view of the world   177–8
Kohlberg Kraus Roberts (KKR)   212
Komatsu   11, 130
Kotter, Jan   173–5
Kutaragi, Ken   218
KwikFit   165
Kwiksave   34

laboratory interventions, organizational
    development   161
Land Rover   59
Langone, Ken   200
Lastminute   75
leader role of managers   167
leadership
    and change   165–75
    and excellence   139–40
    roles   166
Leahy, Terry   213, 216
learning organizations   177–8, 190
legal factors   21
Leighton, Alan   213
Leonard-Barton, D.   179
leveraging resources and capabilities   71
Levi Strauss   11, 190
Lex   147

liaison role of managers   167
licensing   72, 99
Lidl   69
life-cycle model   32–8, 100
lifetime employment, Japan   129
Link, the   207
Linux   150, 184–6
Littlewood's   109
Lloyds-TSB   114
L'Oréal   183
Lorenz, Chris   165
Lowe's   199
loyalty
    brand   82, 83
    customer   73–4
    employee   55
Lucent   208
Lufthansa   114
Luner Glas   210

Macaw   30
manageability issues, parenting strategies
    107, 108
management buy-outs   107
managers, roles   166–8
    see also leadership
manufacturing sector   82–3
Marakon   114
Marcus, Bernie   198, 199
market development   8, 88–9
marketing   93, 156
market penetration   8, 88
market positioning   52–62, 67, 69–70
market power   67, 91–2
market share
    analysis   40–1
    hybrid strategies   67
    Japanese attitudes   130
    market turbulence and
        hypercompetition   78–9
market turbulence   74–80
Marks & Spencer (M&S)
    Beckham, David   181
    Brooks Brothers acquisition by   90
    challenges   109
    clothing   66, 68
    criticisms   138
    excellence   136
    grocery retailing   34, 39, 65, 216
    growth vector   9

Marks & Spencer (M&S) (*cont'd*)
  hybrid strategies   66, 67, 68
  industrial orthodoxy   85
  internationalization   89, 90
  mission statement   10–11
  retrenchment   216
  strategy   1
  theory of the business   15
Marriott's   139
Martin, J. A.   178
Matalan   54, 69, 85
matrix organizations   141
Matsushita   146, 220
Matsushita, Konosuke   126
Matthew Clarke   30
maturity stage of life cycle   35
Maubourgne, R.   199
Mazda   132
McColough, Peter   225, 226
McDonald's   89, 99, 117–19, 182
McGrath, John   196
McKinsey   114
Merck   139
Metro   89
Metro   37
MFI   108
Microsoft
  game-console business   220
  industry standard   80
  market turbulence and
    hypercompetition   74, 79
  platform leadership   184
  software wars   184, 185
military strategy   2–3
Mirror   36, 37
mission statements   10–14
  theory of the business   15–16
  visionary organizations   190
mobile Processor Interface Alliance   207
mobility barriers   38–40
moments of truth   171
monitor role of managers   167
monopoly, natural   72
Montgomery, C. A.   71
moral hazard   165
moral issues   187–8
Morita, Akio   125–6, 131
Morrison   34, 47, 212, 214, 215
Morrison, Sir Ken   213
motivation role of leaders   169

Motorola   75, 183, 207, 208, 222
multinational corporations (MNCs)
  complexity of environment   23
  directional strategies   89, 90
  structuring for complexity   144–6
  see also internationalization
music industry   182

Nalebuff, B. J.   150
Nardelli, Bob   200–2
narrow markets   72
National Health Service   163, 192,
    203–6
National Institute of Clinical Excellence
    (NICE)   203
NEC   146, 219
negotiator role of managers   168
Netto   69
New Look   69
News International   36
newspaper industry   36–7
Newstrom, John   137–8
Nienburger Glass   210
Nike   12, 183
Nissan   127, 132
Nohria, N.   224
Nokia   75, 183–4, 206–9, 220
non-co-operative (aggressive) strategies
    81, 84–5
Nortel   208
Norton, David   119
Norwich Union/AMP   96
not-for-profit companies   7
NTL   22
Nucor   140

O2   207
objectives, corporate   112–20
OfTel   73–4
oligopolies   74
Oliver, Jamie   215
Olla, Jorma   208
One.tel   21, 22
operating environment   6
opportunities   7, 46
  see also SWOT analysis
Oracle   184, 185
Orange   207
organic networks   142
organizational development (OD)   161–3

organizational (internal) analysis
  model of strategy   6
  procedure   19–20
  resources and capabilities   41–6
  SWOT analysis   46–8
organizational structure subsystem   156
organization and strategy   121
  competence   178–80
  competition and co-operation   149–50
  complexity, structuring for   144–6
  critical voices   137–8
  excellence, new perspectives on   138–40
  IKEA   136–7
  Japanese organizations   125–8
  Marks & Spencer   134, 136
  parenting   146–9
  Peters and Waterman's excellent
    organizations   122–5
  strategic human resource management
    128–34
  structure of organizations   140–3
  Walt Disney   134–6
Ouchi, William   127
over-servicing   165
Owen, Michael   180
own-label brands   30

Palo Alto Research Center (PARC)   225–8
parenting   146–9
  strategies   86, 104–11
parenting fit matrix   105
participative management   133
patents   80, 82
Pearson   36
Pelopu, Krishna   199
Penrose, Edith   177
Pepsi   12, 29, 137
Permira   215
personal computer industry   78–80
Peters, Tom
  bureaucratic organizations   141
  In Search of Excellence   121, 122–5, 134,
    137–8, 182
  leadership   168, 169
  matrix organizations   141
  values, organizational   6
pharmaceutical sector   82, 182–3
Philips   74, 75, 146, 150, 220
Phones   4U   21, 207
physical resources, situation analysis   43

Pilkington   9, 152
planning   1, 2
  contingency   23–5
  strategic   147
platform leadership   184
Plessey   147
PLM   210
political factors, environmental analysis
    21
Porras, Jerry   138–40, 149, 225
Porter, Michael
  business services   44
  competence as clustering phenomenon
    180
  competitive environment, structural
    analysis of   26, 28–9
  competitive strategies   53, 54, 62, 64,
    68
  industrial structure   188
  market positioning, supply-side
    perspective   52, 69
  strategy, definition   1
  structural analysis   49
  Value Based Management   115
  value chain   42
portfolio power   92
portfolio strategies   86, 100–4
Prahalad, C. K.   84, 110, 111, 176–7, 178
predatory behaviour   81
Pret á manger   118
pricing policy   39, 69, 82–3
Prince's   30
process interventions, organizational
    development   161
Procter & Gamble   82, 139, 146
product development   88
  see also innovation; research and
    development
product differentiation *see* differentiation
    strategies
product–market scope   7–9
profit
  competitive environment, structural
    analysis of   28–9
  corporate objectives   114
  economic   115, 116
  and market share, relationship between
    67
project-based organizations   141
ProMarkt   108

public sector
  mission statements   13–14
  model of strategy   7
  and private sector, blurring of line
    between   187
punctuated equilibrium situation, market
  turbulence   76

Quaker Oats   114
Qualcomm   208
quality issues   69, 130, 164–5
Queen's Medical Centre, Nottingham   14
question marks   101, 102
Quinn, J. B.   125, 153–4, 155, 159

radical change   152–3, 154–5
railroad sector   14
Railtrack   107
Randall, Geoffrey   214
Raymond, Eric   186
realized strategy   5, 7
Red Hat   185
regulation, exclusivity through   72
rejuvenation phase of life cycle   35
related diversification   89, 91–2, 107–8
relatedness
  of business units   107, 108, 110
  corporate   93–4
relationship skills   93
Renault   127, 183
reputation   30, 72
research and development (R&D)   82, 83,
  84
  see also innovation
resource allocator role of managers   168
resource-based view of the firm   177, 179
resource planning   112
resources and capabilities, organizational
  competitive advantage   70–4
  deployment   112
  model of strategy   6
  situation analysis   42–4
responsibility, corporate   7, 176, 187–8,
  191–3
  stakeholders   188–90
  values   191
  visionary organizations   190
retailing sector
  growth vector   8–9
  internationalization   89–90

parenting strategies   108–10
  see also grocery retail industry
retaliation   27
Reuter's   114
rewards for innovation   160
Rexam   209–12
rigidities, core   179
rivalry
  competitive environment, structural
    analysis of   27–8, 31
  cost leadership strategies   56
  differentiation strategies   58
  focus strategies   59
Robson, Bobby   181
Roddick, Anita   187–8, 190, 191
role modelling   12
Rolls Royce   59
Ronaldo   180
Royal Bank of Scotland   213
Royal Dutch Shell   24–5, 215
Rumelt, R.   16–17
Russell, Steve   195–6
Ryanair   59

Saatchi & Saatchi   45
Safeway
  competitive position   33
  Sainsbury's bid for   212–14
  SWOT analysis   47, 48
Sainsbury
  case study   212–17
  competitive position   33
  growth vector   9
  hybrid strategies   65–6, 67–8
  internationalization   89
  takeover bid for Safeway   47,
    212–17
  telecommunications industry   21
Sainsbury, John   216
Salbu, S.   192
Samsung   207, 220
Sanyo   220
SAS   165, 170, 171
Savacentre   215
scale economies
  competitive environment, structural
    analysis of   27
  demand-led strategy   68
  diversification   92
  hybrid strategies   67, 68

and market share, relationship between 67

natural monopoly 72

Scandinavian Airlines Systems (SAS) 165, 170, 171

scenario planning 23–5

Schumpeter, Joseph 74

scope, economies of 92

search products 64

Seeger, John 104

segmentation 31, 40–1

selling network 82, 83

Senge, Peter 190

Sennett, R. 179, 193

service environments

change 163–5

market development 89

organizational analysis 44–5

Seth, Andrew 214

seven Ss framework 123–5

shareholder value 114–19, 192, 195

Shell 24–5, 215

Sherman, Stratford 221

shippai-gaku ('Failure-ology' Institute) 127

Siemens 207

Silo 90

Silva, M. 122

simple environments 23

Singapore Airlines 96

situation analysis 18, 49–50

environment defined 18–19

identifying the firm's competitive position 32–41

internal environment: resources and capabilities 41–6

nature of environment 22–6

procedure 19–20

scanning the general environment 20–2

structural analysis of competitive environment 26–32

SWOT analysis 46–8

skills, seven Ss framework 124

Slater Menswear 60–1

Sloan, Alfred 221

Smiddy, Paul 215

social and cultural factors 21

socialization 130, 134–5

social welfare and corporate responsibility 187

Somerfield 34, 215

Sony

case study 217–21

change management 158

core competence 110, 178

culture, organizational 131

glocalization 189

innovation 79

joint ventures 150

market turbulence and hypercompetition 75, 79

mobile telecommunications industry 207

Sony Ericsson 99, 220

Southwest Airlines 1

span, economies of 92

specialization strategies *see* focus strategies

spokesperson role of managers 167

Sprint 96

stability pillar of excellence 122

staff, seven Ss framework 124

Stagecoach 96

stakeholders 7, 188–90

standards, industry 80, 150

Staples 68

stars 101, 102, 160

static environments 23, 88

STC 147

Stern Stewart 114

stock markct 113

strategic business units (SBUs) 100, 105

strategic choice 51–2

strategic commitment 81

strategic control 147

strategic fit 6

strategic group analysis 38–40

strategic history 5

strategic intent 130–1, 132

strategic management

model 4–7

in public sector and not-for-profit companies 7

working definition 3

strategic planning 147

strategic vision 7

strategy

approaches 2

definition 1

elements 2–4

evaluation 16–17

strategy (*cont'd*)
  future 184
  model 4–7
  seven Ss framework 123, 124
  and structure, link between 140–3
  subsystems 155–7
  and values, in mission statements
    13–14
strengths, organizational 6–7, 44
  see also SWOT analysis
Stringer, Howard 218, 219
structure, organizational
  model of strategy 6
  seven Ss framework 123, 124
  and strategy, link between 140–3
style, seven Ss framework 124
substitutability test for resources and
  capabilities 71
substitute products
  competitive environment, structural
    analysis of 28, 30
  cost leadership strategies 56
  differentiation strategies 58
  focus strategies 59
suitability issues, corporate-level strategy
  87, 111
Sun 36, 37
Sunday Times 36
sunk costs 72
Superdrug 108
superordinate skills, seven Ss framework
  124
suppliers, power of
  competitive environment, structural
    analysis of 28, 30, 32
  cost leadership strategies 56
  differentiation strategies 58
  focus strategies 59
supply, assured 82, 83
supply-side perspective, market positioning
  52–62
Swiftcall 22
switching costs 27, 28
SWOT analysis 20, 49, 111
Symbian software 207
systems, seven Ss framework 124

targeting 12
Tarmac 147
Taylorism 126

teamwork 129–30
technological factors 20, 43, 56, 182
technology subsystem 156
telecommunications industry 21–2, 73,
  182
television production organizations 142,
  143
Telewest 22
Tesco
  challenges 109
  competitive position 33
  growth 213, 214, 215, 216
  hybrid strategies 66, 68
  internationalization 89
  mission statement 11
  non-food sales 215
  takeover bid for Safeway 47, 212,
    213–14, 216
  telecommunications industry 21
Thatcherism 187
theory of the business 15–16
Thompson GCR 222
Thornton's 11
threats 7, 46–7
  see also SWOT analysis
Tichy, Noel 201, 221, 222, 223
Tillman, Robert 199
Times 36, 37
TK Maxx 69
T-mobile 96, 207
Tokunaka, Teruhisa 218
top-down approach to strategy 2
Torwalds, Linus 184–5, 186
Toshiba 207, 219
Toyota 127, 177
Toys'r'us 68, 89
trade barriers 30
transnational companies 145
  see also multinational corporations
turbulence, market 74–80
turn-round skills 93

Ulrich, David 223
Unilever 82, 146, 148
Unipart 106, 107
United Automobile Workers 132
United Biscuits 147
United Kingdom
  competitive advantage 49
  corporate objectives 113–14

entrepreneurs 158
financial services industry 188
Ford 132
Japanese investment in 132, 145
social welfare and corporate
responsibility 187
United States of America
corporate objectives 113–14
entrepreneurs 158
Ford 132, 133
junk bond market 188
management practice 127
railroad companies, identity 14
social welfare and corporate
responsibility 187
unrelated diversification 89, 93–7
upgrading resources and capabilities
71

Value Based Management (VBM) 87,
114–19
value chain 41–4, 91–2, 142
value-for-money (VFM) frontier 69
values, organizational 6, 13–14, 188,
191
value trap businesses 105, 106
van der Heijden, Kees 25
venture capital 158
Verdict 212
vertical integration 91–2
Vickers 147
Vimto 30
Virgin Group
diversification 93, 94–7, 107
internationalization 89
reputation 72
virtuous circle, hybrid strategies 67,
68
visionary companies 139, 188, 190
Vodaphone 107, 207
Volkswagen 127

Waitrose 216
Wall Street 192

Wal-mart
challenges 109
cost leadership strategy 54–5
excellence 139
internationalization 89, 90
outbids Kingfisher for Asda 108
Safeway takeover battle 212, 214, 216
and Sainsbury's, competition between
66
Walt Disney 134–6, 139, 201
Walton, Sam 55
Wanlass report 203, 204, 205–6
Ward White 109, 110
Waterman, R. H.
In Search of Excellence 121, 122–5, 134,
137–8, 182
leadership 168, 169
matrix organizations 141
values, organizational 6
Wayner, Peter 185
weaknesses, organizational 6–7, 44
see also SWOT analysis
Welch, Jack 170, 200, 221–5
Wertkauf 90
Wheatcroft, Patience 203
White, Lord 148
Whittington, Richard 93
W. H. Smith 90, 96
withdrawal strategy 88
Wm Low 66
Wm Morrison *see* Morrison
Woolworth 108

Xerox
case study 225–8
competence issues 178
identity 14
market turbulence and
hypercompetition 74
stakeholders 189

Yamaha 12
yield management 94
Young, Bob 185–6